Soldiers' Lives through History ↷
The Early Modern World

Soldiers' Lives through History
Dennis Showalter, Series Editor

The Ancient World
Richard A. Gabriel

The Middle Ages
Clifford J. Rogers

The Early Modern World
Dennis Showalter and William J. Astore

The Nineteenth Century
Michael S. Neiberg

The Twentieth Century
Robert T. Foley and Helen McCartney

Soldiers' Lives through History

THE EARLY MODERN WORLD

✴ ✴ ✴

Dennis Showalter and William J. Astore

Soldiers' Lives through History
Dennis Showalter, Series Editor

GREENWOOD PRESS
Westport, Connecticut · London

Library of Congress Cataloging-in-Publication Data

Showalter, Dennis E.
  Soldiers' lives through history : the early modern world / Dennis
Showalter and William J. Astore.
        p. cm. — (Soldiers' lives through history)
  Includes bibliographical references and index.
  ISBN–13: 978–0–313–33312–5 (alk. paper)
  ISBN–10: 0–313–33312–2 (alk. paper)
  1. Military life.   2. Sociology, Military.   3. Military art and
science—Europe—History—16th century.   4. Military art and science—
Europe—History—17th century.   5. Military art and science—Europe—
History—18th century. I. Astore, William J. II. Title.
  U765.S56 2007
  355.1094'0903—dc22   2006039151

British Library Cataloguing in Publication Data is available.

Library of Congress Catalog Card Number: 2006039151
ISBN–13: 978–0–313–33312–5
ISBN–10: 0–313–33312–2

First published in 2007

Greenwood Press, 88 Post Road West, Westport, CT 06881
An imprint of Greenwood Publishing Group, Inc.
www.greenwood.com

Printed in the United States of America

The paper used in this book complies with the
Permanent Paper Standard issued by the National
Information Standards Organization (Z39.48–1984).

10 9 8 7 6 5 4 3 2 1

In loving memory of our fathers, Edwin Showalter (1900–1978)
and Julius Astore (1917–2003).

CONTENTS

Series Foreword   ix

Introduction   xi

    Soldiers in a Revolutionary Age?   xi
    Scope   xii
    Arrangement   xii

Timeline   xv

Prologue: Early Modern Warfare in Practice   xix
    Pavia (1525): Warfare in the Age of Mercenaries and Gunpowder   xix
    Breitenfeld (1631): The Quest for Decision   xxxii
    Leuthen (1757): Professionalism and Enlightened Warfare   xlii

One: The Matrix of War: Policies, Strategies, and Mentalities   1
    The Warmaking State   1
    Duels of Faith and Empire   9
    The Time of the Dynasties   14

Two: Where They Came from, Why, and How   25
    Listening for the Drum   25
    Weapons and Men   33
    Signing On   36
    Alternative Approaches to Recruiting Soldiers   42

Three: Technologies, Tactics, and Training — 51
  Gunpowder Cannons, New Fortresses, and Siege Warfare — 53
  Drill, Discipline, and Muskets: The Rise of Infantry — 61
  The Poor Bloody Cavalry — 71

Four: Command and Leadership — 79
  The Age of Entrepreneurs, 1494–1648 — 80
  The Age of Noblemen, 1648–1740 — 84
  The Age of the Officer, 1740–1789 — 88
  The Relationship between the Leader and the Led — 94

Five: Morale and Motivation — 99
  Religious Belief As Motivation for War — 100
  Morale and Motivation of Officers — 107
  Morale and Motivation of Ordinary Soldiers — 110

Six: Structure and Routines — 117
  Early Days for the Soldier — 117
  Moving into War, Physically and Psychologically — 119
  Camp Life — 121
  Women and Children with the Regiment — 123
  Medicine, Sexual Diseases, and Sanitation — 125
  Rewards of the Job — 127
  The Creation of Standing Armies — 129
  Training, Punishment, and at Ease — 132
  Billets and Quarters: Living Outside of Camp — 134
  Afterward: Veterans — 137

Seven: Europeans in a World of War — 141
  European Reconnaissance and Initial Conquests — 142
  Pebbles in a Flood: Europeans in Asia — 145
  The Sepoy Exception in India — 147
  Westerners: Opportunistic Entrepreneurs or Natural Born Killers? — 150
  The American Experience: Southern Hemisphere — 154
  The Northern Hemisphere and the First Way of War — 156

Eight: Conclusion — 165

Bibliography — 169

Index — 179

✵ ✵ ✵

SERIES FOREWORD

The song "Universal Soldier" has been a staple of peace rallies since the 1960s. Written by Buffy Sainte-Marie and performed by Donovan Leitch in 1965, when it became popular, the song indicts the soldier as war's agent, unlike most other songs of its type, which cast the soldier as war's victim: "He knows he shouldn't kill / And he knows he always will. . . . "

The killing, of course, goes on apace. Sometimes it will be by neighbors once thought of as friends, as in Rwanda during the 1990s. Sometimes it will be by bureaucratic utopians who see the path to the future obstructed by Jews in Hitler's Germany—or by class enemies in Stalin's Russia—or by people who wear glasses in Pol Pot's Cambodia. Sometimes it will be by zealots who expect to gain paradise by dying while killing others, like the Crusaders of the Middle Ages, or today's Jihadis. Most often it will somehow involve soldiers.

Historians are currently engaged in a debate on the existence of a "Western way of war," which distinguishes the West from the rest of the world, and arguably defines Western civilization as well. Underlying that debate, and structuring it, is the question of whether there is a distinctively Western soldier. Victor Davis Hanson writes eloquently of free men voluntarily committing themselves to conquer or die in order that they might return to the homes they saved. Critics such as John A. Lynn in *Battle: A History of Combat and Culture* assert the cultural specificity of approaches to war in both Western and global contexts. The ancient Greeks, for example, sought quick decisions because of particular values emphasizing individual worth and independence. Nineteenth-century Europe's concept of the decisive battle was influenced heavily by a Romantic high culture as opposed to specific military factors, such as rapid-firing weapons and mass armies.

This series, Soldiers' Lives through History, is the first to address comprehensively the cutting-edge experiences of the Western soldier from his initial appearance at the beginning of history to his latest avatars in Vietnam and the Middle East. Richard Gabriel's volume on the soldiers of the ancient world notes that the first archaeological evidence of organized war is in present-day Iraq. Thousands of years later the wheel has turned a full circle. The authors of each volume, Richard A. Gabriel; Clifford J. Rogers; Dennis Showalter and William J. Astore; Michael S. Neiberg; and Robert T. Foley and Helen McCartney, address not only "the face of battle," but also its frameworks. The soldiers' civil origins, their emotional and intellectual makeup, their daily lives in peace and war, and above all their reactions to facing death and dealing it—these are the kinds of themes developed in all five volumes of the series. The authors' intentions are to facilitate understanding of one of history's fundamental questions: Why do humans fight wars? That question's continuing relevance is made plain everywhere, in television and in newspapers, on the Internet, in video games, and not least in the cemeteries where bugles still sound over those who gave all in war and to war. Did they do so as heroes, fools, perpetrators—or perhaps a little of all three, structured by individual factors defying collective analysis?

With this series, Greenwood Press takes a major step in providing substance to the issue of the soldier's identity and the soldier's place in Western civilization. One point that Hanson and his critics share is an agreement that war making in the West has evolved away from any class or caste restrictions on participation. War has become every man's business—and, increasingly, the business of women as well. Most men and women who will read these books have known someone who was a solider, have soldiers in their family trees, and have the potential to be soldiers themselves. In that sense, this series is about all of us: the heirs and successors of the Universal Soldier.

Dennis Showalter

✶ ✶ ✶

INTRODUCTION

SOLDIERS IN A REVOLUTIONARY AGE?

The study of military history in early modern Europe is dominated by the question of military revolution. Simply put, the debate involves two questions: Did the nature of warmaking change so fundamentally that it altered the dynamics of state and society as well? When did this network of changes occur? The vast literature on the subject carries the military reconstruction of so-called early modern Europe back to the Hundred Years War (approximately 1337–1453) and forward into the eighteenth century. Most accounts, however, locate its focus somewhere in the period covered by this book: between 1494 and 1789.

And that is the last time the subject of military revolution is addressed directly in this volume. Apart from the existence of a vibrant specialist literature on the concept, military revolution too easily becomes a macro-issue, a wedge for introducing military history into the amorphous big picture that is discussed in general histories. That is one of the purposes of the study of military revolution, and it is perfectly legitimate on its own terms.

Buying into the mainstream, however, carries the risk of overlooking the sharp ends of war—in particular, those who fought them. The early modern soldier is, in any case, a figure unsympathetic and remote. He is the freebooting *Landsknecht* of the sixteenth century, swaggering in dilapidated finery through the ruins he and his kind create. He is the mercenary of the Thirty Years War (1618–1648), rootless and masterless, brutalizing civilians for a few coins, destroying civilization's works for the pleasure of it. He is the uniformed automaton of the eighteenth century, initiative beaten out of him, fit to do no more than endure battles and floggings until pitched into an anonymous grave.

The authors do not offer an avowedly revisionist interpretation of these images. Our intention is to present a comprehensive, nuanced analysis of the men who were the first to be called "soldiers" rather than "warriors." Our focus on Europe is more than an adherence to the structure of the series. A distinctive "Western way of war" may or may not exist; the subject remains debatable. A much stronger case, however, can be made for the Western soldier as an archetype that has influenced the structure of armies and the waging of war throughout the world since his first appearance in his definitive form on history's stage, beginning in the sixteenth century.

SCOPE

Soldiers' Lives through History—The Early Modern Period begins with the French invasion of Italy in 1494. Widely regarded as the first modern military campaign, the long-enduring Italian Wars featured the first large-scale use of professional infantry, and the last appearance of massed armored cavalry, at Pavia in 1525. It featured an organized supply system and the largest artillery train ever seen in Europe. Above all, 1494 marked the beginning of Europe's gunpowder wars, with their world-transforming social, political, and military consequences. The book ends in 1789, with Europe on the brink of an Age of Revolution that swept away the technocratic, professional armies that had become normative over the previous three centuries by mass armies of conscripted civilians.

In between, the book tells the story of the Western soldier—his evolution from mercenary to professional; the weapons he carried, the way he fought, and how he lived—for it must be remembered that the ordinary soldier spent most of his career in times of peace. The book presents the soldiers' lives in the contexts of the civil societies that produced them and the policies and strategies of the states they served. It also briefly analyzes the extra-European experience of Europe's soldiers—the conditions they faced in Africa, in Asia, and North and South America—and suggests some consequences. Because it is impossible in a small space to describe in detail the experiences of the thousands of men who took the soldier's path over three centuries and more, the text is correspondingly episodic and impressionistic, seeking to reconstruct comparatively the common aspects of the common soldiers' ordinary experiences.

ARRANGEMENT

The work includes eight chapters. The work begins with a triptych of battles, showing the early modern soldier in action in three battles typical of phases in the nearly 300 years of the era, which combine to highlight the changing face of early modern war and the changing demands it makes on those who fight. It presents an exciting backdrop for the entire book by vividly presenting the battle scenes, first at Pavia, in northern Italy, in 1525, featuring dynasties at war, the capture of a king, and mercenaries battling through gunpowder. Second, the battle of Breitenfeld in 1631 presents a great captain-king, Gustavus Adolphus of Protestant Sweden, and the 19,000 men he summoned everywhere he could find them, entering a war against Catholic Imperialists in

Germany. Third, the battle of Leuthen in 1757 describes how the history of a state, Prussia, and a continent depended on the events of a single afternoon at a small Silesian village, Leuthen (now part of Poland), as the soldiers of the army of Frederick the Great fought to drive Austrian troops from Silesia.

Chapter One establishes the wider contexts of early modern warmaking: the policies that sent soldiers to war, the economics that sustained them, and the planning that structured their operations. Chapter Two deals with where soldiers came from, why and how they joined, and the kinds of armies in which they served. That last category is a broad one, ranging from freelance adventurers like the sixteenth-century *Landsknechte* of south Germany to an eighteenth-century Prussian army recruited under something closely resembling the U.S. Selective Service System of the 1950s and 1960s.

Chapters Three, Four, and Five are the core of the work. Chapter Three addresses weapons, tactics, and training. It takes the soldier from the *Landsknecht*'s pike to the flintlock musket and socket bayonet, from the mass formations of the sixteenth century to the three-rank firing lines of the eighteenth, and from imitating the veterans to the systematic training methods characteristic of all effective armies by the time of the coming of the French Revolution. Chapter Four deals with command and leadership: the emergence of the professional officer, who might not always be a nobleman but who could usually act competently under stress in a wide variety of situations. Chapter Five considers morale and motivation, demonstrating that both were as necessary in early modern armies as at any time in history and analyzing how they were generated and sustained.

Chapter Six steps behind the curtains to take a look at daily routines: life in camp and on the march; issues of health and discipline; religious considerations; and relations with a civilian world from which soldiers felt increasingly alienated. Chapter Seven follows Europe's soldiers overseas as they confront enemies and environments entirely alien to any previous experience.

Like its counterparts in the Soldiers' Lives through History series, the book includes a timeline following the introduction as an aid to structuring the events and dates presented in the main text. A selected, topically arranged bibliography of 160 books, articles, and Web sites presents the best resources for those wanting more information on soldiers of the early modern era. A comprehensive general index concludes the volume.

✳ ✳ ✳

TIMELINE

c. 1300	Knowledge of gunpowder comes to Europe via China
c. 1450	Development of Gutenberg printing press makes rebirth of Classical knowledge permanent
1453	Ottoman Turks capture Constantinople using cannons
1482	Leonardo da Vinci joins the court of Lodovico Sforza
1492	First voyage of Columbus to the New World
1492	Ferdinand and Isabella unify Spain and expel Moors and Jews
1494	Charles VIII leads a trans-Alpine invasion of Italy with cannons; Italian Wars end in 1559
1494	Treaty of Tordesillas; Pope divides the New World between Spain and Portugal
1517	Martin Luther posts Ninety-five Theses to start the Protestant Reformation
1519	Charles V becomes Holy Roman Emperor; abdicates in 1556
c. 1520	Construction of *trace italienne* fortresses; persists into eighteenth century
1521	Machiavelli publishes *The Art of War*

1521	Cortés conquers Aztec Empire
1524–1525	Peasants' Revolt in Germany
1525	Battle of Pavia; Habsburgs gain control of Milan and capture Francis I, King of France
1526	Battle of Mohács; Suleiman the Magnificent and the Ottoman Empire conquer Hungary and besiege Vienna in 1529
1527	Sack of Rome by Imperial Habsburg forces
1532	Pizarro conquers the Inca Empire
1533–1534	Henry VIII breaks with the papacy and creates the Protestant Church of England
c. 1543–1687	Copernicus publishes the sun-centered universe; Brahe, Kepler, Galileo, Descartes, and other natural philosophers produce the Scientific Revolution that culminates with Newton's three laws of motion and law of gravity in the 1680s
1545	Council of Trent and Catholic Counter-Reformation
1546–1547	Schmalkaldic War
1555	Peace of Augsburg; Charles V, Holy Roman Emperor, accepts practice of Protestantism
1556	Charles V splits Habsburg Empire between his brother Ferdinand I (Holy Roman Empire) and his son Philip II (Spain, Milan, Naples, Sicily, and overseas possessions)
1559	Treaty of Câteau-Cambrésis; French abandon claims to Italian territory
1562–1598	Religious wars within France
1567–1648	Eighty Years War; attempt by Spain to suppress Protestantism in Netherlands ultimately fails
1571	Naval battle of Lepanto curbs Turkish hegemony in the Mediterranean
1572	St. Bartholomew Massacre of French Huguenots (Protestants)
1576	"Spanish fury" and sack of Antwerp
1585	Maurice of Nassau becomes captain-general of Holland until his death in 1625
1588	Spanish Armada fails to invade England and overthrow Elizabeth I
1598	Edict of Nantes extends religious toleration to French Protestants
1605	Cervantes publishes *Don Quixote*
1618	Start of the Thirty Years War in central Europe

1620	Battle of the White Mountain, Bohemia, and Sack of Prague by Imperial forces
1624–1642	Cardinal Richelieu governs France
1625	Hugo Grotius writes *On the Law of War and Peace*
1630	Gustavus Adolphus of Sweden invades the Holy Roman Empire
1631	Battle of Breitenfeld; victory for Gustavus Adolphus over Catholic forces led by Tilly
1631	Rape of Magdeburg: 25,000 killed as Imperial soldiers sack the city
1632	Battle of Lützen; death of Gustavus Adolphus
1634	Assassination of Wallenstein by order of the Holy Roman Emperor
1634	Battle of Nördlingen; Imperial victory over the Swedes
1642–1661	Cardinal Mazarin controls France
1642–1648	English Civil Wars; Rise of Cromwell and execution of Charles I in 1649
1643	Battle of Rocroi; French victory over Spanish forces
1648	Treaty of Westphalia ends the Thirty Years War and inaugurates an age of so-called limited warfare
1648–1653	Fronde revolt in France
1651	Thomas Hobbes publishes *Leviathan*
1652–1674	Anglo-Dutch Wars
1660	Restoration of Charles II in England; end of Cromwell's New Model Army
1661	Louis XIV's rule begins; ends 1715
1667–1668	War of Devolution
1672–1679	Dutch War between France and the United Provinces
1683	Last siege of Vienna by the Ottoman Empire
1685	Revocation of Edict of Nantes by Louis XIV
c. 1685	Socket or ring bayonet replaces pike in early modern armies; fielding of English "Brown Bess" smoothbore flintlock musket, which remains the standard infantry arm in England until 1840
1688	Glorious Revolution in England; ascension of William and Mary
1688–1697	Nine Years War or War of the League of Augsburg (King William's War)

1700–1721	Great Northern War pits Charles XII of Sweden against Peter the Great of Russia
1701	Elector of Brandenburg becomes King of Prussia
1701–1713	War of Spanish Succession (Queen Anne's War)
1704	Battle of Blenheim; alliance led by Marlborough and Prince Eugène of Savoy stymies French-Bavarian Army
1707	Union of England and Scotland
1709	Battle of Malplaquet; 34,000 casualties illustrates high cost of symmetrical warfare
1709	Battle of Poltava; Russian victory over Charles XII of Sweden
1713	Peace of Utrecht marks the end of Louis XIV's attempt to dominate western Europe
1713	Pragmatic Sanction; Maria Theresa recognized as legitimate Habsburg successor
1715	Death of Louis XIV of France
1733–1735	War of Polish Succession
c. 1740–1789	Age of Voltaire and the Enlightenment
1740–1786	Rule of Frederick the Great of Prussia
1740–1748	War of Austrian Succession; ended by the Treaty of Aix-la-Chapelle and award of Silesia to Prussia
1745	Battle of Fontenoy; Maurice de Saxe (French) defeats William, Duke of Cumberland
1746	Battle of Culloden ends Jacobite threat against Great Britain
1757–1763	Seven Years War (French and Indian War); arguably the first global war
1757	Battles of Leuthen and Rossbach; victories for Frederick the Great over Austria and France
1758	Battle of Zorndorf; Frederick blocks Russian invasion of Brandenburg
1772	First partition of Poland by Austria, Prussia, and Russia
1775–1783	American Revolutionary War
1777	Battle of Saratoga; French recognize American independence
1781	Battle of Yorktown marks the end of Britain's attempt to suppress the American revolt
1789–1794	French Revolution inaugurates *Levée en Masse* and age of nationalistic armies

PROLOGUE: EARLY MODERN WARFARE IN PRACTICE

Countless bands of mercenary warriors, militias, and standing armies trod the soil of Europe during the early modern period. From French soldiers and mercenaries crossing the Italian Alps bent on conquest in 1494 to British regulars crossing the Atlantic to deal with rebellious subjects in the American colonies in the 1770s, a complex and highly variegated spectrum of conflict characterized these three centuries. A thematic approach to warfare, as this book adopts, can help us to distinguish the brightest and most distinctive colors within this spectrum. But an equally revealing approach is to focus on individual battles, complex as they are, to isolate and resolve the various intensities and frequencies of conflict and the ways in which they intermixed with larger societal contexts. Using a different metaphor, if one imagines early warfare and society encompassed within a cathedral, its stained glass windows and altar would commemorate major battles and leaders. From the many thousands of glorious and harrowing scenes captured in our hypothetical cathedral of conflict we have chosen a triptych of battles as representative. Limited though they may be, the scenes these battles provide serve to illuminate the many subtle colorations of soldiers' lives. Let us now direct our attention forward, both in wonder and horror, as early modern soldiers come to blows on our triptych of battles.

PAVIA (1525): WARFARE IN THE AGE OF MERCENARIES AND GUNPOWDER

The battle of Pavia is the first panel in our triptych, featuring dynasties in conflict, mercenaries enveloped in smoke and adapting to battlefields swept by musket fire and charging pike masses, and even the capture of a king. It came on February 24–25, 1525, the climax of a three-decade war that began when Charles VIII of France sent his state-of-the-art army across the Italian Alps to confirm in arms his inherited claim to the Kingdom of Naples. Naples was, at the time, the largest of Italy's states and a promising base for the renewed crusade against the Muslim Ottoman Empire that was Charles's dream. But Naples lay inconveniently far from France. The Italian states proved inconveniently stubborn opponents. And France's difficulty—or, more accurately put, its refusal to cut its losses in the Italian quagmire—provided opportunity for other enemies. The Spanish Habsburgs and their cousins within the Holy Roman Empire had their own dynastic claims, no less ephemeral than those of France. Years of bitter seesaw fighting left Spain in control of Naples, but spillover effects from the fighting resulted in diminished economies, new forms of government, and changed political outlooks that left Italian states demoralized and depleted.

The Habsburg Charles V became King of Spain in 1516. Three years later, he inherited the Imperial crown of the Holy Roman Empire (centered on modern-day Germany) as well. This unification of realms fundamentally altered both Europe's balance of power and its strategic profile. France now faced the near-certainty of invasion across both the Rhine and the Pyrenees—to say nothing of the potential damage that might be wrought by Charles's then ally, England's King Henry VIII.

Yet Charles was cautious. Even with his enhanced power, his preferred option was to move into northern Italy, dominated by the Duchy of Milan. But that region had been a sphere of French interest and a glacis protecting the French south for over twenty years. For Francis I, barely twenty-one when crowned King of France in 1515, steeped in Renaissance ideas of glory and *virtù*, the decision was obvious—particularly when he was challenged in 1523–1524 by a revolt led by the Duke of Bourbon but supported by Charles V and Henry VIII and highlighted by an invasion of Provence: the first invasion of France from Italy in centuries.

For Francis, taking the fight to the enemy seemed preferable to awaiting another trumped-up rebellion, or perhaps an assassin's knife—especially since France's position in northern Italy was not as secure as it had once been. In 1515, Francis had defeated at Marignano a Swiss mercenary army more or less holding Milan hostage, in the process destroying the reputation for invincibility Swiss pikemen had enjoyed for decades. But the very scope of his victory mobilized Italian opposition. Seven years later, at Bicocca, another place lost to history until drenched in blood, a combined Italian, Spanish, and Imperial army nearly annihilated a French force built around Swiss mercenaries.

Theater conditions as well as grand strategy impelled Francis to try again, and in October 1524, he led an army of 33,000 across the Alps. It was twice the size of the forces available to his immediate opponents. It was also a first-class fighting force: Swiss mercenaries determined to prove that Marignano and Bicocca had been accidents served with (though not alongside) a regiment of German *Landsknechte* no less determined to prove that there was a new master of the battlefield. Both Swiss and *Landsknechte*, on whichever side they fought, depended on the shock effect of massed sixteen-foot pikes. Their ranks, however, included an increasing number of men armed with the shoulder-firing arquebus. This low-velocity matchlock weapon was the first firearm of its kind to allow for rudimentary aiming, accomplished by placing its stock to the shoulder or chest and sighting down the barrel. Faster to load than the crossbow, and with a smashing power important in an age when plate armor was common, the arquebus became correspondingly popular among first Spanish, then French and Italian foot soldiers. Like their Imperialist counterparts, the French companies that Francis took south contained various mixtures of arquebuses and pikes. But where for the Germans and the Swiss, gunpowder weapons supported the pike charge, in the southern European companies, pikes protected firearms.

During the campaign, Francis also secured the services of some of Italy's most renowned contract fighters, the arquebusiers of the "Black Bands," whose charismatic leader, Giovanni de Medici, changed sides as a result of a pay dispute. The heart of the cavalry, however, was French: the plate-armored, lance-armed gendarmerie who had overthrown the Swiss at Marignano and who were confident they could repeat the performance against any enemy willing to stand in place. The artillery train, as by now was the norm for a French army, was state of the art in technology and effectiveness.

Higher organization on both sides was rudimentary. The basic unit was the company, whose strength might vary from 500 men for the Swiss or *Landsknechte* to fewer than 100 in other armies. The Swiss and *Landsknechte* combined their mercenary companies into regiments, whose strength again varied from 3,000 to as many as 8,000 or 10,000. Elsewhere, companies were grouped—and as we shall see, regrouped—ad hoc, a system rendering command and control problematic in any complex tactical situation.

The Imperial commander, Charles de Lannoy, Viceroy of Naples, was of Spanish origin and generally regarded as better in the council chamber than on the field of battle. He had received his appointment, indeed, because Charles V believed him more able than anyone else to keep the duchy's complex and conflicting factions in some kind of order. Lannoy had done well at this and in the face of superior force was able to execute the conventional textbook counter of abandoning Milan to the French and falling back on the smaller, better-fortified city of Pavia, leaving a garrison there and using the rest of his troops as the nucleus of a relief force. His decision was facilitated by a serious outbreak of plague in Milan, unrelated to any military operations. With the civilian population dying in the hundreds, Lannoy nevertheless feared the consequences of exposing his troops—but by retreating, he hoped, perhaps, to leave a parting gift for Francis should the king's well-known vanity impel him to stage some kind of triumphal parade through Milan's diseased streets.

In the skirmishing and small-scale fighting that characterized the campaign's opening weeks the French proved sufficiently superior that some of the king's advisors recommended catching up with Lannoy and seeking a decision in the open field. Francis, however, was content. Milan had sent for and accepted a French garrison. The weather had been north-Italian bad: high winds, heavy rain, and unexpected cold. The men were tired—a usual condition of improvised armies at the beginning of a campaign. Besieging Pavia seemed the step that promised the most gains for the smallest uncompensated risk. On October 28, 1524, the leading French units appeared before the city. The artillery train arrived on the night of October 31, as the French tightened their investment—a process delayed by continued heavy rain.

Besieging Pavia

Pavia was not a nut to be easily cracked. The now-flooded Ticino River secured the city to the south. Other approaches were protected by a network of walls and redoubts, which, if not up to the new standards of the *trace italienne* fortifications (discussed further in Chapter Three), were sufficiently state of the art to requite carelessness painfully. The Spanish garrison commander, a veteran of the Italian wars, Don Antonio de Leyva, had about 9,000 men, most of them Spanish and German mercenaries, whose initial loyalty he secured by confiscating the church plate and melting it down for the most worldly of all purposes (save perhaps one)—paying the troops. There was food enough for a long siege, and De Leyva could be expected to hold his battle-hardened men together for a long time.

At this point, if not earlier, Francis's judgment was clearly strained by his perception of the opportunities. The French gunners opened two of what would later be called "practicable breaches," and on November 12, 1524, the king sent his infantry forward. They encountered a network of improvised earthworks defended by small arms that turned the terrain beyond the breaches into killing grounds. The next French effort deserved more success. It involved an elaborate attempt to divert the Ticino by damming the river upstream. The skill of the French engineers and the energy of their laborers were, however, undone by increasingly heavy rains that washed away the barrier while it was still under construction.

The king's advisors recommended that he return to France rather than risk his reputation in a situation he could not influence directly. Instead, Francis detached a force of 6,000 men and sent them south to threaten Naples. At worst he hoped to divert Imperial troops from concentrating against his siege lines. In fact, an unexpectedly quick sequence of responses, plus the onset of winter proper, with heavy snow and freezing cold, led to an operational stalemate.

Diplomatically, the best Francis was able to achieve was a treaty, in which the pope agreed not to assist Charles V and to encourage other Italian states to hold back as well. The value of that document, based on ample past experience, depended on the fall of Pavia. And despite a series of optimistic prognostications from the French camp, the city's walls stood, and its garrison held. On the other side of the line the usual run of camp diseases—typhus, diarrhea, pneumonia—reinforced by the newcomer syphilis, took heavier tolls as the winter worsened. Well might De Leyva have reflected, "If Francis has me, then I also have him."

Meanwhile, Lannoy was evaluating his options and accepting reinforcements— initially cash, but all the more welcome for that. Niccolò Machiavelli's familiar contemporary aphorism that gold will not always provide good soldiers, but good soldiers will always provide gold was reversed in the winter of 1524. As Austrian bankers made funds available to Imperial recruiters, veterans took notice. Georg von Frundsberg was a legend among the German *Landsknechte*. His name and the emperor' money started 15,000 of them on the roads to Italy with the waning of winter. Add a few hundred men at arms signed on from throughout the Low Countries, a few cannon from the Imperial arsenals, wagon trains of ammunition, and more chests of hard coin, and Lannoy's once vestigial army took a new lease on life.

Imperial forces had two possibilities. One was to raise the siege of Pavia by maneuver, striking at Francis's outlying forces, eroding his operational position to a point where withdrawal was his best option, or the Imperialists could march directly on Pavia and force a fight—fresh troops against an enemy weakened numerically and physically by a winter in the open. By contemporary standards, Pavia's garrison had made a determined, even a spirited resistance. Appearing to write it off now risked damaging the morale of soldiers who might have fought for pay but who also expected a fighting chance from their commanders.

The foundation of the forthcoming battle was laid on January 24, 1525, when the Imperial army, by now almost 40,000 strong, marched on Castello de San Angelo. Twenty-five miles from Pavia but only eleven from Lodi, it had served throughout the siege as a sixteenth-century early warning system for Francis. Its defenses were not formidable; its garrison of 2,800 men was little more than a trip wire readily cut, had the Imperialists been willing to pay the price. Now, with the ground frozen hard enough for Imperial forces to bring up heavy guns, the commandant and his Italian mercenaries, staring defeat in the face, surrendered after a token resistance. Even by the standards of later and fiercer wars, the decision was not a pusillanimous one. At odds of over ten to one, few of the Italians would have survived an assault, apart from the *Landsknechte* reputation for giving no quarter to garrisons that resisted. As matters stood, they gave their paroles and went home, honor and life alike spared for another day.

Lannoy and the main Imperial army nevertheless advanced cautiously. Thirty years of experience in the Italian Wars indicated that the best option was to lure Francis into abandoning the siege in favor of seeking battle. Francis and his generals were not to be drawn. Mutual feints accomplished nothing of substance as the Imperials reached the town of Pescara, only four and a half miles from Pavia, on February 2, 1525. They announced their presence by firing artillery salvos—as helpful for De Leyva as it was disconcerting to the French. The garrison's pay was in arrears, and artillery ammunition was running low—not a good combination. In contrast, however, to the doctrines and practices of later centuries, the Imperialists did not seek to lift the siege immediately by breaking through the French siege lines. Instead, they deployed around the city, sending only a small detachment of cavalry into the city with supplies and orders—and as tangible proof that help had arrived.

The French responded by establishing a defensive system beginning with isolated works, some already existing to keep Pavia's garrison hemmed in, then connecting them with entrenchment and barricades. These outward-facing lines of contravallation would eventually become as standard in siege operations as the inward-focused lines of circumvallation. In 1525, they were sufficiently unfamiliar that they have since frequently been described as virtually invincible. That was a significant overstatement. Nevertheless, the main defensive sector in particular, with its south end resting on a Ticino impassable in winter and its north on a strongly garrisoned and fortified hunting palace, the Park of Mirabello, was the kind of barrier that would take a good deal of high-risk, high-casualty storming—a prospect that did not bring joy within Imperial ranks.

The French king's behavior thus far was sufficiently out of character to be disconcerting. Francis had a well-developed image as a man of action, seeking to force the pace to his advantage. Nothing suggested that he was willing to be pinned against a second-class Italian city for months while waiting for something to turn up. In a military context Francis could expect no relief from outside, no significant reinforcement from across the Alps. The army he commanded was France's only field force. Its other troops were held in place by the strategic situation that had impelled the strike into Italy in the first place. And when his campaign of shock and awe did not produce quick, decisive results, Francis's store of ideas was empty.

It has been suggested that Francis had contracted syphilis as early as 1524, and the first manifestation of this disease certainly might have distracted him as well. A more tangible explanation for the king's decision to hold his ground was economic. Imperial forces were suffering too. Lannoy's troops were well in arrears of their pay, and the conditions prevailing in their lines offered little incentive to await its arrival. The Imperialists faced all the hardships of a siege with none of the usually expected rewards. Their very closeness to the enemy bred frustration: In some places, only 100 feet of mud and water separated Imperial lines from their French counterparts. Despite Frundsberg's best efforts, combining inspiring speeches with increasing use of the gauntlet and the gallows, the *Landsknecht* companies in Imperial service were leaking men steadily. There was, moreover, a limit to which coercive discipline could be applied in a sixteenth-century army. The *Landsknechte* and their comrades saw themselves as free men under contract. Push them too hard, and the result could be mutiny—with a corresponding opportunity for the French to sally forth and scatter their demoralized opponents all over northern Italy.

The Imperialists understood that and knew they were working against time. They brought up and dug in their artillery, opening a heavy fire on what seemed a few vulnerable points in the enemy defenses. French guns replied, and the artillery duel became such a regular feature of the siege that senior officers of both armies took to dropping by and watching the show. Francis himself was knocked down, but uninjured, by the shock wave from a heavy cannonball. The Imperialists mounted a series of raids as well, complemented by sorties from the garrison. Designed, like the artillery bombardments, to develop weak spots, their results were frustratingly limited.

Like their successors during the Great War of 1914–1918, these small-scale actions did little but create in senior officers an illusion of progress. Halfway through February, the illusion became unsustainable. The weather was still bad, with snow and rain slashing through improvised shelters. Casualties and desertion were reaching a point of synergy, with one automatically encouraging the other. To complete the crisis, De Leyva reported that with token sums and extensive promises, he could keep his unpaid men on station for no longer than a few more days.

This fiscal crisis provoked Lannoy to summon, on February 21, 1525, a council of war. In later centuries this would be taken as prima facie evidence of weak command. But in the sixteenth century a council was just that: a tapping of the collective wisdom of senior officers at a time when the craft of war was changing too rapidly to give anyone a monopoly on insight. Lannoy set the terms of discussion. Three or four days at most remained to restore more than temporary contact with the garrison of Pavia. Retreat was a high-risk option militarily, to say nothing of its wider political implications. On the other hand, the French positions were too strong, and too well manned, to make all-out attack feasible. The collective decision was therefore to mount a raid into the park and capture Mirabello Castle, its central feature and Francis's reputed headquarters. While the French were recovering from the shock, Lannoy would bring food, ammunition, and what cash he could spare into the park. At the same time Pavia's garrison would launch a sortie, make contact, and escort the supplies back into the city. By the normal standards of early-sixteenth-century operations, that should be enough to convince Francis that the garrison was relieved and to abandon the siege.[1]

Two external factors also influenced the plan's adoption. On February 17, Giovanni de Medici was wounded during a sortie. When he left the army, so did about two-thirds of his men. Many of the Black Bands had been unenthusiastic about the French connection; with Giovanni removed from the scene they saw no reason to remain. Far more seriously, the Swiss were beginning to pull out as well: not because of any arrears of pay—Francis had, by this time, fully absorbed the lesson of the aphorism *point d'argent, point des Suisses*, or "no money, no Swiss"—but to protect their homes against increasing pressure from Imperialist raids. That was the official reason, at least, for the contingent from the Grisons. Old-timers in the Swiss ranks were beginning to see too many signs of an operation going south. Francis eloquently appealed to their contract and their honor. When they stopped laughing, 6,000 Swiss broke camp on February 20, accompanied by the hearty best wishes of the Imperialists.

Early modern armies seldom kept good records, and by this time, strength figures on both sides are at best reasonable estimates. Francis had about 7,000 Swiss, 4,500 *Landsknechte*, who had remained in good part to show up their professional rivals, and 6,000 or so French and Italian infantry. The 2,000 French and Italian light cavalry did not promise to be of much use in a close-quarters fight. The same, however, could not be said for the heavy horse: somewhere around 1,000 lances. A lance at this stage was a small combat team: one fully armored gendarme, two archers wearing lighter armor but still considered heavy cavalry, a light horseman, whose job was general support, and a servant or two. These last were often experienced fighters who could be very useful bringing up fresh horses and water, securing prisoners, or finishing off wounded. After a hard winter, the lances may have counted 6,000 men at maximum and probably a good many less.

The Imperialists outside the city could muster about 18,000 infantry—3,000 Italians and 5,000 Spanish, a little less than half the total armed with arquebuses, and 15,000 *Landsknechte*. Fifteen hundred Spanish and Italian light cavalry and 800 lances of heavy cavalry on the French mode, probably also under the standard strength of a half-dozen each, completed the muster. De Leyva's garrison by this time could produce about 3,000 Spanish infantry and 5,000 *Landsknechte*, plus 1,000 or so Pavian militia who would do well enough behind walls, and a handful of cavalry whose horses had not yet been eaten during the siege.

Speed, not mass, was the key to success in an attack like this. First of all that meant opening sizeable breaches in the park wall. The development of the *trace italienne* had given military engineering an importance it had not enjoyed since the Roman Empire, and the Spanish army stood in the forefront of the new dispensation. Beginning on February 21, 1525, Lannoy had been sending small patrols, a half-dozen or so engineers, over the north wall to decide the best location for a breach. On February 22, one of these reached the south end of the wood but ran into a French patrol, losing four of its seven men in a confused brawl in the darkness. For security reasons Lannoy ended the scouting. But the engineers were able to report that French security was generally lax. They correspondingly recommended opening a number of small breaches near the northeast gate, the Porte Pescarina. Elements of the strike force could then open the gate itself and secure reasonably free passage for the main body. By the time the French reacted the Imperialists would be at Mirabello, awaiting the arrival of the sortie by the Pavian garrison.

As will be seen, the raid and its direct covering forces absorbed most of Lannoy's effective troops. The Imperial forces that remained were ordered to keep the camp fires burning and to attract French attention with small arms and artillery fire. A bit before dawn, the guns would stop; then three shots in succession would give De Leyva the signal to begin his sortie. His orders were simple and direct: break into the park, link up with the relief force, and hold a corridor while it entered Pavia with its supplies. At that, the mission was no bagatelle. Undertaken at night in broken country, it illustrates on a minor scale the level of effectiveness a mercenary army could be expected to demonstrate when necessary.

The Raid and the Battle

Around 10:00 p.m., the main Imperial force began its march to the Porte Pescarina. Along with the usual injunctions for silence and against smoking, the men were ordered to wear their shirts over their armor as a means of identification in the dark. This camisado was another indication that Lannoy was not planning a fight to the finish, but rather a rapid strike and relief. About the same time, the Imperial engineers began work on their breaches. They encountered unexpected difficulty. The wall at that point was not defended, but it was fifteen-foot-high, solid brickwork that did not yield easily to force or skill. Hand tools dulled and broke. Artillery or gunpowder would be faster, but the explosions were sure to alarm the French. Lannoy detailed infantry to assist, and with 2,000 men at work the process of leveling the wall continued.

That many men could not work quietly indefinitely. Around 4:00 a.m. on February 25, French patrols brought news of continuous, unfamiliar noises in the park's northeast sector. The sector commander, who had spent the night on alert against the Imperial artillery feint, now informed Francis of the report, faced most of his guns north, and marched 3,000 Swiss pikemen to the sound of the rams and hammers. By now it was after 5:00 a.m.—again, not bad reaction time for a French army whose internal articulation was still relatively undeveloped. A few minutes earlier, however, Imperial engineers had lowered the wall enough for the strike force to climb over and through. It consisted of around 3,000 man, all arquebusiers. For the sake of speed, there were no wagons or pack animals. Instead, the men themselves carried extra ammunition, supplies, and money. The constitution of this force further supports the hypothesis that Lannoy's relief operation was simply that: a gesture to show Francis that his siege ultimately would fail. Three thousand men equipped for battle could hardly bring in on their persons enough resources to sustain a 9,000- or 10,000-man garrison for any length of time.

The raiders were drawn from throughout the army, a mixed bag of Germans, Spanish, and Italians, partly as a recognition of ethnic pride and partly because assembling task forces of specialists for desperate enterprises was already becoming a Spanish trademark. Meanwhile, engineers opened the main gates for the passage of the covering force: a battery of artillery, in case Mirabello proved tougher to overrun than expected, supported by a body of Spanish and Italian light cavalry that deployed and advanced south to cover the open flank. Around dawn—a relative term since darkness gave way to a thick mist—this Imperial force encountered its French counterpart. With visibility at less than 100 yards the rival horsemen grappled confusedly while the Imperial arquebusiers managed to sidestep the French Swiss coming up to support their cavalry. With no idea what lay to their front, or indeed exactly where they were going, the Swiss ran into, and promptly overran, the Imperial guns advancing in column down the road.

Taken completely by surprise, Francis sent a senior officer, Admiral William de Bonnivet ("Admiral" was a court title, with no connection to the sea), forward with an escort of gendarmes to find out what was happening. He managed to get the Swiss infantry moving to the sound of the cavalry fight, arriving on the scene just as the Imperialist horsemen took the worst of it, broke, and fled. Bonnivet, returning command to the officers on the spot, rode back to inform Francis that another raid had been repulsed. Bonnivet was one of his closest friends, and the king saw no reason to question him in detail.

By now it was a bit after 6:00 A.M. The Imperial guns fired their three-round salvo to launch the sortie from Pavia, after which they resumed bombarding the French lines near the city. The local commander, expecting an Imperial attack as the mist lifted, stood his men to arms and sent an alarm to the king. Thus to the extent Francis and his senior officer expected any further action that day, they were looking in the wrong direction when De Leyva's men from Pavia broke out to the northeast, cut their way into the park, and set up a defensive perimeter, while sending patrols north to determine the position of the Imperial strike force they were supposed to meet. In an era when communications ranged from poor to nonexistent, De Leyva once again was following accepted procedure. His men were well placed to advance quickly, and should something have gone drastically wrong on the other side of the attack, they could retreat back to Pavia with minimal damage.

Meanwhile, the mixed bag of Imperial arquebusiers had made its way through the woods and, at about 6:30 A.M., stormed Mirabello, taking its few defenders entirely by surprise. An added bonus was that Mirabello was the location of the French baggage train: the assemblage of whores, peddlers, gamblers, and hangers-on that accompanied every sixteenth-century army. Some were cut down, partly from blood lust and partly for the crime of being in the way. The rest fled south toward Pavia, spreading panic in their wake.

The Imperial commander seemed to have a better than average grip on his troops. Straggling and looting remained at an acceptable minimum—a Papal legate was one of the collective prizes of war—as the strike force began its march south to rendezvous with De Leyva's sortie. Boggy ground and the French artillery, firing almost at random into the mist, slowed their pace—it might be said as well that an ad hoc force like this was not the best instrument for charging hidden batteries across swamps. But Imperialist reinforcements continued to advance through the breached wall and the open gate into the park, with the *Landsknechte*, Lannoy's best shock troops, leading the way. One column of about 8,000 deployed and moved straight ahead until it encountered Francis's Swiss mercenaries, who had been inactive since helping to scatter the Imperialist light cavalry earlier that morning.

Historically, when Swiss and *Landsknechte* met, blood flowed thickly. The Swiss Confederates, with a well-earned reputation for ferocity to sustain, took it personally that outlanders sought to use their national weapon, the pike, against them. The Germans were no less proud and quickly learned that against the Swiss, quarter would be neither asked nor given: It was kill or be killed. This time proved an exception, as both forces avoided a death grapple. Each was demoralized from the previous circumstances of the campaign. The Swiss had lost many veterans at Bicocca and entertained a certain sense of having been left in the lurch by their homeward-bound kinsmen. The two forces engaged, but at something closer to arm's length than push of pike. The Swiss were slowly forced back by weight of numbers, but even the revered Frundsberg was unable to get the *Landsknechte* to put it all into one big rush.

The second Imperial column, about 4,000 *Landsknechte* and an equal number of Spaniards, with another 2,000 cavalry of various types, advanced toward Mirabello, ready to support either the strike force or the *Landsknechte*, as required. Lannoy was with them, leading the cavalry in person—it was not uncommon for an army commander to take direct command of a subordinate unit in an age when he was expected to demonstrate *virtù* as well as insight.

By now, and unintentionally, the Imperialists were on the way to driving a wedge into the middle of the French army. Its main body, insofar as one existed, was on the Imperial left, where Francis had about 3,000 heavy cavalry, 4,000 *Landsknechte*, the elite Black Bands, and 2,000 French infantry, Gascons generally considered the best of the French foot. On the right, across the park and closer to the city, about 4,000 more were held in check by De Leyva's sortie. A final 5,000 or so, deployed around Pavia's southern boundary, were, for all practical purposes, out of play. Called in some accounts the rear guard, they were in fact designated the "Rearward Battle," after the medieval custom, but fully available for action. Their commander, Duke Charles of Alençon, was simply content to watch the action unfold before him, as opposed to participating—a decision that later earned him the opprobrium of his countrymen.

The French situation as yet, however, was neither hopeless nor indeed even desperate. It improved substantially when the mist lifted just enough to show the column of *Landsknechte* and Spaniards advancing toward Mirabello. The French had a battery of about a dozen cannon in position at the northern gate into the park, the Porta Repentitia, reinforced by another four-gun battery that had accompanied the Swiss into the park at the beginning of the action, gone into position, and stayed there because of the saturated ground. French accounts claim that these guns tore the Imperial column to pieces. But the Imperialists appear to have shrugged off the damage. Sixteenth-century artillery technology was insufficiently developed to guarantee debilitating casualties against a target that was able to increase its pace and open its files. But the five or six hundred casualties suggested as the maximum in most modern sources were no small number, and it seems reasonable that the moral effect of the unexpected cross fire left the Imperialists more shaken than their chroniclers and commanders wished to admit—shaken enough, perhaps, to be vulnerable to another weapon available to the French king: a charge by heavy cavalry.

Contemporary authorities state that it took about thirty minutes for a man to don full armor. Add a few minutes for the effects of tension, and a few minutes more to establish formation, and the time was just about right for the gendarmerie to move from their camps into position facing the Imperialist columns. The French practice was to charge in a single line, three or four ranks deep, the gendarmerie in front, followed by the lightly armored men of the lance. While the gendarmes, and most of their followers, were noblemen, they were also a far cry from the ill-disciplined local levies the English had repeatedly butchered during the Hundred Years War. As a class, they had learned from experience, and three decades of campaigning in Italy had created something of a generational effect. The gendarmerie could keep in line, accelerate their pace gradually, and strike like the wrath of God—the kind of shock whose impact seemed preferable to the more measured tactics being developed in Germany, with squadron following squadron in so-called deep order. At Marignano the French heavy cavalry had shown endurance as well as a willingness to sacrifice, pinning the Swiss in the open by repeated charges, whose high casualties were more than requited by the devastating effect of French guns on the massed pikemen.

Francis, then, was not harkening back to lost feudal glories when he unleashed his armored horsemen to decide the day. They struck the Imperial cavalry under Lannoy: 500 Spanish light horse and about 1,600 heavy, generally and legitimately considered less well armored and mounted than their French counterparts. Lannoy, initially taken by surprise, brought his men into line and met the French charge with his own. In something like five minutes the Spanish cavalry was broken, scattering into the adjoining woods. The French pursued about six hundred yards, then rallied as Francis, flushed with his triumph, reportedly declared, "Now I am truly the Duke of Milan!"

He spoke too soon. In charging the enemy Francis had masked his own guns, which had been firing on the Imperial Spanish and German infantry. As the guns fell silent, Imperial forces regained their integrity and fighting spirit. Lannoy was caught up in the rout of his cavalry, but his infantry commander, Fernando D'Avolos, Marquis of Pescara, was a seasoned veteran who knew an opportunity when he saw one. Sending in all directions for support, he ordered his infantry forward to the edge of the woods, where his arquebusiers, covered by pikemen, opened a steady fire on the French cavalry. The broken, boggy ground made this a small-unit battle, placing the French horse at a severe disadvantage as they were useless in dismounted fighting and accustomed to having substantial targets for their charges. On the other hand, Imperialist control dissolved as powder smoke covered the field and detachments took advantage of particular terrain—even a fallen tree or two could help. In case of defeat, there would be no orderly Imperialist withdrawal in this sector: It was win or die.

The first response came from Frundsberg. As the Swiss continued to fall back in front of him, he led half his men west to Pescara's support. About the same time, the duc de Bourbon, who had been doing an outstanding and overlooked job of coordinating the movement of troops and guns through the Porta Pescarina, sent another

The brutal nature of close combat. Detail of a large tapestry illustrating the Battle of Pavia in 1525. By Barent (Bernard) van Orley. © Erich Lessing/Art Resource, New York.

4,000 *Landsknechte* and a few hundred cavalry south on the same mission. While the terrain was difficult, the combat zone was too small to allow for serious errors of navigation by that stage of the fighting. By 8:00 A.M. the French gendarmes were absorbing withering fire on the right from Pescara's men, in the center from Bourbon's reinforcements, and on the right from Frundsberg's *Landsknechte*, with the recalled strike force moving to the French right rear.

The gendarmes mounted charge after charge in an effort to clear their front, but lances could not easily reach into the hedges and small woods where the arquebusiers were taking cover. At short, almost point-blank ranges the plate armor worn by the French heavy cavalry offered little protection against the large-caliber balls fired by the shoulder arms. Even plates that did not break could splinter, tearing into a man's body the way World War II antitank guns tore into the soft-skinned interiors of armored vehicles. At Pavia, for the first time in the history of warfare, gunpowder shoulder arms achieved critical mass. There were enough of them in a small space to maintain a steady and heavy fire. French cavalry were knocked from saddles by the shock of bullets. Others were set afoot when their horses were shot. Arquebusiers took high risks to dart from cover and finish these unfortunates— less, it seems, for the purses they might be carrying, and less even for reasons of class hatred than from professional memory. Few veterans of the Italian Wars had not heard stories of the fate of foot soldiers overrun by cavalry, and payback tasted no less sweet when served cold.

The governing nobility of France died in its tracks that day. But it did not go down easily, and it did not stand alone. Before launching his initial charge, Francis had summoned the *Landsknechte* in his pay, the Black Bands. They joined the fighting at the double and made for the most obvious enemy: their counterparts in Imperial service. They hit Bourbon's Germans, forcing them back at push of pike by sheer élan. Then Frundsberg struck their flank. Just as Swiss never fought Swiss, *Landsknechte* as a rule preferred to avoid each other in battle. Should that be impossible, the usual result was a fight to the death. Future contracts, bragging rights, and sheer testosterone set the pace in what the *Landsknechte* themselves called "bad war." Pavia was as bad as it got. The Black Bands fought to a finish. Their blood well up, the *Landsknechte* then turned against what remained of the French gendarmerie.

Any hope of a less disastrous outcome ended as the Swiss in French employ continued to fall back against even the reduced number of *Landsknechte* in front of them. After the battle, Francis's Swiss units were scapegoated by both sides. Some sources have them collapsing in panic and their commander falling into Imperial hands. An overlooked factor in their discomfiture was the work of the Imperial strike force, which turned around and reached the field in time for their arquebus fire to demoralize further men who had done all they were willing to do that day.

In the south the Pavian garrison was mopping up its immediate opponents: Swiss pikemen who finally cracked when their compatriots from the fighting in the park reached them. A mass of men, as many as 6,000, fled toward the Ticino River. About half made it across; the rest drowned in bitterly cold water or were cut down by pursuing Imperialists. Alençon, who figured out something was seriously wrong just as it grew too late for him to do anything about it, restored what order he could, abandoned the siege and its works, and fell back toward Milan.

In the park Frundsberg's *Landsknechte* scattered the last of the French infantry. But like the Imperial Guard under Napoleon at Waterloo nearly three centuries later, the French noblemen preferred to die rather than surrender under the eyes of their king. Die they did, by the dozen, as Francis himself became something like a hero, fighting with courage and skill that attracted general admiration. Slightly wounded, his horse killed from under him, he stood surrounded by Spanish arquebusiers until Lannoy rescued him, by some accounts turning his sword against his own men in the process.

By 9:00 A.M. it was all over. French soldiers not already on their way to Milan were heaped in the park, or sat under armed guard, or were scattered any place a badly hurt man can crawl before he dies. The 10,000 casualties included numbers of noblemen comparable only to that lost at Agincourt a century earlier. The bodies of the great and near-great were sold for return home—a postmortem form of ransom. Living nobles unable to pay were paroled on the recommendation of the duc de Bourbon, who still retained his political ambitions. Francis, his wounds dressed, passed into Imperial captivity after informing his mother that "all is lost to me save honor and life." In Madrid he would sign a treaty of peace the next year, which he denounced as soon as he was released.

Lessons Learned at Pavia

The Imperialists are frequently criticized for failing to follow up their victory at Pavia with a full-scale diplomatic offensive. In that context it might be said that when a battle is as unplanned as the victory is unexpected, effective exploitation cannot be expected. It is also true that the Italian states were not interested in exchanging a French ruler for an Imperial one. They were correspondingly quick to open negotiations with Francis when he was again safe in Paris. Issues like the Protestant Reformation and the Ottoman invasion of Hungary put Italy somewhat on Europe's back burner as well: a preliminary to the Wars of Empire described in Chapter One.

Tactically, Lannoy and his subordinates consistently read the confused situation just a bit better than Francis and his commanders and reacted more decisively. Otherwise, Pavia indicated the growing importance of shoulder-fired gunpowder weapons and the risks of employing large forces of heavy cavalry in a limited space. In the next few decades the proportion of heavy cavalry declined throughout Europe, while the arquebus and its successors became an essential part of the weapons mix of all infantry and most cavalry units. Pavia illuminates as well the qualities, good and bad, of the mercenary armies that dominated this period of history. It showed they were more resilient and reliable than is generally accepted, if their original conditions of employment were reasonably met. The general condemnation of the French Swiss in good part reflected the fact that their inglorious behavior, once combat was joined, was so unusual as to be exceptional.

Pavia marked as well the growing importance of infantry, whether Swiss pikemen, German *Landsknechte*, or Spanish foot. No one could ignore the high death toll the French gendarmerie had paid that morning. Pavia further marked the growing dominance of siege warfare as well as new techniques being developed both to defend fortresses and to invest and reduce them. And although at Pavia, France's defeat was nearly total, it was also temporary—indeed, Francis and Charles would renew their Valois-Habsburg dynastic rivalry in three more wars over the following two decades. Pavia's lessons were suggestive, but the battle itself was not decisive.

But this fact did not deter other monarchs of Europe from seeking decision by sowing the dragon's teeth, as we shall see as we turn our attention to the middle panel of our triptych.

BREITENFELD (1631): THE QUEST FOR DECISION

The middle panel of battle descriptions features one of the great captain-kings of the early modern period: Swedish king Gustavus Adolphus. When Gustavus chose to intervene in the war that had been raging in Germany since 1618, he knew he was entering a high-risk environment. The Catholic/Imperial cause was everywhere triumphant. Habsburg forces under the great mercenary captain, Count Albrecht von Wallenstein, and the army of the Catholic League, commanded by Count Johan Tilly, were watering their horses in the Baltic. Emperor Ferdinand II, in March 1629, had issued an Edict of Restitution, ordering the return to Catholic control of all church land secularized by Protestant rulers in the Holy Roman Empire since 1555. Protestant resentment and resistance were the natural result, with some looking to the north for, if not deliverance, at least military aid.

Battle Captains: Gustavus Adolphus and Johan Tilly

Intervention offered Protestant Sweden a chance to preempt the threat implied to its security and sphere of influence by establishing a forward position on Imperial ground.

In July 1630, Gustavus landed in Pomerania at the head of 14,000 men. It was a small force to challenge an empire. Nor was Gustavus universally welcomed as a savior by the Protestant princes and estates of northern Germany. Some local rulers hoped to maintain neutrality. Others, like the Electors of Brandenburg and Saxony, hoped to mobilize German Protestantism to defend itself—preferably by negotiations, rather than by fighting. The Swedish king's first breakthrough came from the independent city of Magdeburg, Protestant until Ferdinand's heavy-handed Edict of Restitution. In July its citizens revolted against Catholic rule and requested Swedish assistance.

Gustavus had nowhere near the deployable resources to support a major military effort on his own. He sought German support by calling for freedom of religious conscience and local liberties. But Protestant solidarity did not prevent him from finalizing, in January 1631, a treaty with Catholic France that provided an annual subsidy of 400,000 talers (with fear of Imperial Habsburg hegemony serving to open French purses). But the Protestant Elector of Brandenburg still refused to risk compromising his neutrality by allowing Swedish troops to enter his territory.

Ferdinand, suspicious of Wallenstein's growing power, turned command of the Imperial forces over to Tilly. Johan Tserclaes Tilly, like every other successful senior officer of this era, was a political soldier, familiar to his fingertips with the constantly changing relationships and allegiances of dozens of principalities. He knew that despite confessional sympathies, the north German Protestants were anything but firmly in Gustavus's camp. He knew that the Elector of Saxony was raising an army—but had also called a meeting of the Empire's Protestant Estates, with the avowed purpose of negotiating grievances with the Catholic emperor.

From Tilly's perspective the most promising scenario in early 1631 involved bringing his troops out of winter quarters and marching against Gustavus. Beaten in the field, the Swedish interloper might return whence he came. Should he remain, Germany's Protestant princes might well treat a defeated Gustavus the way the Italian cities had treated Hannibal in the Second Punic War: sympathize, cheer him on his way when he passed, but do nothing more.

Tilly first sought to smoke out his opponent by moving against one of his outlying positions. The fortifications for the town of Neu-Brandenburg were simple and antiquated. Tilly offered terms; the Swedish commander refused them. On March 19, 1631, Tilly's infantry took the small town by storm. The laws of war offered no mercy to a defeated garrison that forced its opponents to accept the risks and losses of an assault. Yet at Neu Brandenburg, as in so many similar situations, killing unresisting men did not prove as easy as it sounds. About one-third of the garrison of 750 men died fighting or were cut down afterward. The rest were taken prisoner—most of them probably finding their eventual way into one of Tilly's regiments.

The Swedish king responded by pulling together every man he could summon from every outpost and garrison: around 19,000 in all to Tilly's 12,000. The stage seemed set for a battle that would decide control of the Baltic coast and possibly all of northeast Germany. Then Gustavus hesitated. He called a council of war. A majority of his senior officers voiced doubts that amounted to belief that even at long odds, Tilly was a different proposition from any general the Swedish army had previously faced. Gustavus called off the advance—whether because of his own doubts or because he was unwilling to drive his subordinates instead of leading them.

Tilly interpreted Gustavus's behavior as the typical tactics of an ordinary general: trying to wear him down by feints and diversions. He rejected the gambit. Instead, he withdrew across the Elbe and turned on Magdeburg, transforming the blockade into a full-scale siege against a garrison reduced by earlier losses to around 2,000 men. By April 11, many of the city's outworks had been captured. As the Imperialists drove their trenches toward his walls, the city's governor warned that he might not be able to hold out beyond Easter.

Gustavus, unable to march directly to Magdeburg's relief without violating the territory of a still neutral Saxony, mounted a diversion against the Imperialist garrisons on the river Oder. A successful thrust down the river might well draw Tilly away from Magdeburg to protect Silesia, one of the few remaining undevastated regions in the Habsburg Empire. By April 12, the Swedes were at the walls of Frankfurt an der Oder, the main Imperial base. The next day was Palm Sunday, and the entire army attended services. Gustavus took the opportunity to address his men, saying he hoped before long that they would be drinking wine instead of water. When he followed by commanding the infantry to fall in under arms and be ready for orders, some of the old hands began providing themselves with ladders. Siege be damned; this looked like an attack. It was 5:00 P.M. when the king sent a patrol forward to test a weak spot in the old-fashioned city wall. He followed the patrol with a brigade. The rest of the story is told by a man yielding to no one in his admiration for "his Majesty of famous memory." Robert Monro was a Protestant, a mercenary, and a Scot—not always in the same order—who rose to colonel in the Swedish service in the front ranks of one of the hardest-fighting regiments in Gustavus's army, Mackay's Scots. Monro's writings have survived and are valuable for their on-the-battleground view.

In Monro's narrative of the battle he notes that a regiment of "Wild-Geese" (mercenary) Irishmen in Imperial service threw back two attacks by some of the best men in the Swedish army. But at other points the Swedes met only token resistance or were able to break through in close-gripped, hand-to-hand fighting that put the city into Gustavus's hands by nightfall at a cost of around 800 casualties. Their blood up, the victors took payback for Neu Brandenburg. "The most part of the Souldiers were cut off," to use Monro's euphemism—as many as 1,700 men. Another thousand were granted quarter as bloodlust died and men turned to thoughts of loot. Frankfurt was a Protestant town, but that made no difference. "Plate, Iewells, Gold, Money, Clothes. . . . I did never see officers lesse obeyed and respected than here for a time, till the hight of the market was passed."[2]

The capture and sack of Frankfurt generated widespread panic. In Prague and Vienna, fortifications long neglected were put in order. The emperor and the Catholic League embarked on recruiting campaigns. Tilly considered transferring his army to Silesia in order to block a Swedish advance southward. But Gustavus spent the next two weeks in small-scale operations around Frankfurt, and Tilly instead tightened his grip on Magdeburg. On May 2, 1631, a message reached Gustavus: The city could not last much longer.

Its best hope for relief was a direct advance. That meant marching across the territory of still neutral Electoral Saxony. Tilly had somewhat over 30,000 men around Magdeburg. Gustavus had about 18,000. His infantry were "fifteen pays in arrear, and both officers and men mighty discontented, so that I never heard such grumbling." The long-unpaid cavalry "plunder the land to the bare bones, provoking complaints and curses fit to make you shudder."[3] Concern with allowing such marauders into his still relatively unspoiled territory may have influenced Saxon elector Johann Georg's flat refusal even to meet with Gustavus—an insult seldom given by an elector to a king, who was a long step higher on the ladder of sovereigns.

On May 20, Tilly's men stormed and carried Magdeburg's final defenses. The city was subjected to a sack that went down in history as one of the defining atrocities of a war that spawned cruelty. Contemporaries set the death toll at 40,000. The adjusted figures are bad enough. Over 20,000 people were massacred or died when fires set by marauders spread and combined. Tilly, who wanted the city for a base, was enraged by its destruction. Accidental or not, Magdeburg's burning generated horror throughout Germany. For Protestants the city had been a symbol since it defied Emperor Charles V in 1547. For not a few Catholics, after the sack, it became a symbol of another kind: the fate awaiting any challenger to an emperor whose power was growing beyond any restraint. Refugees and survivors spread stories of pillage and rapine that lost nothing in the repetition. Germany was flooded with songs and broadsheets denouncing Ferdinand for seeking to replace the Holy Roman Empire with a Spanish-style absolute monarchy. And Gustavus Adolphus, who a year ago had arrived with neither allies nor invitation, emerged in this popular literature as the "Lion of the North," come from a far land to save the Protestant cause and uphold Germany's religious and political liberties.

That May, the Protestant princes Johann Georg had summoned earlier agreed to create a defensive alliance and raise an army of 40,000 men. In June the Elector of Brandenburg agreed to provide Gustavus with money and quarters. In July Gustavus

The Imperial army under Tilly storming the town of Magdeburg on May 20, 1631. © Bildarchiv Preussischer Kulturbesitz/Art Resource, New York.

began concentrating his forces at Werben, on the Elbe. Tilly marched against the king's position, only to be dissuaded after a few skirmishes by the breastworks, temporary fortifications, often as high as a man's breast or chest, that provided cover, that Gustavus's men had built in twenty-four-hour shifts—an unusual effort for an army of this era, whose men joined partly to escape grunt labor. "Generall Tilly made a shew of on-falling . . . by making all his trumpets to sound and his Drummes to beat." The gesture impressed no one in the Swedish camp. "He's afraid of us! We can take him!" That was the conclusion of Monro and of many another soldier in the Swedish camp.[4]

Tilly then played a political card: issuing the Elector of Saxony an ultimatum to stop recruiting troops and transfer those already enrolled to the Imperial army. Forced to the last ditch, Johann Georg finally called for help from the Swedes. On September 13, the Swedish army crossed the Elbe River at Wittenberg, to be joined two days later by its newly minted Saxon ally. Gustavus was now determined to fight. Not only did he require a victory to legitimate his position in Germany, he also needed to expand the area from which he could systematically draw men and supplies. Johann Georg and the Elector of Brandenburg, also present with the armies, were, if anything, more enthusiastic at the prospect of a battle. The Saxon ruler in particular had an immediate reason. Tilly had moved his main army into Saxony, taken Leipzig, and was allowing his hard-marched and unpaid men to refresh themselves at will in countryside as yet unravaged by war. Pillage, so often descried as a solvent of armies, often had an opposite effect in the Thirty Years War. Men returned to camp ready for action, laden with bulky plunder best disposed of in the informal markets that accompanied armies. It was not as though they had anywhere else to go.

Heading into Action Near Breitenfeld

As his regiments refilled, Tilly considered waiting for further reinforcements. Five thousand veteran troops under Johan von Aldringen were no more than three easy days' march away. But his senior officers urged him to action. The terrain north of Leipzig was ideally suited to a set-piece pitched battle: miles of open country, and only a few low elevations. On September 17, Tilly marched his army into position on one of them: a little rise the locals called Gallows Hill, near the village of Breitenfeld, about six miles from Leipzig. The combined Catholic League and Imperialist armies counted about 32,000 men. About two-thirds were infantry: 13,000 of those in the ranks of the elite League regiments, the *tercios* that had followed Tilly for years and were loyal to him with an allegiance few princes could command. They and their Imperialist counterparts held the center, deployed side by side in four wedges of three *tercios* each, with an extra one on each flank.

On the Imperial left stood the cavalry, 4,000 men, a dozen understrength regiments. Its core was the cuirassiers, big men on large horses whose helmets and body armor, painted black to prevent rust, added to their daunting appearance. Worn down from a season's campaigning, they nevertheless had a blood-bought reputation as the best heavy cavalry in Europe; and their commander, Heinrich Gottfried von Pappenheim, had no peer as a leader of mounted troops. The right of Tilly's line was held by another 6,000 horsemen under the overall command of Egon von Fuerstenberg. Half were Catholic Leaguers, mostly Bavarian heavy horse. The rest, new arrivals to this theater of war, were Imperialists from Italy, who had cut their way to Tilly through the improvised resistance of the south German Protestants. The two dozen cannons at Tilly's disposal were posted in front of the infantry and between the infantry and Fuerstenberg's troopers.

Tilly had so chosen his ground that the sun and the wind were behind his men—a substantial advantage on a black-powder battlefield. As he rode along his line, on a white horse as familiar in his ranks as Robert E. Lee's Traveller would be to a later army, he had no reason to feel anything but confidence. In later years, authors with the advantages of hindsight would describe Tilly's deployment as retrograde, depending on mass in contrast to the flexibility of the Swedes. In fact, the Spanish *tercios*, reduced in strength from over 4,000 to around 1,500 in the course of the preceding half-century, were no longer the relatively inflexible pike-and-musket blocks of an earlier era. An experienced unit—as were Tilly's—could change formation under fire with impressive facility and move with alacrity when required to do so. It could deliver heavy, sustained fire and replace losses at the front from its rear ranks. The usual deployment, about fifty ranks broad and thirty deep, reflected the fact that the mission of the *tercios* was not to perform tactical arabesques. Their role was to fix an enemy in place, grind him down, and hold him while the cavalry enveloped one or both of his wings and either struck home from the rear or smashed directly into the enemy's vitals.

That was Tilly's intention. Ideally, he would have preferred a few thousand more cavalry—enough to match the raw numbers of the Swedes and Saxons. But he was confident in the fighting power and the staying power of his infantry: confident enough to deploy them in a single line, with no reserves, in order to extend his front and increase his cavalry's chances of overlapping one or both of his enemies' flanks. That was contrary to accepted general practice, and for good reason. Second lines were often needed in an infantry fight as regiments lost strength and cohesion. But Tilly believed his veterans could handle anything the Swedes and the Saxons could throw at them, long enough to give his cavalry the time they needed.

By the early seventeenth century, European battlefields were becoming increasingly gridlocked. Firearms had limited tactical maneuverability, but firepower was as yet not decisive by itself. The result was to force aggressiveness into the operational and strategic spheres. As the initial stages of the Breitenfeld campaign demonstrated, commanders found themselves seeking decision by maneuver and attrition. In practice, this meant wearing down an enemy by exhausting or destroying his resources. The risk was exhausting one's own instead, to no purpose.

Most accounts credit Maurice of Nassau, Prince of Orange, with taking the first steps to reestablishing the battlefield as the central arena of war. His reduction of the strength of the basic tactical unit, from the 1,500-man *tercio* to the 500-man battalion, has been widely praised for enhancing cohesion, maneuverability, and firepower. In combat, however, the smaller units had been proven repeatedly to lack the endurance of the restructured *tercios*. Saxon battalions at Breitenfeld consisted of around 1,000 men, formed from a single regiment or several, depending on the strengths of the formations raised by the elector's freelance contractors. Saxony, like many German states, maintained a militia system based on a form of general levy. It could produce numbers in a hurry. Veterans, the old soldiers who were the real source of unit cohesion, were relatively few. Signing on with the Saxons in the circumstances of 1631 was unlikely to be a mercenary's first option.

What of the Swedes? Gustavus understood, more clearly than any of his contemporaries, that shock and not firepower remained the crucial instrument of victory. He understood as well that shock was an element of both fire and movement. The Swedish infantry's basic tactical formation at this period was the brigade, organized in three squadrons, each around 500 men plus officers and noncommissioned officers (NCOs). Whenever possible, brigades were composed of men speaking the same language. A table of organization from early September 1631 shows four German, three Swedish/Finnish, and one Scottish. Brigades, however, were tactical, not administrative, organizations. The regiments composing them were often transferred to keep numbers of men and proportions of weapons consistent.

A Swedish squadron at full strength in the early 1630s fielded about 400 men, half armed with pikes and half with matchlock muskets. A further ninety-odd musketeers were available as skirmishers or for detachment to the cavalry or the regimental guns. A brigade at Breitenfeld had one squadron massed in the center on a front half as wide as the other squadrons. Its pikes were forward, its musketeers to the rear, and its leading files slightly ahead of the line formed by the rest of the brigade: a squadron on each flank, with pikemen toward the center and musketeers on the wings. This T-formation was flexible and articulated. To meet a cavalry charge, the musketeers on its ends could take cover behind the pikes. In a fire fight the center squadron's musketeers could advance on either side of its pikes, screening the pikes of the other squadrons and supported by their musketeers. As a rule, the musketeers deployed in six-deep files and fired one rank at a time. Gustavus, however, had recently introduced so-called salvo fire: six ranks temporarily crowding into three, the first kneeling down, the second leaning forward, the third standing upright, and every musket firing at once. Delivered at point-blank range, followed up by a charge with gun butts, swords, and pikes, a Swedish salvo was meant to be the infantry's ultimate tactical argument.[5] To improve further his infantry's fire power, Gustavus developed cannon light enough to accompany the brigades. By 1631, an infantry squadron usually included a couple of iron three-pounder cannon, light enough to be drawn by a single horse or a few men, strong enough to withstand full charges of gunpowder, and able to fire eight rounds to the musketeers' six. The heavier Swedish guns were organized into permanent batteries, which enabled heretofore unknown concentrations of fire against selected targets.

Gustavus's cavalry in 1631 was a mixture of Swedes and Germans. At this stage its relative lack of body armor was more by necessity than choice. The king's correspondence reflects constant concern at the shortage of breastplates. His emphasis on the use of the sword over the then-fashionable pistol has also been overstated. His attachment of small units of musketeers to his cavalry formations was an effort to increase the firepower of horsemen, who often lacked pistols or were too poorly mounted to take on Imperial cuirassiers directly.[6] What the Swedish king did bring to Germany was an emphasis on delivering the charge at a gallop or a fast trot, making up for lack of mass and firepower by speed and ferocity. Most feared were Gustavus's Finnish troopers, whose war cry of *"hakkaa paalle!"* (chop 'em down!) meant cold steel and no quarter. Gustavus's allies deployed separately, with the Saxons taking the left wing. They formed a single line, infantry in the center and cavalry on the flanks, each deployed by regiments or battalions in a large, open wedge, with the apex pointing at the enemy. It was nothing sophisticated, but the newly raised formations could find their places without falling into confusion. Gustavus, by contrast, built his center around a first line of four brigades, with three more behind them. Each line had its own reserves, and each brigade had a half-dozen light guns. The forty-odd heavier pieces were massed in a so-called grand battery in front of the left center of the line. Field marshal Johan Baner commanded the right, primarily composed of Swedish and Finnish cavalry. The left was entrusted to mercenaries, German troopers under another Swedish marshal, Gustav Horn. On both flanks the mounted regiments were posted in two lines and had detachments of musketeers, 50–100 strong, interspersed among the forward squadrons.

The allies' deployment took most of the morning and left them with their center as well as both flanks held by cavalry: unusual, but reflecting a relationship where neither party was willing to take the risk of integrating their forces. Tilly's artillery played on their lines, but he made no other effort to disrupt Gustavus's movements. As they came into position, the Swedish heavy pieces replied—three shots for one, according to Swedish sources—and did rather better against the heavy Imperial formations. Noon passed, and the guns still thundered. Tilly expected Gustavus to advance and saw no need to sacrifice his advantage of position. The king's original intention seems to have been to begin the action on his right, where the best of his cavalry were posted—partly to deprive Tilly of the weather gauge, partly to threaten his line of retreat, and partly to avoid having to depend on the Saxons to do anything but stand their ground. A small stream, the Lober, flowed between the armies. Gustavus described it as hindering a forward movement at best undertaken in fits and starts. Perhaps he was waiting for the opportune time. Or just perhaps, he was a shade reluctant to put his fate to the touch, to win or lose all in a matter of hours.

It was Pappenheim, the horse soldier with the scarred face, who broke the deadlock. His armored men were suffering under the September sun, their mounts growing restive under Swedish cannon fire and tired under the weight they bore. He could see the Swedes opposite him moving rightward and forward in what seemed a halfhearted fashion. Studying the ground to his front, Pappenheim decided that he could preempt Gustavus: drive off Baner's cavalry, then turn hard right and crush the Swedish center before the king could react. It was a risky maneuver, but Pappenheim was confident in himself and his men. Shortly after 2:00 p.m., he led them forward. Pappenheim's cuirassiers had long since abandoned the sixteenth-century tactic of the caracole, with successive ranks firing pistols and wheeling away. Instead, they expected only the first rank or two of the dozen in a formation to use pistols, disrupting the foe just enough for the rest to break in and ride down anything opposing them. It had worked time and again. But now the musketeers in Baner's first line took toll of the Imperialists as they drew within range. The Swedish troopers "abid(ed) unloosing a pistol till the enemy had discharged first,"[7] and then tended to save their one shot for point-blank range, where no breastplate could stop it.

Prior to the battle being joined, Gustavus advised his men to use their swords on the cuirassiers' horses. It was ungentlemanly, but enough of Pappenheim's men fell to bullet and blade or went down under their own mounts that after three vain charges, he swung the weight of his attack leftward, seeking to turn Baner's flank. The Swede countered with regiments from his second line. No fewer than seven times did Pappenheim rally his troopers and bring them back against an enemy hanging on by what seemed a thread. Baner's musketeers, lacking bayonets and unaccompanied by pikemen to protect them against enemy swords, took ruinous casualties. Pappenheim himself was credited with killing no fewer than fourteen men in hand-to-hand combat during the charges and countercharges. But the musketeers held their ground. The Swedish squadrons always had one more rally left in men and horses. In the end it was Pappenheim's regiments that broke, first one and then others, plundering their own baggage and leaving their furiously cursing general to salvage what he could.

"They have robbed me of my honor and my glory!" Tilly shouted as he saw Pappenheim's charge. The cry was less a recognition of imminent disaster than an expression of frustration. Tilly had won too many battles to attack where his enemy was strong. The raw Saxon army offered a far more promising objective. Then Pappenheim's charge on the left dislocated Tilly's right wing. The newcomers from Italy were unwilling to risk losing their share of glory and plunder. The generals feared they had missed the signal for a joint attack. And Fuerstenberg's regiments charged formations that broke at the first shock. Some of the Saxon cavalry closed on Horn's Swedes and fought well the rest of the day. Within thirty minutes, however, most of the Saxon army had been driven from the field, the elector setting an example of flight at the head of his bodyguard.

Tilly seized the opportunity and sent his *tercios* forward. Prefiguring Frederick the Great's oblique order (detailed in the next section on the battle of Leuthen), they initially marched not straight ahead, but half right, then swung half left toward a Swedish flank opening ever wider as the Saxons peeled away. It was a neat piece of work, the kind of maneuver Tilly's trimmed-down regiments could perform better than any foe they had faced to date. As the infantry's vanguards completed the Saxon panic with a couple of musket discharges, and their main bodies restored formations disordered by the advance, Fuerstenberg rallied his cavalry to cover the Imperialist right. Around 4:00 P.M., Tilly sent 18,000 foot and horse rolling forward against Horn's 3,500.

As they advanced, some of the Imperialists raised the traditional shout of triumph: "Viktoria! Viktoria!" Some participants declared afterward that no more than a quarter hour separated the Swedes from defeat. But Horn was a first-rate battle captain. Initially uncertain of exactly what was happening in the Saxon sector, he had grasped enough of the situation to "refuse" his entire wing, pivoting on the center's infantry and swinging back to redeploy at right angles to his original direction. The maneuver's success was a tribute to the flexibility of the Swedish organization and to the quality of the German regiments under Horn's command. Long hours of training paid off in the short time it took to reform the line. What happened afterward marked Horn as also a first-rate cavalry commander. Instead of waiting to be either attacked or reinforced, he mounted a series of charges against Fuerstenberg's regiments, driving some of them into the *tercios* on Tilly's right, spreading enough confusion to delay the Imperialist attack. The German troopers "did behave themselves valorously divers times that day," commented Monro, no mean judge of courage and skill.[8]

Meanwhile, the Swedish center began to notice "two great Batailes of foote" on their immediate left. Initially, they were thought to be Saxons forced to give ground by Fuerstenberg's charge. Gustavus sent an officer to investigate, who "certified him they were enemie." The king responded by sending two brigades from his second line to reinforce Horn, with orders to charge the enemy and with promises of further reinforcements. Again, Gustavus's men moved faster than Tilly's could respond. Monro was in the counterattack: "They were prepared with a firme resolution to receive us with a salve of Cannon and Muskets; bot our small Ordinance [the regimental guns] being twice discharged among them and before we stirred, we charged them with a salve of muskets, which was repaied [repaid], and incontinent our Briggad [brigade], advancing unto them with push of pike, putting one of their battailes in disorder, fell on to the execution, so that they were put to the route."[9] Horn gave the *tercios* no breathing space, using his cavalry to crowd them together, depriving them of the internal maneuvering room necessary for their tactics to be most effective. But the Imperial regiments were conditioned to take losses and keep fighting. As many times as the battering charges of Horn's men threw them back on their heels, they rallied and came again to "push of pike." The Swedes gained ground, but only a few yards at a time.

Tipping the delicate balance was Baner's cavalry, which had managed to rally and reorganize. Leaving Horn to manage the fight in his sector, Gustavus had ridden to his other flank. As he passed the West Gotland horse, he ordered it to charge Tilly's left. He then put himself at the head of the Swedish East Gotland and Smaland regiments and the Finns under Wunsch and Torsten Stalhandske and led a second attack. This one skirted the imperialist infantry's left flank and plunged into their rear—toward the guns, neglected since Fuerstenberg's cavalry attack had begun.

Earlier, Tilly had mocked the Swedes' ratty-looking little horses. They were big enough now. Troopers who had not lost or discarded their pistols took no time to reload. Their blood was up, and they went in with the saber: Swedish farm boys and the wild men from the Finnish wastelands. Shouts of *hakkaa paalle* rang out as the infantry of Gustavus's first line came into action and completed the overrunning of Tilly's guns. "Beating them from their Cannon, we were masters of their Cannon, and consequently of the field," Monro later wrote. The Swedish heavy artillery had turned most of its own pieces around and was engaging the Imperialist infantry at what, for the time, was point-blank range. A few of Tilly's guns were coming into action against their former owners. By now the lines of battle were almost at a right angle to their original positions. The wind had shifted and was blowing into the faces of the Imperials. But to the Swedish army as well, "the smoake being great, the dust being raised, we were as in a darke cloude, not seeing the halfe of our actions, much lesse discerning . . . the way of our enemies."[10]

There was heavy fighting as Gustavus's infantry closed in through the smoke against the *tercios*. The Imperials knew well enough that it was ruin to run from this kind of close-gripped struggle. Their pikemen in particular stood to a finish, the Holstein regiment giving way only when heavy guns were turned on its ranks. If the Swedish army's maneuverability had structured the victory, their élan completed it: a close-quarters ferocity that finally eroded the *tercios'* will to stand. Around dusk, the trickle of men from the Imperialists' rear files turned into a flood, and soldiers became fugitives, scattering in every direction.

The exhausted Swedes downed arms and rested on their laurels. Gustavus dismounted, knelt, and offered a prayer of thanks, heartily echoed by everyone in range of his voice. Over 7,500 Imperialists were dead or wounded. Another 6,000 were prisoners, mostly taken in the final ruin of the *tercios*. The rest of the army had scattered. All the guns, all the supply wagons, almost a hundred flags and colors, pikes, muskets, breastplates, and buff coats: It was a day's work that had cost about 2,000 casualties, more than replaced within days by former Imperialists who willingly took the colors of the man who beat them.

Victory and the Aftermath

Breitenfeld became a famous victory. Protestants throughout Germany and Europe rejoiced. Gustavus emerged as "the Captaine of kings, and king of Captaines . . . having robbed [Tilly] of glory and clipped the wings of the Empire with his little Royall Army."[11] But Breitenfeld did not lead to the collapse of the Catholic Holy Roman Empire and the Protestantization of Germany. Nevertheless, Gustavus's victory did sustain the continent on a path of Christian confessional pluralism. After 1631, neither a universal faith nor a universal state was able to legitimize its governance of Europe.

Breitenfeld also prefigured the shape of modern war. Since 1618, Germany had involuntarily become a warfare society. States and armies had learned how to mobilize material and human resources effectively enough for even badly defeated forces to reconstitute themselves. Within weeks Tilly had pulled together sufficient outlying troops, augmented by new recruits, that Gustavus once again needed to beware of a Catholic/Imperial threat. When major armies again clashed, in early 1632, it also became clear that the tactical discrepancies between Gustavus and his opponents that had decided Breitenfeld were by no means decisively large. Tilly's defeat had reflected less his army's flawed structure than overconfidence at its command levels. No one who faced the Swedes repeated the mistake of underestimating them. And in turn, Breitenfeld proved the high point of a Swedish army whose flexibility, responsiveness, and cohesion became diminishing assets as the number of Gustavus's originals shrank from combat, disease, and desertion.

Seduced by this one-sided Swedish victory, for the next two decades, generals still sought decision in the field in a series of brutal battles retrospectively grouped together as The Thirty Years War (1618–1648). But as early modern armies grew more symmetrical—more like mirror images of themselves—battles devolved into close-gripped slugging matches, producing casualty lists well out of proportion to any results, long term or short. Breitenfeld, in the end, proved a false tactical beacon in a war that only became grimmer and dirtier—as did its successors, even in the so-called enlightened age of Frederick the Great, the leader who glowers forth from the final panel of our triptych.

LEUTHEN (1757): PROFESSIONALISM AND ENLIGHTENED WARFARE

"Sir, you are an army. We are a traveling whorehouse!" These words, allegedly spoken by a French officer to his Prussian captors on November 5, 1757, aptly sum up the battle of Rossbach. It had been one of the most one-sided encounters of the Seven Years War (1757–1763). In four hours Frederick the Great's army had smashed an allied force nearly twice its size. Five thousand Frenchmen, Austrians, and Germans of the Holy Roman Empire had been killed or wounded. Another 5,000, including 11 generals, were prisoners. Seventy-two cannons, twenty-one flags, and three sets of kettledrums were among the trophies. Prussian casualties amounted to 169 dead and 379 wounded— one-tenth of the losses sustained by the coalition arrayed against them. Such a cheap victory was unprecedented in an era when battles most frequently resembled a process of pushing two candles into a blowtorch and seeing which one melted first.

The Importance of Silesia

Despite his overwhelming success, Frederick was not satisfied. "Rossbach," he declared, "merely freed me to seek new dangers in Silesia."[12] Prussia's king was not indulging in rhetorical flourishes. He had gone to war in 1756 against a seemingly overwhelming coalition of France, Russia, and Austria intent on winning a political victory on the battlefield. Frederick expected that such a victory would forever settle the question of ownership of the rich province of Silesia, which was nestled between Poland and the Austrian province of Bohemia. Seized from Austria by Frederick in 1740, its loss had never been accepted by Austria's Habsburg empress, Maria Theresa.

Thus far, however, Frederick's strategy had been a dismal failure. A year's hard campaigning, highlighted by the murderous battles of Loboswitz, Prague, and Kolin, had failed to drive Austria and its allies from the war. Instead, Frederick had been forced to abandon his effort against Austria to deal with the French threat from the west. While he was winning the battle of Rossbach, an Austrian army commanded by Prince Charles of Lorraine, with field marshal Leopold Daun as his able subordinate, reconquered most of Silesia. Left to hold the province in Frederick's absence, August Wilhelm, Duke of Bevern, had been outfought and outgeneraled at every turn. A man enlightened enough to hire professors to lecture on mathematics to his junior officers and assign foreign enlisted men to teach their native languages, Bevern nevertheless was out of his element in an independent command against long odds. The Austrians took full advantage of their superior numbers to keep him well in check, while systematically overrunning Silesia's fortresses.

Those fortresses did not compare with their massive counterparts in the Low Countries or France. They were simpler, cheaper works, designed more as operational centers than as independent strongpoints and requiring a supporting field army for their long-term survival. On November 13, 1757, Schwednitz, near the Bohemian border, was surrendered after a three-week siege. On November 22, more than 80,000 Austrians attacked Bevern's 28,000 men in front of the fortified Silesian city of Breslau, thirty miles to the northeast, and forced the hard-pressed Prussians across the Oder River, leaving what amounted to a token garrison of ten battalions in the now-isolated city.

Charles and Daun were more than satisfied with their achievements. They had overrun a good half of Silesia, the province lost in 1740. They had done so in late autumn—an unusual campaigning season, despite the atypically mild weather. The Austrian Habsburgs looked like winners, especially to the good citizens of Breslau. Loyalty to Prussia was well enough when Prussia's king could protect them, but it did not extend to withstanding a siege and risking a bombardment that could destroy the city. The fortress commander came under increasing pressure from the citizens to evacuate his soldiers, and deserters from the garrison found it easy to disappear among a civilian population unwilling to report them. On November 25, Breslau surrendered on terms that allowed the garrison to evacuate unmolested. However, only about 600 officers and men rejoined Frederick's army. The rest sold or discarded their equipment and scattered across the province.

Bevern's field force was in little better shape. Bevern himself had been captured while making a personal reconnaissance, perhaps seeking an honorable death at enemy hands. Frederick had so often ordered his subordinate to hold the province or risk his neck that captivity might have been a welcome relief from the all-too-predictable royal wrath. Without their commander, discipline in the Prussian ranks eroded. Hungry men looted villages and set fire to homes, while officers looked the other way.

Learning of the disaster unfolding in Silesia, Frederick had wasted no time in turning his attention to the province. His army of 13,000 men, all that could be spared, began its march on November 13. General Hans Joachim von Ziethen was sent ahead of the army to assume command of Bevern's demoralized soldiers. Frederick expected no miracles from the veteran cavalry officer, but the king knew that Ziethen was at least popular enough with the men to keep what remained of Bevern's army together until he arrived. When Frederick joined Ziethen on December 2, he commanded about 38,000 men. One-third of these were veterans of the victory at Rossbach. The remainder were the overmarched, underfed, and badly beaten men of Ziethen's command.

Bevern's poor performance had nullified Frederick's original plan. The duke was supposed to hold off Charles and Daun and thereby set the stage first for a major battle under Frederick's personal command, then a pursuit into Bohemia, even in the depths of winter. This grand design, intended to convince Austria of the wisdom of making peace, no longer seemed achievable. Frederick nevertheless was determined to strike the Austrians before they had time to consolidate their Silesian victories. Militarily, he could not afford to begin a new campaigning season with a major enemy army less than 200 miles from his capital, Berlin. Politically, the laurels of Rossbach were unlikely to survive a winter of stalemate on what Frederick insisted was Prussian territory. Economically, Silesia's material and human resources were too vital a part of Prussia's war economy to be abandoned, even temporarily.

To drive the Austrians from Silesia, Frederick would need to motivate his battered army to fight one more time and win. The king's behavior during the first days of December laid much of the foundation for the subsequent mythology of "Old Fritz." It depicts a monarch moving from campsite to campsite, warming himself at his men's fires, listening to their stories and complaints, and promising promotion and reward for courage on the field. To the senior officers of Bevern's misfortunate command, who expected at the least massive reproaches, the king instead offered fellowship and preferment. Future performances, Frederick implied, would cleanse past records. Camp discipline was sufficiently relaxed to allow the victorious veterans of Rossbach to mingle with the survivors of Breslau, telling their stories of victory and plunder to the rest of the army. Extra rations and additional liquor were distributed to the troops as far as stocks allowed.

These changes represented a more or less calculated exercise in reverse psychology, a contrast to Frederick's normally harsh, demanding approach. Their failures had created a sense of anticipatory dread among the officers and men of Bevern's army, similar to the feelings inspired by the threat of "wait till your father comes home." Instead Frederick's unexpected and unconventional behavior inspired old soldiers and recruits, cynics and idealists.

On December 3, Frederick capped his performance by ordering the army's generals and regimental and battalion commanders to his headquarters at Parchwitz. This in itself was unusual for a monarch noted for keeping his own counsel. When Frederick finally appeared, instead of a battle captain radiating confidence, the Prussian officers saw their king in a uniform even more worn and snuff stained than usual. Instead of a master craftsman ready to ply his trade, they saw a tired, aging man whose voice was too low pitched to be heard beyond the range of his audience.

The army was marching, Frederick declared, to attack the Austrians at Breslau. The only alternatives were victory or death. "We are fighting for our glory, for our honor, and for our wives and children," the king proclaimed. "The threefold Austrian numerical superiority, the strong Austrian positions, must yield to the bravery of the troops and the execution of my orders. Those who stand with me can rest assured I will look after their families if they are killed. Anyone wishing to retire can go now, but will have no further claim on my benevolence."[13] As a coda, lest anyone think the king had gone soft, he announced that any cavalry regiment failing to do its duty would be dismounted and used as a garrison force. Any infantry regiment that flinched when meeting the enemy faced the loss of its swords and colors plus the public disgrace of having the ornamental braid cut from its uniforms. Like all great performances, Frederick's "Parchwitz Speech" blended sincerity and artifice in such a way that they were impossible for anyone to separate. Not even Sir Laurence Olivier, nor Kenneth Branagh, could have recited Henry V's "we few, we happy few" speech before the battle of Agincourt (1415) more convincingly, and the king's words lost nothing in the repetition.

Frederick was conscious enough of what he hoped to achieve that he gave his army a day to consider the urgency of the situation before breaking camp on December 4 and marching toward Breslau. That evening, the Prussians benefited from what Frederick, at least, regarded as good news. The Austrians had left their positions in front of the city and accepted Frederick's challenge by advancing toward the village of Leuthen. Their decision to move has often been condemned, and not without reason. The terrain around Leuthen offered no obviously favorable defensive positions. Frederick and his generals, moreover, knew the region well from peacetime maneuvers.

Charles and Daun, however, had practical reasons for their decision to seek battle. Charles was not the stereotypical royal nonentity who owed his rank to his position as Empress Maria Theresa's brother-in-law. He was a seasoned field soldier who had been fighting the Prussians since 1741. Daun, for his part, was a master of the feints and maneuvers characteristic of eighteenth-century warfare. He was also a man who took no unnecessary risks. Earlier in the year, the prince and the marshal had between them fought Frederick to a near-standstill in front of Prague and defeated him at Kolin. The season's events in Silesia thus far indicated that the Prussian army was far from being unbeatable. The Austrian commanders, in short, seemed to agree with Frederick's view of the situation. In their minds, one decisive battle would end the war, only with Austria emerging as the victor.

Finally and significantly, the Austrians had more chips to bet. Despite the hyperbole of his Parchwitz speech, Frederick anticipated a fight on equal terms. He had 39,000 men and 170 guns, and he believed that the Austrians in front of him were no stronger. In fact, Frederick faced an enemy 66,000 strong, with 210 pieces of artillery on ground chosen by its commanders. But the Austrians' tactical situation was less favorable than their numerical advantage. Surprised by Frederick's rapid advance, Charles ordered his soldiers to bivouac for the night of December 4 in battle formation along a 4.5-mile front, extending from the hamlets of Nippern in the north to Sagschutz in the south. December's early sunset combined with an overworked road system to keep many Austrian regiments moving until late in the evening, then left unfed. Fatigue and hunger were poor preparations for combat. The next morning, morale among the regimental officers also faltered as they saw their lines of battle forming on the open, rolling ground around Leuthen. Habsburg troops had performed best against the Prussians with some terrain advantage. What Daun and Charles now seemed to have in mind was a toe-to-toe death grapple, with the Austrians' principal edge being superior numbers.

The Battle at Leuthen

The Prussians sounded reveille at 4:00 A.M. on December 5, 1757. Between five and six o'clock, the army was on the march, two columns of infantry in the middle, cavalry on each flank, and a strong advance guard. Frederick himself led the way with a task force of light troops: three irregular battalions, a handful of riflemen, and a half-dozen regiments of hussars. The day dawned clear but cold. When a veteran trooper complained of the temperature, Frederick advised him to be patient; things would get hot soon enough. His one-line jest was hardly necessary. As they marched, some of the regiments sang hymns.

First contact between the armies came near the village of Borna, where the Prussian vanguard encountered a mixed force of Saxon light cavalry and Austrian hussars. One quick charge scattered the Austrians and netted the Prussians 600 prisoners. Frederick ordered the captives paraded past his own men, then rode forward to a small hill. He found himself facing the center of an Austrian line that, deployed as it was in the open, at first sight appeared even more formidable than its numbers warranted. Two minor terrain features, however, combined to offer an opportunity. The Austrian left was in the air; unsecured, it ended well short of a network of ponds and marshes that could have served as a geographic anchor. In the same sector a series of low hills offered at least some cover for the Prussians to execute a right wheel across the Austrians' front, followed by a quick turn to fall on the enemy's exposed flank.

The king's maneuver was a conventional tactician's nightmare. The Austrian flank he proposed to attack was open only in a technical sense. It did not come to an abrupt end with a single soldier; the Austrians had reinforced it with improvised barricades and artillery positions. The attacking force would need to be strong enough to break through at the right point and not become hung up by Austrian reserves. Reaching this area successfully in turn depended on drawing the Austrian commanders' attention away from the threatened sector. That meant dividing an already inferior Prussian force so precisely that the enemy would be deceived as to the decisive point of the attack.

Frederick began his tactical sleight of hand by deploying the cavalry of his vanguard, eventually supported by infantry, as though he intended to strike the Austrian right. The Prussians took their time developing the feint. By 11:00 A.M. the movement was still incomplete. Its effect on the cautious Austrians was nevertheless mesmerizing. Previously, they had been confident in their ability to finish off what they derisively called the "Berlin Security Detachment." Now, with an absurdly small force of Prussians preparing what seemed a suicidal attack, Charles and Daun took the proffered bait. First, they dispatched most of their reserves to the apparently threatened sector, then they took position there themselves. Frederick might be at bay, but he was not a foe to be taken lightly.

Meanwhile, Frederick turned the bulk of his army south. Even the detailed Prussian official histories fail to clarify the complex pattern of halts, advances, stops, starts, and sidesteps involved in that process. That the maneuver succeeded at all, much less in the remarkably short span of one to two hours, is a great tribute to the Prussian army's drill masters. Europe's armies in the mid-eighteenth century were replete with brave, well-disciplined men and with officers ready to lead them into the heaviest fire. No army other than Prussia's was likely to be able to execute this kind of complicated shuffling in the face of an enemy without tying itself into hopeless knots. The effects of adrenaline and anxiety on individual judgments was likely to generate enough of what military strategist Carl von Clausewitz would later call "friction" to render such a movement an unthinkable risk for anyone other than Frederick the Great.

Frederick's men pulled off the maneuver, but they had help from an obliging enemy. As the Prussian rightward movement became apparent, Charles took no action. In earlier battles of the Seven Years War the Austrians had been reluctant to abandon strong defensive positions, natural or artificial. They did not want to risk maneuvering against a Prussian force known for its ability to improvise. Here, on open ground, nothing stopped them but command inertia. Charles, in particular, convinced himself that the Prussians were retreating. The move against his right, to which he had so promptly responded, was no more than the posturings of a rear guard. Far from mounting an attack of his own, the prince seemed to have been pleased at the prospect of bluffing Frederick off the field. "Our friends are departing," he observed as the Prussians swung across his front. "Let them go in peace."[14]

Geography reinforced both the Austrian commander's wishful thinking and his tactical paralysis. The high ground that Frederick put between himself and the Austrians was not impressive in height, but the terrain was deceptively rolling. The exact Prussian line of march remained concealed from the Austrian commanders' view, a fact that was checked after the war in an effort to help determine the reasons for Charles's inactivity. A horseman carrying a flag along Frederick's route could not be seen from the hill Charles and Daun occupied, even by men looking for him.

Frederick thus was able to prepare his attack unobserved and undisturbed. Shortly after noon, the leading Prussian troops had moved far enough past the Austrian flank for the king to order them to swing to the left and deploy for battle. The initial breakthrough would be made by three infantry battalions, two of the Twenty-Sixth Infantry Regiment and one of the Thirteenth. Their right flank was covered by a four-battalion column: three of grenadiers and one of musketeers from the Eighteenth Infantry Regiment, plus a battery of Brummers, heavy twelve-pounder guns brought down from the Silesian fortress of Glogau. The rest of the main body's infantry deployed in a staggered line by battalions, extending west at intervals of fifty paces. Ziethen, with fifty-three cavalry squadrons supported by a half-dozen infantry battalions, took position on the infantry's right rear as a screening and exploitation force.

Military historian Christopher Duffy justly called the tactic "a textbook example of the Oblique Order," holding back one wing of an army while concentrating the other against an enemy's flank or a similar vulnerable point. Frederick made his immediate intentions clear in a brief speech to his first assault wave: "Boys, do you see the whitecoats over there? All you've got to do is go for them with the bayonet and run them out. I'll support you with the whole army. It's win or die!"[15]

Frederick had learned from his previous experiences that speed was vitally important on a modern battlefield. Acting before an enemy could react was a valuable step toward victory. Haste, however, often made waste as well. The war's earlier battles had shown that the Austrians could not simply be turned out of their positions by a series of limited attacks. This time, the Prussian army would hit its enemy with the controlled power of a hammer blow, everything focused behind the three battalions that began their advance on the Austrian positions around 1:00 P.M.

The Austrians in the threatened sector had neither been entirely idle nor remained completely ignorant of the impending attack. Their commander, General Franz Nádasti, was a veteran Hungarian hussar who had faced the Prussians too many times to be caught unprepared. As the Prussians crossed his front, Nádasti sent repeated requests for support to Charles and Daun. But the messages remained unacknowledged—everyone in the Austrian army knew (or thought they knew) that Hungarians tended to start at ghosts and shadows.

Frederick had not left the composition of his attack's spearhead to chance. The Twenty-sixth Regiment was one of the army's best. Recruited from Pomerania, its ranks included a large proportion of Slavic Wends, who spoke their own dialect and possessed the kind of strong group loyalty that, when properly tapped, can yield a formidable fighting unit. The Thirteenth was a Berlin outfit, known for its rigid discipline as the "thunder and lightning" regiment, with an NCO corps that was the terror of recruits and a combat record that affirmed the worth of hard peacetime training. The royal grenadiers, drawn from the best of the army's hardened veterans, saw their natural place as the head of any forlorn hope and victory as their natural achievement.

Nádasti, on the other hand, had been assigned most of the army's *Reichstruppen*. These formations, recruited from the small German states of the Holy Roman Empire and middle-sized Austrian allies, such as Württemberg, were widely and legitimately regarded as unreliable, even after they had a season of victorious campaigning under their belts. Nádasti's original decision to deploy them on the far left of his line was defensible enough. As long as the Prussian attack was expected to come from the front and strike farther north, the army's weakest links would be posted where they were likely to face the least action. Given Frederick's new axis of advance, Austria's German allies were positioned at exactly the wrong spot, for Nádasti and the whole Austrian army.

Once they recovered from their initial shock at the Prussians' appearance, the Imperial colonels on the spot did the best they could with what they had. Turning ninety degrees to the left, they deployed to take advantage of a shallow ditch facing the Prussian line of attack. Most of the men in the new first line were Württembergers—Protestants whose willingness to fight the Lutheran Prussians had been widely questioned in the Austrian camp. They nevertheless held out for a few minutes, blazing away until they saw the Prussian lines continuing to push forward through the smoke. Then the Württembergers ran for their lives, carrying with them the Bavarians Nádasti had redeployed to support his suddenly vulnerable flank.

Prussian infantry, effectively supported by artillery, drove steadily toward the village of Leuthen as the leading elements of Frederick's main body came into action behind the first wave. These men were commanded by Prince Moritz von Dessau, a general who knew what hard fighting was. A color-bearer of the Twenty-sixth heard him shout, "Boys, you've won honor enough! Fall back to the second line." The answer, at least the one recorded for posterity, was, "We'd have to be yellow-bellies to fall back now! Cartridges! Cartridges!" Such heroic rhetoric is always suspect. It is, however, a matter of record that the Twenty-sixth Infantry's officers won no fewer than fourteen *Pour le Mérites* that day: Prussia's highest military decoration. Frederick himself donated 1,500 silver talers from his own pocket for distribution among the rank and file. "Your Majesty can trust his crown and scepter to that regiment," Prince Moritz later remarked. "When they run from the enemy I don't plan to stay around either."[16]

The Twenty-sixth's call for ammunition highlighted another modification of Frederick's prewar tactics. Earlier in 1757, at the battles of Prague and Kolin, the Prussian infantry had advanced without firing. The resulting heavy casualties had convinced most of the regimental officers that keeping muskets shouldered meant sacrificing one of the Prussian infantry's great material advantages in breaking enemy morale—its firepower. Sheer numbers of shots fired per minute were less important than a formation's ability to deliver sustained fire over the course of several hours. At Leuthen the Twenty-sixth went into battle with the regulation sixty rounds per man. By the time they passed the Austrian first line, many of the men had exhausted their supply. But Frederick had learned from experience. At Leuthen he had ammunition wagons brought up from the artillery park and posted directly behind the advancing infantry. When the Twenty-sixth dispatched an officer in search of replenishment he found the source close at hand. Its cartridge boxes filled once more, the Twenty-sixth closed with Prince Moritz's advancing troops. First the Prussian grenadiers' column, then three more infantry battalions, reinforced the drive northward.

Nádasti had not been idle as his infantry collapsed. Instead of attempting to restore the forward line directly with fresh battalions, he tried to change the battle's course by sending his cavalry against the Prussian musketeers. This was Prussian general von Ziethen's moment, and he almost botched it. His horsemen initially had trouble deploying among the ditches and small woods in their assigned sector. Instead of striking one concentrated blow, the Prussian cavalry regiments attacked the Austrians by ones and twos. Ziethen had to commit all fifty-three of his squadrons before the melee was resolved in Prussia's favor. But he redeemed himself by ensuring that the victorious Prussian troopers turned on the retreating enemy infantry instead of pursuing their mounted foes. Running fugitives offered a more inviting target, especially to the Second Hussars, Ziethen's own regiment, which had a major hand in rounding up more than 2,000 demoralized Württembergers and Bavarians.

With his left flank disintegrating Charles finally realized the real direction of the Prussian attack. His solution came from the textbook of common sense. While the Prussians were busy with the remnants of Nádasti's force, Charles proposed to form a new line at right angles to his original position, one flank resting on the village of Leuthen and the other protected by cavalry from his reserve. The prince began by redeploying a few infantry battalions from his second line. Then he dispatched his infantry reserves. Finally, and belatedly, convinced that nothing at all was likely to happen in the northern sector of his original position, Charles ordered his whole army to execute a left turn and meet Frederick's attack face-to-face.

The Austrian position now extended on both sides of Leuthen—not a bad idea, given the solid construction of the village's buildings and the general tendency for built-up areas to act as magnets for even the best disciplined attacking troops. Perhaps the Prussians could be tied down in a house-to-house fight, buying time for the redeployment Charles had ordered. Quick reaction, however, was not one of the Austrian army's strong points. Neither was traffic control. Battalions arrived seemingly from everywhere, without specific orders, their men often breathless and sweating from forced marching, then chilled by long halts. Too often, instead of forming into battle lines, the Austrian infantry remained massed in the killing zone of Prussian artillery now positioned on the high ground overlooking Leuthen.

Despite the punishment they were receiving from the Prussian artillery, the Austrians were still holding their ground when the final Prussian advance began around 3:30 P.M. By this time Leuthen was full of stragglers and fugitives, but the men remaining in ranks fought on. As the battle turned against the Austrians, the Prussians stormed Leuthen. Inside the village's churchyard, a German regiment supplied by the bishopric of Würzburg held out against repeated attacks until artillery knocked down the churchyard's walls and the Prussians closed in with musket butts and bayonets.

As the Prussians finally cleared Leuthen, the Austrians mounted a massive cavalry counterattack. Seventy fresh squadrons closed on the Prussian left flank, which was made vulnerable as their infantry had closed toward Leuthen. Then Lieutenant General Wilhelm von Driesen earned his footnote in history by launching a counterattack with his forty cavalry squadrons. He charged as the Austrians rode across his front, giving the Prussians a tactical advantage that compensated for inferior numbers. First to engage the Austrian cavalry were the Bayreuth Dragoons, who, for a short time, fought the Austrians alone. The remainder of the Prussian cavalry took its time supporting the dragoons, according to one account, because of regimental jealousy. The cuirassiers, who regarded themselves as the elite of the mounted arm, allegedly sat back to appreciate the discomfiture of their social inferiors. Once they charged, however, the heavy Prussian horsemen drove the Austrians eastward, into their own infantry still fighting around Leuthen.

That collision was enough. The Austrians panicked and fled by battalions. The few units that stood their ground were mowed down by the advancing Prussian infantry. Prussian troopers, again taking advantage of easy prey, sabered the fugitives until night put an end to the slaughter. Frederick, in another departure from eighteenth-century custom, attempted to organize a pursuit of the fleeing enemy. He was able to collect no more than a small task force of grenadiers and cavalry, which by 7:00 P.M. reached the bridge across the Wistritz River at Lissa but could go no farther in the dark. With snow falling heavily the king rested for the night with a number of wounded Austrian officers who had taken shelter in the local castle. "Good evening gentlemen," he addressed them. "Certainly you weren't expecting me here."[17]

As individual Prussian regiments rallied and reorganized, the men marched in silence, each busy with his own thoughts. Then someone struck up a hymn, "Now Thank We All Our God." The tune and the words were known to everyone—Lutheran or Evangelical, Catholic or Protestant, Christian or unbeliever—in the ranks of Frederick's army. Man after man took up the words of what has ever since been known to Germans as the "Leuthen Chorale." For the pious it was an affirmation of God's power over the king's enemies. For the skeptics it was as good a way as any of proving one was still alive.

The Aftermath

The Austrians had come to fight, and they exacted a high price for their defeat. More than 6,000 Prussians were dead or wounded—one-fifth of the men Frederick had taken into battle. Few victories in the Age of Reason were cheaply purchased. But the spoils of Leuthen were substantial, even compared to Rossbach. Fifty-five flags and standards, 130 guns, and more than 12,000 prisoners were among the major Prussian trophies. Three thousand Austrians were dead and another 7,000 wounded. Whole regiments had disappeared from Charles's order of battle, either scattered in the first attacks or overrun in the final grapple. A senior Austrian officer reported that Charles and Daun were "sunk in the depths of despondency," with the prince still unable to believe what had happened and Daun attempting to detach himself emotionally and professionally from the disaster. So total was their defeat that the retreating Austrians abandoned the garrison of Breslau—no fewer than 17,000 men—whose commander was forced to surrender on December 20.

Frederick had benefited from an obliging enemy. The Austrian commanders saw what they wanted to see regarding the thrust of the principal Prussian attack, instead of using their strong and efficient light cavalry to divine what the Prussians intended. Even Frederick remarked that "a single patrol . . . would have uncovered the truth almost at once." Even more surprising than this omission was Nádasti's failure to place outposts on his open flank. A light cavalryman with his experience in independent command against the Prussians should have at least considered the possibility of attack from an unexpected direction. As for the rest of the debacle, the failure to hold Leuthen and the defeat of the final Austrian cavalry attack merely serve to illustrate the truth of the aphorism that in war, luck is usually a byproduct of design.

The battle of Leuthen demonstrated eighteenth-century linear tactics at their best. Frederick's infantry combined fire and movement in textbook fashion. Some individuals fired more than 180 rounds, yet nowhere did the advance bog down in short- or medium-range exchanges of musketry. The Prussian cavalry protected the flanks, delivered two tactically significant charges, and turned the Austrian defeat into a rout. The artillery not only kept pace with the army's movements, but also deployed and redeployed its guns to take maximum advantage of the ground. The heavy twelve-pounders in particular wreaked havoc on the Austrians bunched around Leuthen. Their distinctive bellowing sound also did much to heighten Prussian morale at critical moments.

Nevertheless, Leuthen, while the greatest of Frederick's victories, was in no way a "crowning mercy." The Austrian army, though badly hammered, still remained an effective fighting force. Ziethen and his hussars were unable to do more than harry the retreating enemy across the Bohemian frontier. To the normal difficulties accompanying operational pursuit under eighteenth-century conditions was added a certain lethargy on the part of the Prussians. Leuthen had been a moral statement as well as a military victory. The Prussian army had given all it had. Not until the adrenaline had worn off were either the officers or the rank and file likely to be alert in seizing new opportunities. Even Frederick's body reacted to the months of stress; the king was laid low with colic in the battle's aftermath.

Because Leuthen failed to convince Austrian empress Maria Theresa to make peace, its traditional status as a decisive battle has increasingly been called into question. In fact, Leuthen was decisive in two ways. It kept Prussia in the war. Defeat, or even a draw, might well have compelled Frederick to seek terms while he still retained some negotiating power, rather than risk another campaign at a strategic disadvantage. More important, Leuthen encouraged Frederick to continue his original grand strategic design of seeking political victory on the battlefield. For the remainder of the Seven Years War, as long as a Prussian army remained in the field under his command, Frederick accepted no military or diplomatic setback as final. In his mind the chance always remained of a victory even greater than Leuthen, one that would turn the tide definitively in Prussia's favor.

Was this vision or delusion? The historical fact is that Prussia ended the Seven Years War as a full member of Europe's great power club of France, England, Austria, and Russia. The costs and consequences of that achievement remain subjects of controversy. What is certain is that the history of a state and a continent turned on the events of a single afternoon at an obscure Silesian village: a fitting scene for the final panel of our triptych of early modern battles as well as a salutary reminder that "limited" warfare restricted to professional armies could nevertheless have profound implications for Europe's political order and, by extension, even globally. In many ways the Seven Years War was a deadly drama played out on a global stage, but that is a story best held in reserve for a later chapter.

NOTES

1. The case for the operation's initially limited concept is convincingly made in Angus Konstam, *Pavia 1525: The Climax of the Italian Wars*, Osprey Military Campaign Series, 44 (London: Osprey, 1996).

2. Robert Monro, *Monro, His Expedition with the Worthy Scots Regiment Called Mac-Keys*, ed. William S. Brockington, Jr. Foreword by Geoffrey Parker (Westport, CT: Praeger, 1999), 160.

3. Lars Grubbe to Axel Oxenstierna, c. May 11 (21), 1632, quoted in Michael Roberts, *Gustavus Adolphus: A History of Sweden, 1611–1632*, vol. II, *1626–1632* (London: Longmans Green, 1958), 494.

4. Monro, *Monro*, 180–182, 184–185.

5. The discussion of Swedish organization is primarily based on Marcus Junkelmann, *Gustav Adolf (1594–1632): Schwedens Aufsteig zur Grossmacht* (Regensburg, Germany: Pustet, 1993), 231–235, and Richard Brzezinski, *The Army of Gustavus Adolphus*, vol. 1, *Infantry* (London: Osprey, 1991), no. 235.

6. Brzezinski, Vol. 2, *Cavalry* (London: Osprey, 1993), no. 262.

7. Monro, *Monro*, 193.

8. Monro, *Monro*, 194.

9. Monro, *Monro*, 193.

10. Ibid.

11. Monro, *Monro*, 195.

12. Frederick II, *Oeuvres de Frédéric le Grand*, ed. J.D.E. Preuss, 30 vols. (Berlin: Imprimirie Royale, 1846–1857), IV, 156.

13. O. Herrmann, "Prinz Ferdinand von Preussen über den Feldzug im Jahre 1751," *Forschungen zur brandenburgisch-preussischen Geschichte*, 31 (1918), 101–102.

14. Christopher Duffy, *The Army of Maria Theresa: The Armed Forces of Imperial Austria, 1740–1780* (New York: Hippocrene Books, 1977), 186.

15. E.F.R. von Barsewisch, *Von Rossbach bis Freiberg 1757–1763. Tagebuchblätter eines Friderizianischen Fahmenjunkers und Offiziers*, ed. Jürgen Olmes (Krefeld, Germany: H. Ruhl), 36.

16. Barsewisch, *Von Rossbach*, 41, 38.

17. Curt Jany, *Geschichte der Preussischen Armee vom 15. Jahrhundert bis 1914*, ed. Eberhard Jany, 4 vos. (Osnabrück: Biblio, 1967), II, 458.

One

✷ ✷ ✷

THE MATRIX OF WAR: POLICIES, STRATEGIES, AND MENTALITIES

Warmaking in Europe from the fifteenth century was defined by expanding complexity. Historically, Europe had been a network of limited, overlapping societies, with power devolved among feudal lords, urban elites, and religious institutions. Medieval monarchies were more than the proverbial traveling shows, with kings owning no more than the highways on which they journeyed. Medieval states, in order to exercise power on any scale, nevertheless depended on cooperation: harmonizing their interests with those of local authorities.

THE WARMAKING STATE

That system gave way, beginning in the late 1400s, to centralization of power. The process, frequently described in terms of top-down coercion, is better understood as a system of contractual relationships, with their roots in custom and advantage. Those local and regional elites that cooperated systematically with the emerging central governments tended to benefit from the process—not least because they were simultaneously constrained to cooperate with each other by at least limiting private violence and its accompanying destruction. However distasteful that behavior might be initially, eventually, it generated a spectrum of direct and indirect benefits that fostered band wagoning. Being last on board a ship of state able to set a course under its own power had obvious disadvantages.

This changed agreement developed into an understood contractual relationship. Rulers extracted resources from societies in exchange for protection and stability. That included controlling local hostilities whose scales had tended to increase to a point where they involved the crown itself, as in England's Wars of the Roses. Such agreements had to be sustained continuously, and that facilitated the rise of permanent standing armies.[1]

Initially, most governments preferred to raise armed forces ad hoc, on an emergency basis. "Do not buy guns," Yul Brynner advises the farmers in *The Magnificent Seven*: "Hire men who can use guns." It was easier to secure financial and political support with an enemy at the gates. It was more efficient to engage professional warmakers under mutually understood conditions—also contractual—than to create armies and fleets from scratch, or even to build on the minimal establishments that were all subsistence economies could sustain over long periods of inactivity.[2]

Contract armies in turn became larger in several contexts. Operationally, the development and extension of bastioned-fort systems in western Europe, with the accompanying increase in manpower requirements for their attack and defense, combined with the changing shape of the battlefield to put an increasing premium on discipline and training: qualities best developed and sustained in stable systems. Large numbers of discharged soldiers could not easily be reintegrated into the closed societies and depressed economies characteristic of early modern Europe, especially when war was such a general phenomenon that many veterans considered civilian employment a mere stopgap until the drums beat again. Organized forces were preferable—if, at times, just barely—to bands of marauders.[3]

As armed forces grew, temporary contractual relationships with their commanders generated a corresponding risk of creating not overmighty subjects in the traditional sense, but entrepreneurial challengers for supreme power, as epitomized by the career of Albert von Wallenstein. True, there was only one Wallenstein—but one was enough, an outsider made so wealthy and powerful by war that he was in a position to challenge the Holy Roman Emperor himself. States began integrating military enterprisers into an elite that, in general, was significantly flexible. Since as a class, that group was largely blue-blooded and sought status and stability as the fruits of their enterprise, the process was easy enough at upper levels.[4]

The second stage involved developing standing armies under central control. That process revolved around a second set of contractual relationships, this one between rulers and armies. In what David Parrott calls a "semi-entrepreneurial" system, the military enterprisers' descendants and successors became contractors, raising soldiers under state auspices. The profits might be less, but they were as certain as anything could be in the protean early modern era. Financial rewards were increasingly accompanied as well by social advantage: the granting of military ranks that became permanent at the higher levels offered entrée—or at least the possibility of entrée—into a civil society that increasingly recognized aristocracies of service as well as those of birth.[5]

Officers were only part of the system. States used the resources they were able to mobilize to pay the contractors above all—but increasingly, as well, to guarantee pay, employment, and increasingly some form of pension to their soldiers. The soldiers in turn gave passive loyalty by refraining from coercing the states and societies they served and active loyalty by fighting when so ordered—for as long as the state fulfilled its agreement by providing subsistence without making excessive demands for heroism and sacrifice. Jan Glete calls the result a "fiscal-military state," whose complex structure of contractual relationships could integrate and sustain a broad spectrum of otherwise-discordant domestic interests behind a particular war effort. Organizational capacity was sustained by the active participation of both elite groups and broader sections of the population, who hoped or expected to profit by participating in their state's innovative behavior. Thus a state like Sweden was able to mobilize its limited resources effectively enough to sustain great-power status for a century and regional-power status for a century more. A loosely organized Dutch Republic with a weak central government, committed to economic rather than military development, nevertheless developed, in the sixteenth and seventeenth centuries, a complex network of investment and administration that enabled long-term maintenance of two chartered companies able to conduct war and commerce in the East Indies and the Atlantic, plus an army and a navy able to stand up to the best of Europe's great powers.[6]

The developed fiscal-military state had its rough edges. Considered in the abstract, the system was best adapted to wars of limited duration and limited intensity. It could sustain longer and fiercer conflicts, but only in an episodic fashion, with such items as soldiers' pay becoming increasingly random. In the final analysis, public resources were still significantly limited. The precious metals of the New World and the spices of southeast Asia were a form of windfall profit, frequently interrupted by the vagaries of long-distance voyaging and the direct intervention of enemies. State administrations were still a long way from being able to mobilize and control private resources systematically: The kind of loyalty making that possible was a consequence of the democratic and nationalist revolutions of a later century.[7]

Financing the Military State

As armies increasingly developed a monopoly of effective force, they correspondingly tended to become economically self-sustaining: They raised their own wages. This practical fiscal independence took three forms. Most basic were scorched-earth operations, a development of the medieval *chevauchee*. The latter had been employed essentially for military purposes: denying resources to an opponent, challenging the legitimacy of a ruler unable to protect his subjects. The primary object of early modern scorched earth was destruction. It reached its peak—or nadir—in the French scouring in 1689 of the Palatinate, a frontier province on the Rhine River between France and Germany. This campaign, because of the relatively greater efficiency of the forces involved, came closer to crippling permanently the region's infrastructure than any similar event of the Thirty Years War.[8]

Though soldiers usually profited from scorched earth to a degree, it was on a one-time basis. Such was not the case for what John Lynn calls the "tax of violence." In its simplest form this was a process of "want-take-have": the seizing of resources by force or the threat of force. Armies usually imposed the tax of violence domestically and, in principle at least, situationally. The economic impulses of hunger and privation were reinforced by wider grievances, usually centered on pay tendered late or not forthcoming at all. Armies on the march might plunder the countryside and loot ostensibly friendly towns as though they were enemy strongholds taken by storm. Fine points of obligation and responsibility tended to be obscured by a sense of alienation between military and civil communities. Since the soldiers had the weapons, half-joking demands for feather beds and butchers' meat easily crossed the line into social and criminal offenses ranging from fouling living spaces with excrement to assault, rape, and, occasionally, murder—or what amounted to the same thing: "fair fights" between soldiers and civilians, where the toughest local brawler was usually overmatched.

The tax of violence reached its heyday in the first half of the seventeenth century. Thereafter, while it never disappeared, it steadily declined in extent and degree. Officers who derived much of their command authority from the assent of the commanded were reluctant to test that fragile authority by interfering with off-duty amusements. Experience showed, however, that discipline sacrificed on the march or in garrison was not easily restored for battle. To be effective over long terms, moreover, the tax required a reasonably prosperous, reasonably concentrated host community—France as opposed to Sweden; the Netherlands rather than Poland-Lithuania—societies with something to lose but also able to complain about it. Governments seeking to reassert authority badly shaken by the standing armies created to sustain it took the side of their civilian subjects. Arguably for the first time since the days of Rome, officers were punished for tolerating disorder. Soldiers were required to compensate their victims—at least in theory.[9]

The tax of violence retaught to administrators, military and civilian, the folly of shooting a cow that does not wish to be milked or a sheep that does not stand still to be sheared. In the early stages of the Thirty Years War in Germany, contributions emerged as an alternative. These amounted to requisitions imposed over a substantial area—often an entire small state—to be raised by local authorities and delivered systematically over a set period. The amounts involved, and the balance of cash to kind, theoretically negotiable, were initially set by the military commander under the threat of turning the soldiers loose on the civil infrastructure. The French administration in the age of Louis XIV systematized the process further, accepting contributions as a substitute for physical destruction and moving an increasing proportion of the cash, at least, directly into the state's war chest. Initially little more than a form of extortion, contribution agreements acquired legal regularity and grew less obviously one-sided. Originally a means of compelling civilian populations to sustain any army quartered on them, the protection they implied became enough of a reality to make negotiating one a reasonable policy choice for conquered or occupied territories.[10]

The fiscal-military state had no guarantee of survival, let alone flourishing. For most of the sixteenth century it remained questionable whether rulers could develop the institutional and moral authority to make their aggrandizement permanent. Mighty subjects, even overmighty ones, were still useful in both foreign and domestic conflicts. Every government in Europe suffered a crisis of legitimacy during the Reformation. But the experience of another fiscal-military power, arguably the greatest of them all in its heyday, shows that both of those problems could be submerged by another factor of early modern warmaking: geographic extension.

Power by Geographic Extension

Habsburg Spain was the first European power to develop a global vision: a set of ambitions that may have lacked a blueprint, but nevertheless constituted a proactive grand strategy. That strategy was in part a product of what has traditionally been called the

Age of Discovery but is better understood as the Age of Reconnaissance. Its basis was being able to go somewhere and return on a systematic basis. Its key was a combination of developing maritime technology and improving maritime administration.[11] The Age of Reconnaissance in turn evolved into an age of awareness. Official reports and adventurers' tales generated a literature of books, pamphlets, and, not least, maps—increasingly accurate maps, at least by the standards of the Middle Ages—fostering a global consciousness that began reshaping military thinking.

Europe's globalization also reflected and responded to an increasingly comprehensive confrontation between Christianity and Islam. This was no affair of outpost skirmishes but a product of mutual religious revival in service of the most important conflict of all—one that must end in victory for the true faith. Europe initially stood on the geostrategic defensive against an Ottoman Empire grown rich and powerful by embracing the expansionist ideology of Islam. The Ottoman sultans drew support from a network of outlying powers: in the west the rulers of Egypt and Morocco and the chieftains of North Africa's corsair states; in the east a network of Muslim maritime polities challenged by the Age of Reconnaissance.

The Ottoman storming of Constantinople in 1453 was a catalyst on both sides. For Islam it foreshadowed the beginning of the end for the Kafirs of the crusading west and the Sultan's fleets and armies thrust deep into the Balkans and the Mediterranean. His successors' turning against Mamluk Egypt and Savafid Persia—the latter a religious confrontation between Sunni and Shiite as well as a struggle for secular power—gave the Sultan control of Mecca and Medina, transformed the Black and Red seas into virtual Ottoman lakes, and exponentially enhanced the moral authority and the military power of the Ottoman Empire that under Suleiman the Magnificent turned westward again in the 1520s.

This time, nothing came easily. The Knights of Malta, by now crusaders and corsairs in one, successfully held on behind fortifications built in the new style in the 1522 siege of Rhodes. In 1529, the city of Vienna stood in arms against an Ottoman army suffering from logistical overextension and handicapped by a series of victories along the way that delayed progress until late in the campaigning season. The garrison included a high proportion of veterans experienced in modern siege war and carrying state-of-the-art firearms. The Ottomans were able neither to employ their artillery effectively nor utilize their particular skills of mining. The breaches that were opened proved too narrow to storm successfully against a defense inspired by a high-test mixture of professionalism, desperation, and religious exaltation. After six weeks, Suleiman abandoned the enterprise.[12]

That did not mean he and his successors abandoned the aspiration of overrunning the west. For the next or a half-century Ottoman ambitions focused on the Mediterranean—in the process drawing a second power onto the world stage. Europe's Mediterranean front was held by Spain. A combination of the Muslim challenge and the unexpected material wealth of Mexico and Peru enabled the transformation of a military establishment whose context was European, and whose orientation had been essentially defensive, into a power-projection force with a global dimension that is often overlooked but whose major impact was continental. Spanish troops and warships were committed at the peripheries of Spain's European holdings on the principle that those possessions were sufficiently mutually dependant that none were expendable. Italy, Flanders, Ceuta, Cartagena—it made no difference: What Spain had, it held.

Turkish assault on Constantinople in 1453. © Erich Lessing/Art Resource, New York.

By the last quarter of the sixteenth century, that defensive strategy had developed into something more ambitious and assertive. The Spanish crown, vitalized by the young king Philip II, employed a sophisticated spectrum of pressures and incentives to bring northern Italy's ruling houses and leading families under Spain's control. In the decade after the death of Portugal's childless king in 1578, Spain annexed not merely the peninsular kingdom, but its overseas empire, second at the time only to that of Spain itself. Even the long-running insurrection in the Netherlands seemed to be on its way to a military/political solution, with the southern provinces increasingly reconciling themselves to Habsburg rule, while the northern ones depended more and more on external aid to continue their resistance.

Thus, rather than being a reaction to fear of loss, Spain's growing assertiveness reflected an affirmative, proactive approach. The mentality underpinning this shift has been described as "messianic imperialism." Geoffrey Parker and Paul Kennedy in particular stress the religious dimensions of psychological hubris and physical overstretch. In the first half of the century, defense of the Catholic faith had been a major ideological consideration. The last quarter was, however, increasingly characterized by a military

The honors of war are shown in this painting by Diego Velazquez, *The Surrender of Breda*, 1625. Note halberds and pikes in background. This Spanish victory was later reversed at the end of the Eighty Years War. © Erich Lessing/Art Resource, New York.

approach. Spain's English policy in the Elizabethan era, for example, was initially considered in terms of ending its support of Spain's overt enemies, with diplomacy and dynastic marriage taking precedence over armed force. Even after the disaster of the Armada in 1588, Spain's government thought of England in direct, military terms: invasion and conquest.

That the Habsburgs attempted too much, with an administrative system that sprang too many leaks under pressure, is unquestionable. It is no less clear that Philip II not so much misunderstood the concept of prioritizing, but rejected it on principle. Yet the decisions that led to Spain's spectacular geopolitical decline in the seventeenth century at bottom reflected a proactive, coherent response to the globalization of the monarchy's grand-strategic world. That the strategy had major conceptual shortcomings was to be expected: nothing along such lines had ever been attempted. That any kind of global policy would be limited by the technologies of transportation and communication was even more predictable. Not until World War II did it become possible to implement a worldwide strategy in anything but outline form. Even then, it required the resources of an emerging techo-superpower. Spain's failures were Homeric—but the underlying signifier of Spanish policy was that it was attempted at all.[13]

Sea Power

Globalization was not confined to the Iberian peninsula. An England whose strategic vision had for centuries been focused immediately north and west, toward Britain's Celtic fringes, and directly across the channel into France began broadening its horizons in the mid-sixteenth century, from a combination of increasing overseas trade, a growing sense that sea power could provide near-absolute security from continental interference, and not least, from the accretions to the Matter of Britain provided by the sea dogs of the Elizabethan era. By the seventeenth century this mixture was strengthened by an early version of navalism: the notion that sea power could make war support war through the acquisition and control of trade routes and colonies.

Practice did not begin matching theory until after the Revolution of 1688. Prior to that period, England, though hardly poor in an absolute sense, lacked the administrative systems to concentrate the kingdom's resources for public purposes. The Early Stuarts' failure in this respect was exacerbated by domestic conflicts that for a half-century racked the British Isles in a complex interfacing of religious, regional, and economic tensions that left England unable even to control the channel consistently in its mid-century series of wars with the Dutch Republic.

The Glorious Revolution, which overthrew the reign of King James II, through a union of English Parliament supporters and William of Orange from the Netherlands, resolved the long-vexing issue of sovereignty in favor of Parliament. With sovereignty went control of financing, and government revenues increased exponentially in the reign of William and Anne. The gentry of England no longer feared the crown and were correspondingly willing to expand both tax systems and private credit for public purposes—specifically, a standing navy, the first of its kind in the history of modern Europe.[14]

In his seminal *The Safeguard of the Sea*, N.A.M. Rodger makes the point that even compared to armies, navies were so technically, socially, and economically demanding that they could ultimately be established and sustained only by positive public support. In that sense England achieved a still-unrecognized step forward in the development of the "power state" a good 100 years before its counterparts.[15] The Treaty of Utrecht in 1713 gave Britain Gibraltar and Minorca and control of Mediterranean access to the Atlantic. Britain dominated the English Channel and the North Sea and controlled the North Atlantic's principal trade routes and fishing grounds. Britain had established firm positions in North America, the Caribbean, and the East Indies. The Royal Navy was in the process of establishing sustainability: a network of defended bases, maps and charts of hitherto unknown waters, habitable ships and antiscorbutics, which all contributed to realize and concretize Britain's global perspective.

That did not mean exclusive focus on what later generations came to call a "blue-water" strategy. By painful processes of trial and error, successive governments learned that fleets could not by themselves reduce such emerging land powers as Habsburg Austria and Bourbon France, nor was money sufficient to secure reliable allies and clients for continental military operations. England had to provide a human ante as well: the ground forces that provided the core of the anti-French coalitions in northern Europe and—less successfully—in the Iberian peninsula.[16] These, however, were a secondary element of a global strategic vision that by 1715 established Britain as the sustainer of military balance on the continent and the dominant power at sea. Other states—the Dutch Republic, Spain, and, above all, France—might develop surge capacities and assert their position in one region or another. For the next century and beyond, however, Britain's overseas dominion essentially defined the limits of the European continent.

DUELS OF FAITH AND EMPIRE

The globalization of conflict characteristic of the early modern European experience was balanced, then supplanted, in the sixteenth century by a pattern of domestic war that both transcended and highlighted political boundaries. Fundamental questioning of religious issues long antedated the posting of the Ninety-five Theses by Martin Luther in 1517. Religious wars were nothing new. Albigensians, Hussites, and Holy Roman Emperors had repeatedly challenged Rome's authority and claims in arms. But the Protestant Reformation and the Catholic counterpart that paralleled it combined to raise a fundamental question: Would a 1,000-year heritage continue to shape Europe's behavior, or must the continent's spiritual order and the institutional structures based on it be restructured from the ground up?

Debates that began as theological and intellectual constructions acquired legal dimensions as authorities sought to define acceptable belief and behavior. The issues at stake, however, transcended custom and law alike. Medieval Europe had been characterized by a high degree of individual and small-group violence at all social levels. Much of this was appetitive, temporarily satiated by riots and affrays at one end of the spectrum, tournaments at the other. Religious enthusiasm gave local violence unprecedented staying power.

Religious enthusiasm infused and informed local politics as well. A factionalism still incompletely subsumed by the development of the fiscal-military state found new outlets in faith-based disputes, whose addressing increasingly took military forms. Central authorities, neither able nor willing to assert and enforce policies of toleration, were swept along partly by the tide of events and partly because of their own developing religious convictions—and fears. One interpretation of Christianity, and only one, held the key to salvation—but which one? It was a question to disturb the sleep of the most ostensibly committed secularist.[17]

Systematic violence began in a Germany where authority was already significantly devolved: where rulers seldom could mobilize effective force on their own and where religious dispute was most intense at the grass roots. Beginning in 1524, a series of regional uprisings spread across the southwest. Rural in orientation, drawing their support primarily from serfs and tenant farmers, they combined religious, social, and economic grievances. Their principal targets were local landlords, whether lay or ecclesiastical, but their behavior was shaped by an anticlericalism combining vicious iconoclasm and vague eschatology, projecting a new world order based on the word of God as revealed in the gospels.[18]

Despite its near-total lack of appeal in the towns, the Peasants' Revolt posed enough of a threat to the existing order to bring a combined army of Imperial and Habsburg troops into the field. Its crushing victory at the battle of Frankenhausen in May 1525 set the stage for a brutal repression of heterodoxy—which nevertheless persisted in reappearing across Germany for the next decade. The suppression of social and religious insurrection in turn gave rise to permanent rival organizations of Catholic and Protestant princes, each with a semipermanent army. For Emperor Charles V, the Schmalkaldic League of Protestant princes within the Holy Roman Empire represented a mortal threat to his authority by its existence. To secure a free hand against it, he was eventually willing to make peace not only with France, but with the Ottoman Sultan. His overwhelming military victory over the League at Muehlberg in April 1547 nevertheless was not enough to shatter a Protestantism whose roots had sunk deep since the first days of Martin Luther. The best Charles could achieve was the compromise peace of Augsburg in 1555. By its terms Germany's princes were allowed to determine the religious faith of their own lands—as long as the faith was either Catholic or Lutheran.[19]

The German experience suggested that no matter how transcendent their respective claims, no matter how zealous their respective adherents, neither major religious confession was able to overwhelm the other by any feasible combination of persuasion and force. That pattern was even more obvious in France, where the next sequence of religious wars broke out with the death of King Henry II in 1559. A female-headed regency, even though the woman was Catherine de Medici, opened the door to three decades of rivalry between and among the crown and the major noble families. As in Germany, the struggle was in part political. But the great Catholic clans, the Guises and Montmorencys, were no less committed to their faith than the Protestant—chiefly Calvinist—families concentrated in the south and west. If anything, the religious aspects of the conflict grew deeper with time, as mutual excesses were underwritten by developing theologies.

As in Germany, no faction could achieve a pattern of decisive success on the battlefield. Absent that, negotiations and assassinations, truces and betrayals became the order of the day. The Protestants proved unable to increase their ranks by conversion but were secure in a network of fortresses and fortified towns whose reduction was beyond the resources of the Catholics. The partial revival of the monarchy in the 1570s made the conflict three-sided and correspondingly even less susceptible of resolution by negotiation. Not until France was on the edge of bankruptcy and chaos did the nominal conversion to Catholicism of Henry of Navarre, leader of the Protestant faction, bring about a peace of exhaustion.[20]

Among the theaters of religious war, the Netherlands offered the best case study of long-term stalemate. Discontent with rule from Habsburg Spain, and the heavy taxes that entailed, was a political focal point for the rhetoric of Calvinist preachers. Their activities in turn encouraged local authorities to take a hard-line, repressive policy. In 1566, Protestant iconoclasts swept through the northern provinces, smashing images, monuments, and stained glass windows and setting authority at defiance. Madrid responded with large-scale military intervention, sustained by the seemingly inexhaustible wealth of the New World, and committed to action by a monarch willing to pay any price to reassert control over the region. To provide logistic support, the crown developed the so-called Spanish Road, a corridor of possessions and clients extending from Milan to the Netherlands. Its maintenance was a cornerstone of Spanish policy for the next half-century. The Army of Flanders that it supported was the most effective force sustained in the field for a long term by any great power.

Spain did achieve a certain success: The southern Netherlands, modern Belgium, were reconfirmed in—or restored to—Catholicism in the face of comprehensive and deep-rooted Protestant convictions. Yet the ferocity of the resistance mounted by the emerging Dutch Republic set at defiance Spain's best efforts at conquest and conciliation alike. Militant, determined civilians acquired military skill by experience and osmosis, while Spanish soldiers grew ever more reluctant to make more than minimal commitment to a so-called forever war. When all was said and done, a century of war in the Netherlands left Spain the first Sick Man of Europe, overextended and vulnerable to a France whose own recovery of great-power status in the early seventeenth century was relative.[21]

In 1528, King Francis I of France challenged Habsburg emperor Charles V to a duel that would decide three decades of war. Charles responded by offering to face the Frenchman without armor, in a rapier-and-dagger match. Duels under such conditions were familiar in the era: They usually meant death for one, sometimes both, adversaries. Francis, perhaps prudently, sidestepped the challenge. Twenty-first-century readers may wish that the precedent of rulers settling issues of state directly instead of by million-strong proxies had gone further. The incident nevertheless highlights the fact that war in the late Renaissance had a secular as well as religious dimension.

Some quarrels were based on competing claims to the same territory or the same title. Some were based on personal antagonism: hatreds cultivated over decades or the product of direct encounters between equally arrogant protagonists. Their consequences far transcended that dimension. In 1494, Charles VIII of France invaded Italy, inspired in principle by grandiose ambitions of organizing a new crusade against the Ottomans but in fact by a more mundane claim to the throne of Naples. Habsburg Emperor Maximilian, a Papacy interpreting French conquests as a threat to its own Italian territories, and Spain, still not a Habsburg land but nevertheless suspicious of its neighbor across the Pyrenees, joined forces to block the initiative. For fifty years the peninsula became a battleground, with the focus gradually shifting northward to the richer prize of the Duchy of Milan. Fornovo and Ravenna, la Bicocca and Pavia—some of the battles are still remembered. The sack of Rome in 1527 by largely Protestant German mercenaries in Catholic Habsburg service highlights the indecisiveness of the fighting, sustained in later years more by French unwillingness to acknowledge defeat than by any hopes of turning the tide.[22]

That intention was reflected instead in the extension of the fighting into western Germany and the Netherlands, where Habsburg and French territories connected and where Henry VII of England briefly pursued his own dynastic ambitions as a Habsburg ally[23]—at the price of war in his backyard with a Scotland whose army had significantly improved from its feudal-levy days. The English victory at Flodden in 1513 broke Scotland's back as an independent power—not least because of the death of the king and the near-literal annihilation of the nobility.[24] Events on the continent, however, replicated those in Italy. Victory's baton passed back and forth with no strategic decision until, in 1559, the Peace of Chateau Cambresis formalized the Habsburg-Valois standoff. A few weeks later, Henry of France was mortally wounded in a joust. Philip of Spain vainly sent his personal physician to his fellow monarch's side. Like the proffered challenges with which the war began, this gesture symbolized the personal nature of war at the beginning of the early modern era.

The Thirty Years War

The Thirty Years War (1618–1648) grew out of a complex set of still-obscure circumstances whose nature remains subject to debate. Chief among its direct causes were the revived hegemonial ambitions of the House of Habsburg relative to Germany and an internal German order that no longer reflected either theological or political realities. Facilitating the war's expansion were the continued willingness of France to challenge Habsburg pretensions; the enduring war in the Netherlands; and above all, the rise of Sweden from a Baltic to a European power.[25]

The religious parity established by the peace of Augsburg had endured officially, despite increasing challenge from a Calvinism that made significant headway in central and south Germany, including Bohemia. Its adherents resented their exclusion from the system, and when Emperor Matthias placed his heir apparent Ferdinand on Bohemia's throne, Ferdinand's new subjects advised restraint in religious matters. Ferdinand, a zealous product of the Catholic Reformation, ignored the advice, and a group of Protestant nobles threw his advisors out of a window in the royal palace of Prague.

This defenestration, a conscious imitation of an event triggering the Hussite Wars of the fifteenth century, was arguably intended as a warning rather than a challenge. Ferdinand, who seceded to the Imperial throne in 1619, regarded it as unacceptable defiance—particularly when Calvinist prince Frederick of the Palatinate put himself forward as a challenger for Bohemia's crown.

As yet, however, neither the German Protestants nor the Dutch and English were willing to become involved, and Frederick's improvised army was shattered at the White Mountain near Prague in 1620. The Palatinate was overrun by troops from the Spanish Netherlands and Catholic Bavaria. Bohemia was forcibly recatholicized, its aristocracy largely replaced by "new men" religiously and politically loyal to the Habsburgs.

Ferdinand's ruthless exploitation of his victory generated the response of a league of German Protestant princes, with some ephemeral support from the Dutch and English and more concrete aid from Lutheran king Christian IV of Denmark. His ill-advised initiation of war in 1626 resulted in a series of defeats at the hands of Imperial forces and a rival Catholic League dominated by Bavaria. In 1629, with Catholic cavalry watering their horses in the Baltic, Denmark opted out of the war's front row.

The Protestant coalition promptly collapsed, and again, a possible chance for reconciliation existed. It vanished when Ferdinand insisted on a return to the religious boundaries of 1555. In three-quarters of a century Germany's religious structure had altered significantly, albeit unofficially, in favor of the Protestants tolerated by an Empire too divided to strive for anything else. Even though the situation had altered, Calvinists, Lutherans, and not a few Catholics were unwilling to see the Empire acquire the kind of political and theological power that redrawing the religious map implied.

Gustavus Adolphus

The Protestant crisis attracted external attention as well. Swedish king Gustavus Adolphus, brave to a fault in battle, was a cautious and thoughtful statesman. His growing interest in undertaking military operations in Germany reflected a Baltic policy suffering from overstretch. Sweden had sought aggrandizement by force on the

Baltic littoral on and off for a century, with varying degrees of success. In 1621, Gustavus went to war against Poland, initially to secure Sweden against invasion by occupying the southern shore of the Baltic. His appetite grew with eating. By 1626, Swedish control extended as far east as the Dvina River and westward into Pomerania. By year's end, the entire Vistula watershed was under Swedish control, and the Swedish army was using its new combination of firepower and mobility to teach the Poles some expensive tactical lessons.[26]

They proved all too apt pupils, integrating infantry and artillery into their traditionally cavalry-based system. The next two years featured small-scale campaigning, destructive rather than decisive, in a region at the best of times barely able to sustain its population. Both sides became correspondingly drawn to the wider conflict to the west. In 1629, a contingent of Imperialist troopers contributed to a Polish victory in a swirling, wide-open cavalry battle south of Danzig. By that time, Gustavus perceived the limits of his current strategy. Poland was too big and too amorphous to be defeated by the blitzkrieg-style operations at which the Swedes excelled. As much to the point, Habsburg power was moving dangerously close to a Swedish sphere of influence too new to be considered stable.[27]

In June 1630, Gustavus Adolphus landed in Pomerania at the head of 14,000 men. He was not welcomed as a Protestant savior by the princes and estates of north Germany. Gustavus was a foreigner, with a reputation for practicing the kind of hard war that meant hard knocks and hard fighting for anybody siding with him. Some local rulers hoped to maintain low-profile neutrality. Others, like the electors of Brandenburg and Saxony, hoped to mobilize German Protestantism to defend itself—preferably by negotiations as opposed to force of arms. Not until August 1631 did Gustavus feel strong enough to advance south into Saxony. Even then, he understood that he was expected to deliver a major victory before he could expect systematic support from German Protestants. On September 7, at Breitenfeld in Saxony, Gustavus conducted a battlefield seminar on the use of firepower and mobility, crushing and scattering a veteran Imperial army of half his own effective strength.

Gustavus followed up his victory by planning a campaign for the next year that involved raising over 200,000 men, organized in no fewer than seven armies, for a co-ordinated attack against the Habsburg Empire and its Catholic supporters. Neither German will nor German capacities were remotely equal to such a challenge. Instead, Gustavus undertook a rapier thrust into Saxony against a reorganized Imperialist army also looking for a fight. On November 6, 1632, the Swedes eked out a victory—but lost one-third of their force and their king, pistoled by an Austrian cavalryman.

The death of Gustavus removed the one possible force multiplier that might have averted or modified the war's devolution into a Hobbesian stalemate: a war of all against all, defying efforts at peacemaking and leaving much of Europe between the Rhine and the Vistula physically and emotionally devastated. The Dutch Republic had taken up arms against Spain as early as 1622 and sought help from a France still committed to resisting Habsburg ambitions. Initially, French participation was covert, underwriting the presence of a Sweden whose resources were rapidly diminishing. In 1635, chief minister Cardinal Richelieu took a direct hand but was unable to prevent a slide into entropy, eventually fixed in place in 1648 by the Peace of Westphalia. Never again would a universal faith or a universal empire be able to legitimize its governance of Europe.[28]

THE TIME OF THE DYNASTIES

The Peace of Westphalia, by recognizing the sovereignty of states within the Holy Roman Empire, set the seal on a general legitimization of sovereignty—an affirmation enduring to this day. *Sovereignty* means the exclusive right to exercise authority over a region or a people. Until very recently, it was understood in international law as absolute. Above all in the context of warmaking, sovereign states could act as their rulers saw fit. The concept of *jus ad bellum*, or "just war theory," was correspondingly attenuated, applied more often to validate than to critique states' discretionary powers of wreaking. For the next century European diplomacy centered on establishing the boundaries of sovereign states and their respective positions in the international order.

The defining figure of early modern dynastic war was Louis XIV; the defining institution was the French army. At the end of his reign Louis reproached himself with having loved war too much. This self-reproach had a wider implied context. War had shaped the behavior and the mentality of his kingdom, and by extension, its neighbors as well, in ways foreign to the Europe of 1495 or 1648.

Louis inherited a state policy with an essential goal: take down Habsburg Spain. Developed in a context of French security, it evolved during the Thirty Years War into a springboard for French hegemony. The "rational actor" so beloved of international relations "realists" would have had little trouble accepting the argument that the Peace of the Pyrenees, in 1659, was at least as promising a foundation as the Peace of Westphalia for constructing a New European Order. Louis acquired a Spanish wife at the price of accepting her renouncing her Spanish inheritance. It was true that renunciation was contingent on a dowry that remained unpaid. It was true as well that the weight of legal and religious opinion supported the argument that inheritance was a sacred right, impossible to surrender. It is even more fundamentally true that both of these arguments sustained Louis's commitment to *gloire* as the linchpin of not only his power, but his legitimacy.

Gloire is easier to describe than define. It was, first of all, a gendered quality, reserved for men. It involved fulfilling a code of honor and doing so with panache: the kind of flair that generated public reputation. By implication, a man without *gloire* was without honor as well. This is at the opposite pole from a Western concept, developed in two world wars, that honor is best understood as a thing in itself, arguably most pristine when separated from reputation. But *gloire* was more than a personal concept. It justified position in the world—authority exercised and power held. Failure to uphold rights implied that those rights had lapsed, thus opening the way for others to claim them. Domestic political stability in turn depended heavily on the ruler's ability to provide security from external threats and challenges.[29]

In that sense, *gloire* suggests comparison to the Mandate of Heaven as it developed in China. Its possession both demonstrated and conveyed legitimacy. Without it the most elaborate theories of divine-right monarchy remained intellectual and theological abstractions. The internal challenges to the French monarchy, culminating at mid-century in the series of uprisings known as the Fronde, essentially manifested the crown's lack of *gloire*. The near-contemporary overthrow of England's Stuart monarchy was an even clearer illustration of a throne devolving to the level of its challengers.

Even more than the Mandate of Heaven, *gloire* was dynamic, requiring constant renewal and constant manifestation. At substate levels this gave rise to a culture of formal dueling. Internationally, it made wreaking a constant. The War of Devolution and the Dutch War, the Nine Years War of 1689–1697, and the War of the Spanish Succession all had their practical aspects, iterated and reiterated in the scholarly literature. The series of coalitions against France were relationships of convenience rather than affinity. Yet in their essence these were all wars of *gloire*.[30] Less pretentious monarchies like Habsburg Austria, smaller ones like Piedmont and Bavaria, might participate less enthusiastically than the grand monarchy, but they understood and accepted the rules and terms of the game. England, with its developing blue-water, commercially focused, strategic alternative, might be ambivalent. Its monarchs and its parliament in the final analysis nevertheless sustained a continental commitment, for lack of something better, and accepted military expenditures that absorbed as much as three-fourths of state revenue in times of war. The sober syndics of the United Provinces might eschew *gloire* as a concept but could not deny it as a fact. The profits of the Dutch fiscal-military state sustained a large, permanent, professional army and paid for enough foreign auxiliaries to keep around 100,000 men in the field during the wars of Louis XIV. When someone wants to fight, it is difficult not to oblige him.

Wars of *gloire* tended toward a form John Lynn calls "wars as process."[31] This was not limited war in the generally understood sense; it was not even controlled war. The devastation of the Palatinate between 1683 and 1689 exceeded in scope and system any comparable event of the Thirty Years War. War as process meant, rather, forever war. With no fundamental motive to strive for an endgame, there were no compelling reasons to challenge the structural and institutional factors favoring indecision. As wars expanded geographically, concentrating forces grew correspondingly difficult. Warmaking on land and sea remained heavily determined by weather: For one-third or more of each year, armies were confined to winter quarters and fleets to secure harbors. Operational tempo was slow, reflecting armies' rudimentary internal articulation, navies' limited means of communication and coordination, and logistic systems that, on land or sea, were limited and fragile. Fragility also characterized state finances, with the result that war was still expected to support war directly, through the by now well-established system of requisitions and contributions. That in turn fostered distribution rather than concentration of force, in order to spread out the burden on subsistence economies highly likely to collapse if overstrained. Once dispersed, armies increasingly built around infantry and artillery were difficult to concentrate quickly given the sparse nature and limited capacity of road networks, even in developed regions like the Low Countries. Concentration, moreover, brought little benefit. At sea the Anglo-Dutch Wars (1652–1674) were an ongoing case study in the problems of engaging and controlling large, heterogeneous fleets. On-land battles and sieges alike seldom yielded more than local, temporary results, even when one or both adversaries was willing to take high risks.[32]

The exact balance of policy and circumstance in wars of process remains controversial. *Gloire* suggests a way of reconciling them. Wars of process in a sense resembled the so-called flower wars of Aztec Mexico in that killing enemies, conquering territory, or even exploiting resources was instrumental, rather than essential. In one case the desired outcome was acquiring and manifesting what Polynesian cultures call mana. In the other it was capturing prisoners for sacrifice: acquiring mana at one remove by pleasing the gods. In both cases, with no fundamental motive to strive for an endgame, there were no compelling reasons to challenge the structural and institutional factors favoring operational indecision. In Europe, that pressure would come later, in the next generation of dynastic war.

By the 1720s the consolidation of Europe on the model of sovereign states and centralized authority was, for practical purposes, completed. Domestic challenges now involved control of government, with participants usually willing to resolve disputes without taking up arms. Internationally, the major parameters of dispute had been similarly defined by experience—a process facilitated by the gradual resolution of the complex questions of dynastic inheritance that had so often triggered conflicts in the previous century.

The inability of any European state to increase its power indefinitely significantly limited by later standards meant that wars were frequently waged by alliance systems. It is rare indeed when all the parties to an alliance achieve their aims, nor, at a time when alliances were relationships of convenience rather than principle, did states necessarily wish to see any neighbors aggrandize themselves disproportionally. The ancien régime's increasingly elaborate structures of domestic and international intrigue facilitated that concern by systematizing and legitimizing back-channeling and double-dealing, especially when executed with style.[33]

The concept of *gloire* was also changing. It had never legitimated war as such. Unjustified war was arguably the greatest possible denial of the ruler's responsibility before God, which was the core of most theories of absolute monarchy. That was a major reason why the developing "laws of war" took such a latitudinarian approach to finding reasons for going to war. More pragmatically, making war without sanction, or at least its pretexts, exacerbated the suspicion and hostility of neighbors, while giving domestic critics a metaphoric sword. The alternatives of negotiation and diplomacy were combining not to replace intrastate conflict as the eighteenth century waxed, but rather to narrow its focus.[34]

The face of war was altered as well by developments in mentalities. Every era defines ultimate truth in its own way, whether that be the biological determinism of the nineteenth century or the Internet-based relativism of the twenty-first. Eighteenth-century intellectual life was shaped by a search for first principles, for integrating social phenomena into an order deriving its rationale and its expression from the world of mathematics. In the context of this mechanistic world view, it was not surprising that military theorists and practical soldiers sought to express the conduct of war and the behavior of armies in universal rather than craft-specific terms—terms, moreover, comprehensible and acceptable to the wider societies to which they belonged. It was even less surprising that they did so in the context of what Blaise Pascal called *l'esprit géométrique*—the spirit of geometry.

The geometric spirit was essentially about control. In the context of eighteenth-century warmaking, control meant management on one hand, dispassion on the other. The growing emphasis on training and discipline discussed in the body of this work reflected a wider cultural emphasis on order, precision, and harmony. Executing complex fire-and-movement tactics under the conditions of a flintlock battlefield required close and flexible supervision. Passion was discounted at all levels. Adrenalin could adversely affect everything from a soldier's ability to load and fire by the numbers, to a cavalry general's ability to keep his men in hand during a charge, to a commander's recognition of the precise time to mount an attack—or initiate a retreat, should the situation call for it.[35]

Put together, the changing approach to *gloire* and the rise of *l'esprit géométrique* offered a nurturing environment for the development of war as process into limited war. The near-random chaos of the seventeenth century, so vividly depicted in the writings of Grimmelshausen, gave way to warmaking as a passionless instrument of state policy. Logistics and finances, weather and geography, continued to constrain warmaking's parameters. The exponential increase of infantry firepower provided by the introduction of the flintlock musket, and the accompanying refinement of linear tactics, enhanced battlefield gridlock. The limited wars fought by eighteenth-century armies reflected a mind-set as well—a mind-set predicated on never getting too high and never getting too low. Erratic genius could be more dangerous than predictable mediocrity in a multiple-risk environment. Tomorrow was another day. One campaigning season would be followed by another. And victory lay in nuances.[36]

Conventional historiography has, until recently, tended to conflate *limited* with *indecisive*. Whatever case can be made for the intrinsic indecisiveness of war as process, the rulers and the commanders of eighteenth-century Europe were increasingly committed to achieving decision. On a diplomatic level the often-cited balance of power embodied a dynamic of resolution as well as an ethos of stability. Europe's development after 1648 into what has been called a republic of states, all meriting recognition as equal sovereign powers within a community of common values, did not hinder near-continuous discussions of eviscerating or eliminating some of the participants. Spain, Sweden, and Poland were all, at one time or another, leading candidates for dismemberment in the eighteenth century. The Austrian Empire was increasingly expected to be parted out to its neighbors' advantage once Maria Theresa assumed the throne. The desperate efforts of Charles VI to secure his daughter's inheritance through a network of international treaties is a classic example of applying yesterday's solution to today's problem: The inheritance trope predominant in the Age of *Gloire* was a secondary factor in the Age of Reason.[37]

The mid-century Diplomatic Revolution is an even better example of the international structure's dynamic of resolution. Its principal author, Austria's Count Wenzel Kaunitz, may have in principle sought Prussia's emasculation rather than its annihilation and to that extent was able to present himself and his government as defending Europe's new established order. It was, however, painfully obvious to everyone involved that the process of reducing Frederick the Great's Prussia to a badly carved rump was unlikely in the extreme to turn back time to 1740.[38] That the international order established in 1763 survived another thirty years primarily reflected the continued existence of states like Poland and the Ottoman Empire, whose weakness provided opportunities for aggrandizement in an essentially predatory diplomatic environment.

The search for resolution was also manifested at war's operational levels. In part, this reflected the growing homogenization of Europe's armies: their acculturation to common patterns of training, organization, and tactics. Armies kept abreast of each others' innovations, not least through a pattern of middle-ranking officers moving from service to service. In contrast to forces developed in different frameworks, symmetrical opponents seldom offer each other obvious windows of opportunity. A mirror image can be defeated, but to do so requires a combination of planning and opportunism that has defied even capable generals before and since. Frederick of Prussia was not the first to conclude that victory must be won at the beginning of a war, by getting inside an enemy's loop of competence and turning his strengths to weaknesses. The alternative was attrition: the kind of drawn out, exhausting war an early modern monarch might accept but that no early modern government could afford.[39]

The man who described himself as "the Field Marshal and First Minister of the King of Prussia" was "enlightened," at least, in a pragmatic sense. He understood the essence of the transformation of states, in Charles Tilly's words, "from wasps to locomotives," in terms of their internal power.[40] Drawing on a state's legal subjects for the means of making war nevertheless involved a synergy of coercion and cooperation. Society's productive classes, peasants as well as landlords, local merchants as well as international bankers, could not be taxed above certain levels without risk—not so much popular risings in the traditional sense, but using the state's demands to assert claims against the state.

Models of decisiveness were not lacking in eighteenth-century warfare. The open terrain and the low force-to-space ratios characteristic of eastern Europe led, in structuring that region's armies, to an emphasis on speed, mobility, and shock—which meant that cavalry played a more important role than in the West's firepower-based systems. When the two types met, as in the Austro-Ottoman and Russo-Ottoman wars that dotted the eighteenth century's first half, the battlefield results could be decisive—for either army. Extra-European conflicts also offered multiple examples of tactical decision, both against asymmetric adversaries, like the Indians of northeastern North America, and non-European forces that acculturated to Western military models, like those of the larger south Indian states.

Was it, however, possible to achieve decisive results in conflicts between states whose armies were constructed on the Western model? The most comprehensive and sophisticated association of decision with limited war was developed by Prussia's Frederick II. Even before assuming the throne in 1740, Frederick developed the hypothesis that Prussia needed a systematic, long-term foreign policy to secure its interests as one of Europe's major powers. He proceeded by traceable stages to the conclusion that expansion by annexation—specifically, of Austria's province of Silesia—was an ultimate necessity. The alternative was that followed by the increasing number of lesser German states that, in the course of the eighteenth century, eschewed military competition for a cultural and intellectual version. Often not much less expensive than wreaking, the new course was easier on infrastructure and demographics. Its appeal to Frederick was precisely nil.

Frederick supported this contention by appealing to a "reason of state" that lay outside the moral principles applying to individuals. His concept of a monarch's role rejected fundamentally its representational and heroic elements. His concept of war was that it should be short, decisive, and brutal—less to conserve scarce resources than to deter future challenges from the defeated party or anyone else. The nineteenth-century debate between Hans Delbrück and the unformed historians of the German General

Staff over whether Frederick practiced a strategy of "attrition" like his counterparts or a strategy of "annihilation" prefiguring Napoleon and the elder Moltke suffers from present-mindedness and tunnel vision. Frederick's strategy was above all political. War's optimal goal was to establish, by an initial victory or series of victories, the wisdom of negotiation as an alternative to continued conflict. War's aims should correspondingly be clear, positive, and above all susceptible to discussion. Since Frederick interpreted the behavior of states as subject to rational calculation, governed by principles that could be learned and applied in the same way one maintained a clock, there should be no reason to repeat the lesson of the battlefield.

Between 1740 and 1763, Frederick applied these principles with single-minded determination. Frederick had no imperial pretensions, no dreams of riches from distant colonies, no visions of being a Third Rome. In the mind of its king Prussia's essential interest lay in securing its position at the head table. Prussia confronted Europe in arms and emerged victorious—but at a price that left the state shaken to its physical and moral foundations. Frederick above all consistently miscalculated Austrian intransigence—or Austrian irrationality. Maria Theresa, her diplomats and generals, responded to Prussia's challenge and Silesia's loss by a diplomacy that, by 1756, confronted Frederick with a coalition of forces far superior to anything Prussia could field. This was accompanied by a quantum improvement in the Habsburg army's quality—a process beyond Frederick's control. Still a work in progress by 1763, the Austrian army nevertheless kept the field well enough arguably to win the war by not losing it.

Frederick drew conclusions from experience. After 1763, he essentially maintained Prussia's still tenuous great-power status by negotiation and deference. The army underwrote Prussia's diplomacy by emphasizing its alternative. The Seven Years War finally convinced the king that perceived capacity and perceived readiness to make war were far more important to Prussia's security than the waging of war itself. Standards of discipline and appearance became increasingly rigid, increasingly comprehensive in ways inviting comparison to the British Navy in the late age of sail, and for similar reasons. A smart ship and a smart regiment were understood to assert power by virtue of their respective grooming. Reviews and maneuvers developed from testing grounds for war to public displays of power, designed to deter any state—or any domestic dissident—thinking of trying further conclusions with Old Fritz and his grenadiers.[41]

As Prussia accepted the wisdom of limitations, pressures for decision grew in other politicomilitary systems. In the American Revolution Britain confronted a new type of war. Its outcome was by no means inevitable. On a macro level Britain enjoyed political stability, possessed Europe's finest system of public finances, and governed a world-spanning empire that already had provided broad exposure to unconventional situations. Geographically, three-fourths of the colonists lived within seventy-five miles of a coast generally favorable topographically and environmentally for maritime operations. Operationally, the main revolutionary armies adjusted to European methods and measured themselves by European standards in crucial areas like discipline and tactics—a policy likely to work to the advantage of a British army with a record of broad and successful experience in North America.

Initially, prospects for a short war seemed correspondingly favorable. Britain, however, was able neither to reknit the frayed bonds of political allegiance, nor put away its opponents on the battlefield. In the words of American general Nathanael

Greene, "we fight . . . get beaten, rise, and fight again." Even with French, Spanish, and Dutch help the revolutionaries could not defeat the British head-to-head. But by not losing, they were able to make the case in London, and to American skeptics as well, that independence was preferable to a third form of modern war, emerging alongside wars of process and limited war: attrition warfare, decided by various combinations of accident and design that eroded the resources and the will of one side to the point where it resigns the game as much from frustration as for military reasons.[42]

Improving Operational Effectiveness

Wars of *gloire* and wars of process, limited wars and wars of attrition, shared a common factor. They discounted operational effectiveness. Indecision developed into a standing reproach to increasingly professionalized armed forces. Nowhere did that process bite deeper than in France. The army of Louis XIV had possessed the highest institutional standards in Europe. It had set the trends and established the patterns of land warfare for three-quarters of a century. It showed some signs of arteriosclerosis during the War of the Austrian Succession. Retooling with the coming of peace was at best superficial. During the Seven Years War, the French army sank to the bottom of Europe's first rank and, embarrassingly, remained there.[43]

The causes of French decline in good part reflected wider problems facing ancien régime France. Financing and logistics, favoritism and court interference were alike exacerbated by the lack of support for France's mid-century wars in political circles. On one level, however, the rising generation of military reformers on the whole accepted the system as opposed to challenging it. There were, moreover, a broad spectrum of immediate possibilities for improving the army's effectiveness at the operating level.

In the beginning was the divisional system. Eighteenth-century armies possessed no articulation, or interconnection, above brigade level. Under the auspices of the duc de Broglie, France introduced the division: a grouping of several brigades, plus cavalry and artillery. The direct impact of that innovation to the army must not be exaggerated. French divisions under the ancien régime still tended to be administrative or ad hoc formations, whose operational possibilities remained largely theoretical. It was, however, clear that an army organized in divisions could expand its marching areas and rates of movement. Administratively, divisions would be able to carry a higher proportion of their requirements with them and could make up the rest locally, without devastating an entire zone of operations.

Tactically, a division had the potential to engage an enemy by itself, at least long enough for other divisions to come to its support. And a divisional organization offered wide possibilities for relieving pressure on army commanders. The Seven Years War had shown that even a captain of Frederick the Great's caliber was just barely able to control an army with state-of-the-art size and speed. Subarticulation offered an alternative to the requirement of genius at the top levels.[44]

The second contribution to improving the army's effectiveness was made by J.A.H. Comte de Guibert. As a young man, he served in the Seven Years War and was only twenty-one when he published his *Essai général de tactique* in 1772. This work and its successor, *Défense du Système de Guerre Moderne* (1779), systematically advocated emphasizing mobility in war, for a reason associated with Romanticism's development of ethnic consciousness. Since the Middle Ages, it had been an internal cliché of armies that men from different regions possessed different military qualities. Guibert argued that the national character of France predisposed its soldiers to the attack rather than the defense, to shock action rather than fire tactics. While reaffirming the line as the basic formation because it allowed for maximum development of firepower, Guibert advocated the increased use of columns both for battlefield maneuver and for attack. He integrated this idea with an emphasis on the use of skirmishers, specially trained light infantry, both to screen French movements and to disrupt the enemy's tactical order.[45] By the outbreak of the French Revolution the army had a dozen battalions of them, as good as any in Europe but hardly representing a paradigm shift in favor of maneuver, shock, and decision. That development, and its impact on Europe's soldiers, is the subject of another volume in this series.

NOTES

1. Cf. N. Henshall, *The Myth of Absolutism: Change and Continuity in Early Modern European Monarchy* (London: Longman, 1992); and the Marxist approach by P. Anderson, *Lineages of the Absolutist State* (London: New Left, 1974). B. M Downing, *The Military Revolution and Political Change: Origins of Democracy and Autocracy in Early Modern Europe* (Princeton, NJ: Princeton University Press, 1992), also emphasizes the aspect of conflict.

2. Fritz Redlich, *The German Military Enterpriser and His Work Force: A Study in European Economic and Social History*, 2 vols. (Wiesbaden, Germany: Franz Steiner, 1964–1965).

3. Geoffrey Parker, *The Military Revolution: Military Innovation and the Rise of the West, 1500–1800* (Cambridge, UK: Cambridge University Press, 1988), 8 ff.; and John Lynn's respectful critique "The Trace Italienne and the Growth of Armies: The French Case," *Journal of Military History* 55 (1991): 297–330.

4. See Thomas Barker, *Army, Aristocracy, Monarchy: Essays on War, Society, and Government in Austria, 1615–1789* (New York: Columbia University Press, 1982).

5. David A. Parrott, *Richelieu's Army: War, Government and Society in France, 1624–1642* (Cambridge, UK: Cambridge University Press, 2001).

6. Jan Glete, *War and the State in Early Modern Europe: Spain, the Dutch Republic, and Sweden as Fiscal-Military States, 1500–1660* (London: Routledge, 2002).

7. J. A. A. Thompson, "Money, Money, and Yet More Money! Finance, the Fiscal-State, and the Military Revolution: Spain, 1500–1650," in *The Military Revolution Debate: Readings on the Transformation of Early Modern Europe*, ed. Clifford J. Rogers (Boulder, CO: Westview, 1995), 273–298.

8. John A. Lynn, "A Brutal Necessity? The Devastation of the Palatinate, 1688–1689," in *Civilians in the Path of War*, ed. M. Grimsley and C. Rogers (Lincoln: University of Nebraska Press, 2003), 79–110.

9. John A. Lynn, *Giant of the Grand Siècle: The French Army, 1610–1715* (Cambridge, UK: Cambridge University Press, 1997), 184–196.

10. For an excellent case study, see George Satterfield, *Princes, Posts, and Partisans: The Army of Louis XIV and Partisan Warfare in the Netherlands (1673–1678)* (Leiden, Netherlands: Brill, 2003), 42–88. Cf. also Ronald Ferguson, "Blood and Fire: Contribution Policy of the French Army in Germany (1688–1715)," Ph.D. diss., University of Minnesota, 1970.

11. J. H. Parry, *The Age of Reconnaissance* (Berkeley: University of California Press, 1963).

12. Recent works with academic quality and general reader appeal are Caroline Finkel, *Osman's Dream: The History of the Ottoman Empire* (New York: Basic Books, 2006), and Roger

Crowley, *1453: The Holy War for Constantinople and the Clash of Islam and the West* (New York: Hyperion, 2006). Virginia Aksan, "Ottoman War and Warfare, 1453–1813," in *War in the Early Modern World, 1450–1815*, ed. Jeremy M. Black (London: UCL Press, 1999), 147–176, is an excellent specialist overview.

13. Geoffrey Parker, *The Grand Strategy of Philip II* (New Haven, CT: Yale University Press, 1998).

14. This presentation is derived largely from the two magisterial volumes by N. A. M. Rodger, *The Safeguard of the Sea* (London: W. W. Norton, 1997) and *The Command of the Ocean: A Naval History of Britain, 1649–1815* (New York: W. W. Norton, 2005), 1–200. Still standard for financial mobilization is J. Brewer, *The Sinews of Power: War, Money, and the English State, 1688–1703* (New York: Knopf, 1989).

15. Rodger, *Safeguard*, 430 ff.

16. John B. Hattendorf, *England in the War of the Spanish Succession: A Study of the English View and Conduct of Grand Strategy, 1702–1712* (New York: Garland, 1987).

17. Cf. Steven Ozment, *The Reformation in the Cities: The Appeal of Protestantism to Sixteenth-Century Germany and Switzerland* (New Haven, CT: Yale University Press, 1975); and R. Po-chia Hsia, *The German People and the Reformation* (Ithaca, NY: Cornell University Press, 1998).

18. Tom Scott, *Freiburg and the Breisgau: Town-Country Relations in the Age of Reformation and Peasants' War* (Oxford, UK: Oxford University Press, 1986), is a representative case study.

19. For Teutonically detailed background, see Gabriele Schutter-Schindler, *Der Schmalkaldische Bund und das Problem der causis religionis* (Frankfurt, Germany: Lang, 1988).

20. The best account in English is Mack Holt, *The French Wars of Religion, 1562–1629* (Cambridge, UK: Cambridge University Press, 1995).

21. Geoffrey Parker, *The Dutch Revolt* (Ithaca, NY: Cornell University Press, 1977); and Pieter Geyl's evocative and still useful *The Revolt of the Netherlands (1555–1609)*, 2nd ed. (New York: Barnes and Noble Books, 1958). Looming behind them is Jared Israel's formidable *The Dutch Republic: Its Rise, Greatness, and Fall (1477–1806)* (Oxford, UK: Oxford University Press, 1995).

22. No good English survey of the Italian wars exists. F. L. Taylor, *The Art of War in Italy, 1494–1526* (Cambridge, UK: Cambridge University Press, 1921), remains useful, and Maurizio Arfaoli, *The Black Bands of Giovanni: Infantry and Diplomacy during the Italian Wars* (Pisa, Italy: Pisa University Press, 2005), goes well beyond its stated temporal limits.

23. George G. Cruickshank, *Army Royal: Henry VIII's Invasion of France* (Oxford, UK: Clarendon Press, 1969).

24. Gervase Philips, *The Anglo-Scottish Wars, 1513–1560* (Woodbridge, UK: Boydell Press, 1999).

25. The best overviews in English are Geoffrey Parker and Simon Adams, *The Thirty Years' War* (London: Routledge, 1984); and Ronald G. Asch, *The Thirty Years' War: The Holy Roman Empire and Europe, 1618–1648* (London: Macmillan, 1997).

26. The best treatment of Gustavus as king and general remains Michael Roberts, *Gustavus Adolphus: A History of Sweden, 1611–1632*, 2 vols. (London: Longmans Green, 1953–1958).

27. See the account in Robert L. Frost's excellent general history, *The Northern Wars: War, State, and Society in Northeastern Europe, 1558–1721* (London: Longmans, 2000), 106 ff.

28. Extremely useful for operational and institutional details is William B. Guthrie, *Battles of the Thirty Years War: From White Mountain to Nordlingen, 1618–1635* (Westport, CT: Greenwood Press, 2002); and *The Later Thirty Years War: From the Battle of Wittstock to the Treaty of Westphalia* (Westport, CT: Greenwood Press, 2003).

29. John Wolf, *Louis XIV* (New York: W. W. Norton, 1968), is constructed around the theme of *gloire*.

30. John A. Lynn, *The Wars of Louis XIV, 1667–1714* (London: Longman, 1999).

31. Ibid., 367–376.

32. Russell Weigley surveys decision and its limits in *The Age of Battle: The Quest for Decisive Warfare from Breitenfeld to Waterloo* (Bloomington: Indiana University Press, 1991). Jamel Otwald, "The 'Decisive' Battle of Ramilles, 1706: Prerequisites for Decisiveness in Early Modern Warfare," *Journal of Military History* 64 (2000): 649–677, is a state-of-the-art case study.

33. Johannes Kunisch, *Staatsverfassung und Maechtepolitik: Zur Genese von Staatskonflikt im Zeitalter des Absolutismus* (Berlin: Duncker and Humblot, 1979).

34. Peter Wilson, "War in German Thought from the Peace of Westphalia to Napoleon," *European History Quarterly* 28 (1998): 5–50.

35. Cf. H. Kleinschmidt, "Mechanismus und Biologismus im Militaerween des 17. Und 18. Jahrhunderts," *Aufklaerung* 11 (1999): 51–73, and Thomas F. Arnold, "The Geometry of Power: War in the Age of the Early Modern Military Revolution, 1500–1800," paper presented at the 1994 meeting of the Society for Military History. Isabel Knight, *The Geometric Spirit: The Abbe de Condillac and the French Enlightenment* (New Haven, CT: Yale University Press, 1968), offers a general perspective.

36. Erik A. Lund, *War for the Every Day: Generals, Knowledge, and Warfare in Early Modern Europe, 1680–1740* (Westport, CT: Praeger, 1999).

37. James M. Sofka, "The Eighteenth Century International System: Parity or Primacy?" *Review of International Studies* 27 (2002): 147–163.

38. See Lothar Schilling, *Kaunitz und des Renversment des Alliances: Studien zur aussenpolitischen Konzeption Wenzel Antons von Kaunitz* (Berlin: Duncker and Humblot, 1994).

39. Peter H. Wilson, "New Approaches under the Old Regime," in *Early Modern Military History, 1450–1815*, ed. G. Mortimer (New York: Palgrave, 2004), 135–154.

40. Charles Tilly, *Coercion, Capital, and European States, AD 990–1990* (Oxford, UK: Oxford University Press, 1990), 96.

41. Dennis E. Showalter, *The Wars of Frederick the Great* (London: Longman, 1996).

42. Cf. from different perspectives with similar conclusions, Piers Mackesy, *The War for America, 1775–1782* (Cambridge, MA: Harvard University Press, 1965); and Jeremy M. Black, *War for America: The Fight for Independence, 1775–1783* (New York: St. Martin's Press, 1991).

43. Lee Kennett, *The French Armies in the Seven Years' War* (Durham, NC: Duke University Press, 1967).

44. Steven T. Ross, "The Development of the Combat Division in 18th Century French Armies," *French Historical Studies* 4 (1967): 84–94.

45. Surprisingly, there is no modern analysis of Guibert. Robert S. Quimby, *The Background of Napoleonic Warfare: The Theory of Military Tactics in Eighteenth-Century France* (New York: Columbia University Press, 1957); and Azar Gat, *The Origins of Military Thought: From the Enlightenment to Clausewitz* (Oxford, UK: Clarendon Press, 1989), partially fill the gap.

Two

✵ ✵ ✵

WHERE THEY CAME FROM,
WHY, AND HOW

Armies in early modern Europe existed in the matrices of an economy that was muscle powered and a society that was labor-short. Europe may have moved ahead of much of the rest of the world in developing strength enhancers: macro-technologies of wind and water power and their micro counterparts like the mouldboard iron-bladed plow and harness systems designed to maximize the pulling power of oxen and horses. In the final analysis, however, a day's work depended on what a man could do with his own arms, legs, and back.

LISTENING FOR THE DRUM

Joining Military Service

Conventional wisdom describes Europe as becoming overpopulated during the thirteenth century. In terms of numbers, perhaps. The labor effectiveness curve was nevertheless steep on both ends: adolescents and old men were useful enough but essentially marginal. Apart from the collective scourges of epidemics and bad harvests, the labor force of any community, urban or rural, was disproportionately subject to constant erosion through accidents and work-related ailments like hernias. Numbers, in other words, did not directly translate into economic contributions. The Black Death and the accompanying causes of fourteenth-century population decline led to a corresponding decline of general welfare in good part because, though an individual's opportunities might be enhanced, not enough effective labor power existed to take advantage of the opportunities opened for social and economic change presented by fewer people. Strong and healthy men were never expendable in late medieval–early modern Europe.

Economic facts and cultural perceptions were not always congruent. Arguably, the major challenge any society faces is affirmatively socializing its young adult males: giving them reasons to contribute their labor and their genes willingly and predictably. Success usually involves some combination of work, sex, and power. In the Middle Ages, that meant access to land in the country and employment in the city; marriage legally and religiously recognized; and a chance to share authority as one's years advanced. All of those things were put at risk by a population expansion that strained existing frameworks beyond their adaptability and whose consequences were exacerbated by social and religious factors. Beginning in fourteenth-century Flanders, popular unrest increased in scale and violence, until the German Peasants' Revolt of 1524–1526 and the Hungarian, Croatian, and Slovenian risings of 1514–1515 and 1573.

As Europe's population began to recover in the late fifteenth and sixteenth centuries, the focus of overcrowding shifted to the towns. Their growth, fueled initially by the physical mobility encouraged by the Black Death, on the whole remained disproportionate to that of the countryside. Their rapid expansion, however, produced too few consumers to stimulate production, as opposed to service jobs and casual—often very casual—labor. In the towns, as in the country earlier, social differentiation and religious enthusiasm fostered simmering tensions across Europe.[1]

Though massive outbreaks, like those of the Florence wool carders in 1378, were infrequent, urban environments generally were sufficiently tense that increasing numbers of men from all social classes not only went armed, but sought formal training in violence. This extended to the use of knives and bare hands, whose techniques have changed little. Some Renaissance illustrations of knife fighting are essentially the same as the posed photos in contemporary self-defense magazines. The recommended methods of wrestling, or unarmed combat, can still enhance the chances for a twenty-first-century citizen to walk away from a fight. The sword, however, was the urban weapon of choice. Training in its use normally involved sharp rather than rebated weapons because men who carried steel knew that it might be necessary to wield it in earnest. The formal codes of dueling were more frequently violated than observed. Readers may recall the battering swordplay featured in Richard Lester's 1970s movies *The Three Musketeers* and *The Four Musketeers*. Personal combat was a matter of life and death.[2]

Hiving off the community's so-called dangerous elements into one or another army made corresponding sense. Military service was a recognized way to reduce the number of unruly young men who threatened the patriarchal, hierarchic, everyday order by removing them from the community. It could involve choice as well, particularly for those who fell off the social ladder or never found its first rung. By no means were all of these from what modern jargon dubs the underclass. At society's upper levels a declining child mortality rate meant an increasing number of sons surviving to an age requiring something to be done for them and with them. Urban guild regulations made it increasingly difficult for journeymen to set up their own establishments—acquiring master status by marrying a master's widow was a staple of bawdy humor and an uncomfortable everyday prospect for too many twenty-somethings. Teachers grew tired of beating the same fragments of knowledge into unwilling heads. Clerics lost vocations.

Jugglers, actors, and puppeteers found themselves in uniform as a consequence of injury, rheumatism, or loss of the touch that made an audience throw money.

Like Jane Eyre, such men might well reason that if they could not have liberty, they could at least seek new servitude. A soldier was fed, more or less, and paid, albeit rather less than more. A soldier had opportunities for overnight prosperity—opportunities losing nothing to camp mythology. Prisoners could still be ransomed, with the usual rate being a year of his income. Growing assertion by the state that prisoners were not their captor's personal property, combined with the fact that captives were increasingly acquired in group surrenders, diminished the common soldier's chances of spectacular gains in that quarter. But since a commoner's right to hold a nobleman for ransom had always been at dispute, the alternative possibility of a general share-out, involving a lump sum that could be five times a man's annual pay, offered the same kinds of attraction prize money did to sailors. A contemporary comparison might be an annual bonus as opposed to a winning lottery ticket.[3]

Plunder was an even greater attraction than ransom. Prospects for making anything from captures of equipment or flags was limited here as well by the claims of the state and the army. But looting a captured town, scavenging an overrun baggage train, and even sweating coins out of peasant hoards could add up to tidy sums in portable wealth. Converting booty into cash and getting the cash safely home were other matters entirely. Few ordinary Europeans of any calling were familiar with the details of international banking or had personal contact with a Jew, much less a Lombard. Nor were even small-scale financiers particularly anxious to work with soldiers. A correspondingly

In the painting by Jacob A. Duck, *One Reward of Service*, Spanish soldiers plunder a house. © Erich Lessing/Art Resource, New York.

large amount of plunder was lost—discarded on a long march or hidden in a vain hope of returning for it.

English records for the Hundred Years War, the best of their kind, show no indication that returning soldiers bought, leased, or otherwise acquired land with profits from their campaigns.[4] The same held on the continent. Cadastral, or land, records, however, do not tell the whole story. Geoffrey Parker states that a man might have enlisted with nothing, yet return home with enough ducats in his purse to become one of the notables who ruled his village.[5] Whatever his campfire dreams of one day farming his own acres, an early modern ex-soldier was unlikely to have the will not for hard work, but for steady work. The peasant's life was a structure of routine, the soldier's a series of fits and starts. Veterans might be sufficiently debilitated by wounds, illness, and privation to lack the strength for year-round field labor. Starting at the bottom as an apprentice in anything remotely resembling a guild was an even more dead-end enterprise. By default, then, and by choice as well in many cases, former soldiers who established themselves in civilian life did so by using their capital to open taverns, brothels, and similar marginally respectable recreational facilities or through such positive processes as buying into a going concern or marrying a daughter or widow.

Prudent husbandry was not a virtue highly regarded in most military environments. A typical veteran might reminisce, "I spent three-fourths of my gains on dice, liquor, and women. The rest I wasted!" Such sentiments are not unknown today. Socially and culturally, especially for young men at the margins, a major reason for following the drum was to break with the conventions of one's rearing: to wear outrageous clothes, to drink and brawl, and to swagger at will among the women. "Live fast; go out young and hot" did not originate with the modern gangbanger. Panache was part of the soldier's lifestyle, even in a force with the sober-sided reputation of Oliver Cromwell's New Model Army. Campfire legend says that as punishment for indiscipline, one of its regiments was ordered to cast lots: ten men to be selected in the first round, then cast again, with five to live and five to die. One of the unlucky ten offered a sum equal to around $5,000 to anyone willing to draw for him and accept his lot. A fellow trooper promptly stepped forward and drew a winner. "Look you," he declared, "'tis gallant pay, and nothing venture, nothing have!"

James Graham, Marquis of Montrose, makes the point more elegantly in his well-known couplet: "He either fears his fate too much / Or his desserts are small / That puts it not unto the touch / To win or lose it all." Often described as a prebattle toast, it was in fact part of a love poem—an ironic reflection of the familiar connections between Ares and Aphrodite. But the two men of war expressed the same truth: An early modern soldier's life offered a perceptible degree of acculturation to the nobility, at least that element of it that served in arms.[6] The very act of volunteering was described as lifting the new recruit out of the common ruck, not only by taking up arms, but even more by exercising choice—something considered a major, frequently envied, prerogative of the upper classes.

"For if we go it's one to ten / But we return all gentlemen," promises the most familiar English recruiting song. Soldiers copied their social betters in everything from fighting formal duels instead of brawling to keeping mistresses instead of patronizing anonymous whores. The swords that infantrymen in many armies carried until well into the eighteenth century were more than increasingly vestigial weight on a long march.

A Prussian regiment deprived of them as a punishment before the battle of Leignitz went into action shouting "honor or death!" and charging the Austrian line without orders, opening the way for the cavalry. Frederick the Great not only returned the swords, but purchased new hat tresses for the whole regiment—at his own expense, which, given the king's parsimony, suggested that he was impressed indeed.[7]

The Roles of Commoners and Aristocracy in Service

More was involved here than manipulation of those "baubles" with which Napoleon cynically described soldiers as being led. The laws of war in the Age of Chivalry applied only to knights and squires. Commoners of any kind—from archers to urban militia to peasants forced into service—were outside the system because they had no honor. Thus English archers could freely be ordered to kill prisoners at Agincourt. Commoners in arms also had no protection. Their survival if captured was a function of the victors' whim and the exigencies of the wider military and political situation. Economics might play a role as well—if slave dealers were on hand.[8] The changing nature of war was suggesting a paradigm shift to the real advantage of Europe's subordinate classes.

That attitude did not carry over into a general willingness among the urban upper classes to take up arms either as pastime or profession. The developing urban elites in particular preferred increasingly to hire men to do their fighting. Beginning with Niccolò Machiavelli, this mind-set has attracted scorn alike from conservatives, who interpret military service as proof of virility, liberals in the nineteenth-century nationalist mode, who consider bearing arms an element of citizenship, and Marxists, regarding reluctance to face danger in person as a particularly good reason to denounce the bourgeoisie. Examined at closer range, the picture is more complex. Civic elites were willing enough to join internal security forces like the civic guards that are the subject of so many paintings or to serve in sieges and similar emergencies. But the fascination, and the increasingly complex, demanding processes, of alternatives like making money, or developing the specialized knowledge associated with the secular learned professions of law and medicine led to a corresponding distancing from warmaking as a life choice.[9]

The aristocracy, which had been the backbone of European military systems for centuries, was undergoing a similar process of "civilianization." Militant behavior flourished in the Renaissance as a means of proving virtù, but martial values were increasingly discounted.[10] A father might see to his son's instruction in the arts of the duel but was less likely to provide instruction in the crafts of war. Some accounts describe this development as a reaction to changes in warmaking. Gunpowder weapons challenged both traditional and modern notions of chivalry. More practically, government intervention and the increasing impersonality of battle diminished the prospects of ransom. Other scholars point to the growing success of central authorities in curbing substate violence, suggesting that belligerence diminished in proportion. In a similar context the emerging early modern state is often described as diluting the aristocracy with so-called new men: nobles of the robe, as they were called in France, sons and grandsons of commoners, administrators, and bureaucrats with neither interest nor skill in arms.

Each of these points has merit. Their common denominator, however, limits the aristocracy's collective agency. Describing the secular masters of Europe as acted upon by abstract social and economic forces overlooks the cumulative pattern of thousands of individual decisions to eschew warmaking as a way of life. That pattern can be traced to the high Middle Ages, when increasing numbers of landholders concentrated on managing their "honors," with occasional involvement in small-scale private violence or its surrogate, the tournament, and even less frequent summonses to feudal military service broadly defined. Not least of its nurturants was the sober, late-night recognition that a man could get killed in war, whether "ignobly" by English arrows or Swiss pikes or in honorable combat with a social equal who had developed his warrior skills by constant military service.[11]

Significant as well was the comprehensive growth of affordable, everyday comfort—everything from silk underwear to glass windows—that made ordinary life more a pleasure that could be savored than a trial to be endured. The development of court life, and the administrative and diplomatic functions accompanying it, put premiums on alternative sets of skills. An old-school nobleman at the court of fifteenth-century Burgundy eloquently expressed the consequences, urging his wife to see to their son's cultural development while describing his own shame at being able to do no more than say "Messire Jean has spoken well, and I agree with his position."[12] Even standards of personal appearance were changing, as early forms of plastic surgery grew increasingly able to repair the effects of edged weapons on ears, cheeks, and noses.[13]

Nobles were still considered—not least by themselves—natural leaders in war. It was just that fewer of them were reporting for duty—especially relative to the size and composition of armies. Nobles could always be found to command regiments and accept higher appointments.[14] The "gentleman volunteer" of lesser birth and smaller fortune, willing as a youth to accept a de facto apprenticeship to arms as an alternative to his civilian prospects, was a different matter. That is not to say that Europe's aristocracies had grown effete—merely that their priorities had shifted.

The relative shortage of noblemen in arms was highlighted by fundamental changes in the structure of armies: changes calling for a different spectrum of skills and talents than had been the case in the days of Philip Augustus and Richard of England. Historically, the aristocracy had been concentrated in the heavy cavalry. Even the best units of commoner foot soldiers and light horse often followed leaders from their own class. But privilege had its drawbacks. It was expensive—increasingly so, as armor provided its wearer greater safety but at an exponentially higher cost. A gentleman was also expected to provide for his entourage: the mix of attendants and combatants that went by the name of "lance." Institutionally, armored cavalry developed from the all-purpose fighters who had ridden with Charlemagne six centuries earlier into an increasingly specialized arm, much as tanks in the late twentieth century evolved into weapons designed almost exclusively to fight each other. Whatever sovereign mastery of the battlefield knights may once have enjoyed was steadily diminishing. The number of nobles in the ranks of the heavy cavalry diminished accordingly.[15]

At the same time the growing demands of the battlefield were considered to put an increasing premium on providing direct moral leadership for the lower orders who filled armies' ranks. What had been an exception became a rule as noblemen moved into positions of authority throughout the infantry and cavalry. Aristocrats continued to define themselves by birth: As early as 1664, the French government was revoking patents of nobility granted over the previous thirty years for military service. What men were, however, depended increasingly on what they did.[16]

Courage showcased by patronage was only part of the process of developing aristocrats into officers. That required new skill sets and new personal qualities. The development of the *trace italienne*, or Italian style, whose low walls and angled bastions replaced the castles of old, and its even more elaborate successors made fortress warfare too complicated to depend entirely on rules of thumb. As armies grew larger, their still-rudimentary internal articulation meant that administrative, operational, and tactical deployment alike had to be managed from the top. The alternative was chaos in camp and in battle. Management in turn required mastery of the details of troop types and armaments. It required as well skill at mathematics: How many men required how much space to do what? Primary responsibility in both areas initially rested with technicians: commoners who had learned the mechanics of siegecraft and fieldcraft by long experience. The new stratum of aristocratic leaders, however, grew uncomfortable with depending on outsiders whose primary loyalties seemed to rest with their specialist guilds.[17]

Developing Soldiers' Characters

Periodic attempts to establish formal military schools had limited success, and most of that was by serving as orphanages and as socializing institutions for sons of noble houses. The printing press, however, enabled large-scale production of books and pamphlets on a wide variety of war-related subjects. The semientrepreneurial patronage system of acquiring a commission steadily developed in the direction of formal apprenticeship systems. That reflected a general pattern: The emerging Age of Science and the succeeding Enlightenment alike favored a hands-on, practical approach to knowledge of even theoretical subjects. Jonathan Swift's vicious satire of the floating island of Laputa, whose sages concerned themselves with such arcanae as making excrement edible, highlighted the fact that *l'esprit géométrique* was not a synonym for *l'esprit théoretique*.[18]

Courage too was redefined. The near-solipsistic heroic individualism that was the bedrock of the chivalric mind-set gave way to an emphasis on setting an example. The orgasmic bravery required in a charge—or a duel or tournament—was replaced by self-discipline: the ability to endure whatever an enemy might produce. Courage came increasingly to be defined as what might be called conspicuous steadiness: taking position in front of one's formation and showing insouciant indifference to risk, whether awaiting the enemy's tactical pleasure on a stricken field or leading a forlorn-hope assault on a "practicable breach" in a Vauban fortification.[19]

Direct patronage had its limitations as well. Even in the Middle Ages, the sons of noblemen were expected to learn the skills and attitudes of knighthood outside their parental homes. Acquiring a commission in an early modern army steadily developed along the same lines. In France, for example, an aristocrat might serve at his own expense as a volunteer, learning his craft by osmosis in companies commanded by a relative, a family friend, or a captain wishing to expand his client or patron network. Or he might choose to become a cadet and be paid for service in a training company. The fast track was service in a guard or household unit. A year in that exalted atmosphere was enough to qualify one not merely for a commission, but to request the right to purchase a regiment.[20]

Mercenary Soldiers and Their Portable Political Loyalties

That right segued into the grass roots problems of recruiting, organizing, and maintaining armies in the context of social and demographic developments on one hand and changes in warmaking on the other. Europe's armies in the early modern era were characterized above all by an exponential growth in size. That reflected the growing symmetry in tactics, technology, and discipline—a similarity fostered by the Brownian movement of officers at all ranks from army to army.

For juniors this was a counterpart to the so-called travel year, the period traditionally required of a journeyman in any craft when he acquired new techniques in new places. For colonels and generals, at a time when state identities were still developing, changing service could mean professional opportunity, with no more loss of status than contemporary free agents suffer when changing sports teams. Frederick Herman von Schomberg was born in the Rhineland in 1615. He began his military career in the Dutch army in 1633, as a gentleman volunteer. The next year, he transferred to Swedish service. By the time of his death in action at the battle of the Boyne, Schomberg had served in the armies of over a half-dozen states, was naturalized in four of them—as French, Portuguese, Swedish, and Dutch—and had earned a reputation as being among the ablest soldiers of his time, able to fight a battle, conduct a siege, and manage high policy with equal aplomb.[21]

Lower social echelons were no less widely welcomed. The Dutch Republic and its ruling House of Orange became something like an academy for gentlemen wishing to learn the craft of war. Even Catholics were welcome, forming a majority of the mercenary French regiments officially recruited from Huguenots. The officers of the Scots regiments that won so many accolades in so many armies during the Thirty Years War disproportionately had their first experience under Dutch colors. Above all, England, lacking anything beyond token land forces in this period, saw its traditional military families and its ambitious younger sons cross the channel in hundreds to serve their apprenticeships in the Dutch army. Some stayed a campaigning season or two as a rite of passage. Others became solid professionals, whose presence on both sides contributed disproportionately to the ability of both crown and parliament to keep armies in the field during the first months of the English Civil War.[22]

For everyone, service in foreign parts could reflect religious and political developments at home. The revocation of the Edict of Nantes in 1685 brought French Huguenots into the service of the Dutch Republic, the English monarchy, and most of Germany's Protestant states.[23] The peace terms concluding the Williamite War allowed free passage from Ireland for those preferring exile to defeat. As many as 20,000 of all ranks and classes sailed for France. For over a century the Wild Geese were fixtures in the armies of France, Spain, and Austria, replenishing their ranks with the tacit connivance of an English government that allowed ships that smuggled in goods to southeast Ireland to sail back with holds full of prospective soldiers. With work scarce over most of the eighteenth century, service under foreign flags not only defused potential social crises, but siphoned off hotheads and troublemakers.[24]

This was not a climate conducive to maintaining any kind of qualitative advantage. The obvious response was to seek to increase numbers. To a degree that solution reflected a Thirty Years War, which, in its later stages, had been characterized by armies too small to be effective either in the open field or in suppressing the proliferating small and middle-sized strongpoints that sprang up throughout Germany as a response to repeated devastation.[25] It reflected as well a developing pattern of states conducting major campaigns simultaneously in theaters too far apart to be mutually supporting. While the early modern increase in available public funding discussed in Chapter One was modest by later standards, it seemed like endless wealth to governments whose treasuries had historically been consistently near-empty. Apart from what might be called a natural tendency to overspend, no one was sure exactly how much the new armies would cost, and in what ways. In most cases, optimism triumphed over caution.

Again, France was the exemplar. A peace establishment of around 10,000 at the end of the sixteenth century increased fifteenfold over the next 100 years. John Lynn has highlighted the significant differences between paper strengths and men in ranks, between the ability to raise armies and the ability to maintain them. Even in that context, however, early modern armies in a short span of years grew to sizes unprecedented since the days of Imperial Rome. The corresponding issue in practical terms became how best to secure enough soldiers in the demographic, economic, and social contexts presented earlier in this chapter.

WEAPONS AND MEN

The changing moral role of the developing officer class highlighted a related phenomenon: The decline and disappearance of what might be called the medieval version of the techno-warrior. By the fifteenth century, armies were largely composed of specialized building blocks, recruited from the same region from men with particular skill sets that, for practical purposes, were nontransferable. The longbowmen of the Welsh marches and England's border shires could not even be replicated in Kent or Sussex, to say nothing of Picardy or Bohemia. The light cavalry of the Christian-Muslim frontiers, the *stradiots* of the Balkans or Spain's *genetours*, could not be replicated by mounting Flemish townsmen on cart horses. Italians and Belgians were universally valued as marksmen, with crossbow or arquebus: a skill acquired and maintained in urban environments of competition and practice.

Martial qualities were also described in moral terms. Gascons enjoyed much the same reputation in French service as Texans in American uniform: boastful party animals, larger than life, difficult to stomach—but able to walk the walk in private quarrel or pitched battle. Germans were considered at the head of the list when it came to endurance. The Swiss and the Spaniards were noted for their dash and ferocity in the attack. Nor was imitation accepted as the sincerest form of flattery. The Swiss considered themselves to have a legitimate monopoly on pike tactics, and when they faced *Landsknechte* using similar methods, quarter was, as a rule, neither given nor expected.[26]

At the beginning of the early modern period a state-of-the-art army was precisely tailored to the requirements of a particular campaign. Units not taken on could usually count on finding employment in another structure. These organizations had their own internal dynamics, their own ways of maintaining discipline and sustaining morale. They might be a bit unusual, as when a contingent demanded that its chiefs stand in the front line of the day's battle. As a general rule, however, building blocks did not require—or welcome—external interference. There was a correspondingly limited call for systematic external inspiration. A soldier fought for pay, for comrades, and ultimately, by choice. He drew moral support, when it was needed, by looking from side to side.

Blaise de Montluc rose during the sixteenth century from a gentleman volunteer to a marshal of France, in the process smelling enough burned powder and spilled blood to make him a hands-on authority on military effectiveness. He recommended this tactical deployment for a particular engagement in 1522: Our Italians can pair off against their Italians. Put some of the French companies opposite the Germans; the rest can face the Spaniards. Who deployed where specifically would depend on the captains' tastes and experience.[27]

The Pike

Change came as armies grew larger. More was involved in the growth process than macro-level considerations of policy and finance. Historically, economics of scale had played a limited role in European warfare. Mere numbers of armed men did not confer operational advantages in a tactical environment that usually and quickly became a series of individual combats along a stable front line. Emphasizing quality—skill and spirit—made corresponding sense. Beginning in the fifteenth century, however, an interlocking series of innovations in weaponry generated a paradigm shift in favor of mass.

It began with one of the least technical weapons ever designed: the pike. As developed by the Swiss and copied by the *Landsknechte*, it was most effective when employed in large numbers. Particularly in its shorter, thirteen-foot version, it was an offensive weapon par excellence—a fact highlighted by the Swiss eschewing of body armor, initially from poverty but increasingly from bravado. Pikemen in general generally followed suit—partly to ease the loads they carried, partly because personal armor was of limited use against a full-bodied pike thrust. Offensive tactics thus became a survival mechanism, and pikemen in masses became increasingly able to sweep away any of the other players, from heavy cavalry to bowmen, in the complicated game of rock-paper-scissors that was the sixteenth-century battlefield. That in turn facilitated the pike's "battle space dominance" at the expense of the relatively small specialist units growing more difficult to employ effectively and more difficult to sustain, like their successors in the world wars of the twentieth century: the rangers, the commandos, and the paratroopers.

The pike was not an easy weapon. It was cumbersome to carry and awkward to deploy. The rapid maneuvering essential for its offensive effectiveness demanded practice. In the Swiss cantons, young men mustered on holidays for pike exercises. *Landsknecht* companies included a drillmaster, the *feldwaibel*, whose title and function endured for centuries. Movements in combat were directed by massed drums, beating rhythms rather than tunes. Ultimately, however, the pike called for attitude as opposed to finesse. It demanded muscle and courage from its users. It was correspondingly easy to increase the size of pike formations by recruiting on the basis of size and apparent strength—a general, almost a casual process compared to the relative care with which "building blocks" were formed.[28]

Firearms

Initial attempts to counter the massed pike charge involved field fortifications. By themselves, these proved insufficient—not least because it proved difficult to get the men behind them to stand their ground. A solution emerged with the development of history's first general use infantry fire weapon. Whether slings, arrows, or the *pila* of Rome's legions, the predecessor of the arquebus, the first practical shoulder-firing gunpowder weapon, and its successors, the matchlock and the flintlock musket, had depended for their effect on skill. In fact, this skill was often accompanied by specific physical development approaching malformation, as the overdeveloped arms and shoulders found on the skeletons of English longbowmen indicate. The crossbow, weapon of choice for individuals and social groups who had to fight occasionally but whose resources, time, or interest were limited, was easier to use only by comparison— resembling, in that sense, the handguns of the late twentieth century.

The shoulder firearm, particularly in its initial form of the arquebus, was neither more accurate nor longer ranged than the crossbow. Their weights were about the same, though the arquebus was useful as a club in hand-to-hand fighting. The gunpowder weapon was, perhaps surprisingly, cheaper, reflecting its primary technical advantage of simplicity. There were no bowstrings to snap and no elaborate winding apparatus to break: just a metal tube open at one end with a touch hole and a flash pan at the other, attached to a piece of wood. The gunpowder did the work, and it rapidly became apparent that no amount of the kinds of training available in the sixteenth century would do much to improve an individual arquebus's accuracy. The arquebus, in short, was foolproof. And that was what armies increasingly recruited to carry it.[29]

Weapons That Leveled Skills

A synergy was developing among early modern Europe's population pyramid, its social and intellectual dynamic, and its way of war. On one hand, only marginal elements could conveniently be spared for military service. On the other, armies developed new ways of maximizing the effectiveness of their shallow manpower pool. To offer one example, they began providing personal equipment. This represented a fundamental change from the *Landsknecht* model requiring each man to furnish his own clothing, weapons, and armor. Exact statistics vary, but a suitable outfit would cost a laborer about a year's pay. When demographic and social factors favored recruiting, captains could be selective. When conditions were less favorable, equipping recruits was a useful way of accommodating promising volunteers down on their luck or who had never had any.

A similar process of leveling took place in the cavalry. Beginning with the wars between the Swiss cantons and the Duchy of Burgundy in the later fifteenth century, the superiority of pike over lance became increasingly obvious. Part of this reflected the speed and ferocity of a pike charge. But even when matched by similar qualities, the lance gave the pike a technologically determined advantage. A lance could not be much longer than nine feet or so and still be held steady in a charge. The pike had a four- or five-foot advantage—compounded by the fact that horses could not be easily forced onto a wall of sharply pointed sticks.

A potential solution emerged with the development, in the early sixteenth century, of the wheel lock pistol. Short enough and light enough to be fired from horseback one-handed, it was cocked by cranking a small wheel until an early form of safety catch engaged. Troopers carried anywhere from two up to six or eight in holsters and belts, much like the border guerrillas of the American Civil War, and for much the same reason: Reloading in combat was a chancy business. Unlike their successors, however, these horsemen, generally known as *Reiters,* did not depend on shock for effect. Their preferred tactic was the caracole: successive ranks of horsemen closing to point-blank range, firing a volley, then wheeling to the back of the formation until their turn came again.

When it worked, the caracole could be devastating against either men-at-arms or pikemen. When it did not, individual survival chances were nevertheless improved over hand-to-hand mêlées. Heavy cavalry still wore full upper-body armor (which could deflect pistol or arquebus fire at long or medium ranges). The pistol, however, steadily replaced the lance, and with it came alternate tactical emphases. Order was more important than speed. Steadiness overshadowed heroism. And numbers trumped genealogy. The pistol was most effective used in masses. The slower pace of movements meant that horses did not need to be as high bred as a knight's destrier. His rider did not require the elaborate training of a man-at-arms. As their numbers shrank relative to commoners and their influence dissipated in a homogenized tactical system, increasingly, the old aristocracy abandoned service in the ranks of the new model heavy cavalry in favor of assuming command positions throughout an army.[30]

SIGNING ON

Shakespeare's Sir John Falstaff brought to vibrant life the most familiar general image of recruiting in early modern Europe. In a series of scenes with much the same resonance to London audiences as more modern successors such as *M*A*S*H, McHale's Navy,* or *Dad's Army* had for their television-watching cultural descendants, Falstaff produces a gaggle of "discarded unjust serving-men, younger sons to younger brothers, revolted tapsters and ostlers tradefallen. . . . I had the most of them out of prison. There's but a shirt and a half in all my company, and the half shirt is two napkins tacked together." But Sir John was riding the crest of another new phenomenon.

The standard early modern form of recruitment was becoming entrepreneurial. A state or prince would directly commission, or contract with, an established soldier to enlist a specific number of men under specific terms of service, advancing some cash— as little as possible—for expenses. This "colonel"—his actual title varied—would in turn select captains and send them to particular areas to recruit companies, the principal unit of muster, "by beat of drum" until the ranks were full.

In its heyday, the first half of the seventeenth century, the classical mercenary model of military entrepreneurship was characterized by four features.[31] One was multiple ownership of regiments because of cumulative contracting. That tied into a second factor: the tendency to maintain mercenary regiments on a long-term basis. That in turn connected with a third factor: an increasing separation of separating ownership and management. Capable and charismatic senior officers were not easily come by in a pool confined to relatives. Finally, mercenary regiments were increasingly likely to serve in areas remote from their raising, as part of armies that had limited concern for their welfare. Gustavus Adolphus, for example, was open in his belief that even the best mercenary units were completely expendable. Survival prospects for individuals or small groups somehow shaken loose from their units were illusory in the context of local irregulars and peasants eager to even long-building scores.

A colonel's record could be correspondingly decisive in securing enlistments and replacements; joining a stable, tested organization offered better prospects for both officers and men than starting every year or so from scratch. No less important was the status of the general contractor. Possession of enough cash to offer generous bonuses and still have some left for display at least suggested that the regiment being raised would be reasonably treated and used during its service. And profits made from one regiment could provide basic financing for another, even though that process increasingly depended more on possession of investment capital and access to commercial credit.

The synergies among the above points indicated an economy of scale. That in turn generated another characteristic of the developed mercenary system: the creation of entire armies. The defining figure here is Albert von Wallenstein, who parlayed his successful command of the Habsburg field army into control of enough land to provide its logistics system. A better administrator than a battle captain, as much a businessman as a soldier, Wallenstein remained the archetype of the martial entrepreneur, whose reputation drew fighting men from all over Europe.[32] Schiller's *Wallenstein's Camp* may be more romance than history. Yet there is an enduring appeal as the mercenaries sound off: Holk's Riflemen, "Friedland's Wild Hunt our title still"; a dragoon "from distant Erin"; an arquebusier from the Federsee and another from a Swiss canton; a Croatian irregular—the face of Europe in arms, met to brag and drink and gamble and, above all, to fight under a general they trusted. For many an old soldier this was as it should have been.

In the real world, such freelancing was well in the past. "Pure" mercenary regiments seldom recruited as speculative enterprises. Their commanders had previous, often well-established ties with their employers, sometimes on the basis of religion, more often as a consequence of experience. As Irishmen gravitated to the colors of Spain and Austria, Scots could count on finding themselves in the service of Sweden or Holland. Actual recruiting procedures were about the same, whether Scots were taking the coin of Gustavus Adolphus in 1630 or Frenchmen were signing on with a royal regiment in 1712. Captains could usually call on local authorities to provide assistance while the company was being formed: housing, for example, and extra musicians. Enlistment, however, was voluntary—at least in the sense that the captain had no legal authority to compel enrollment.

In the *Landsknecht* days, as suggested earlier, the process resembled a rural hiring fair, where conditions may have favored the employer but whose applicants had some preexisting qualifications that offered some room for negotiation of terms and conditions. (Dedicated Web surfers may see a certain irony in the contemporary use of the term *hiring fair* by colleges and universities seeking adjunct faculty in a buyers' market.) As wars grew bloodier and terms of service longer, showmanship and artifice came to the fore.

Recruitment Methods throughout Europe

F. Lee Ermey, a Marine drill instructor turned actor *(Full Metal Jacket)*, memorably described himself as "a stand-up comic" whose major challenge was to get the attention of his charges. Early modern recruiters assumed similar personae. Irish dramatist George Farquhar established contemporary archetypes in *The Recruiting Officer*. Published in 1706, repeatedly revived for stage and television in recent years, it features Captain Plume asking a crowd of yokels what they think of "a purse of gold out of a Frenchman's pocket after you have dashed out his brains with the butt of your firelock, eh?" The play is dominated, however, by Sergeant Kite (a kite is a bird of prey that prefers carrion), who exhorts his audience: "If any 'prentices have severe masters, any children undutiful parents: if any servants have too little wages or any husband too much wife, let them repair to the noble Sergeant Kite."[33] With some cosmetic editorial work, the sergeant describes his career path:

> I was born a gypsy; there I learned canting and lying. I was bought by a nobleman; there I learned impudence and pimping. I turned bailiff's follower; there I learned bullying and swearing. I at last got into the army, and there I learned whoring and drinking. So that if your worship pleases to cast up the whole sum, you will find the sum total will amount to a recruiting sergeant.[34]

Recruiters usually held open house in taverns, seeking to create a convivial, masculine atmosphere that encouraged signing an enlistment contract, accepting "the King's shilling," and sometimes merely drinking the local ruler's health at the recruiter's expense. Misrepresentation was so common as to be universal and ranged from promises of rapid promotion, or even commissioning, to describing membership in some kind of elite unit when reality was ground-pounding in the infantry. One British cavalry regiment warned prospective recruits that because the regiment's horses were young, the men were not allowed to hunt more than once a week.[35]

Spain's norms for enlistment, typical for the period, were "able-bodied, over 16 and under 50, single, and sane." Today's readers may find room for doubting that last provision. There is also room, however, for questioning just how successful these performances were in cozening innocents. There were those, certainly, who drifted in to see the show and next day found themselves with an aching head, bound for glory under armed guard. There were teenagers whose parents paid through the nose and under the table to have their sons returned to them. But the public theater was familiar enough that "Recruiting Sergeant" plays became part of the folklore in England's East Midlands. By and large, those who entered Sergeant Kite's nest were at least willing to consider the prospects of a life change and, in that sense, possessed agency. Even Hobson's choice is a choice of sorts.

In the sixteenth-century Spanish service, again reasonably normative, the majority of recruits over an extended period were between twenty and forty years old, with men in their twenties predominating.[36] Since time was usually important for both operational and economic reasons, captains sought to complete the process quickly: about three weeks was the norm for the Spanish army, either in the peninsula or elsewhere. For the same reason, recruiting usually concentrated in the towns, with countrymen coming in to join as they learned of the opportunity.[37] In France, siegneurial recruitment was common: Officers would take up to six months' leave, return home, and come back with a trail of recruits from family estates. Wives, mothers, and siblings participated in the process. A captain's sister won praise from no less an exalted expert than a marshal of France: "There is not a trick that she does not know."[38]

With some regional and administrative variations, this was the system practiced throughout sixteenth-century Europe. It worked well enough in the context of surplus—or disposable—manpower, as discussed earlier. France, for example, relied heavily on mercenary contingents in view of consistent inability to develop a reliable native infantry but seldom found difficulty meeting its needs outside the realm's borders. When, however, demographics were unfavorable or, as in the case of Germany and France during the Wars of Religion, disputed political legitimacy created parallel loyalties, terms of engagement and service could be modified, and standards of age, size, and fitness became more flexible. Adolescents of fifteen could be taken into French companies if they suggested potential to grow and fill out.[39]

The next step in filling depleted ranks involved turning to so-called masterless men: vagabonds and pimps, the chronically unemployed, even brigands—though these last seem to have more often been men living from hand to mouth, pilferers of laundry and chickens, than hardened "gentlemen of the road." The Spanish government raised an entire regiment of them in Catalonia as part of the preparation for the abortive invasion of England in 1577–1578.[40] From sweeping the streets and countrysides, it was a short step to emptying the jails. "Emptying" is an exaggeration. The custodial/rehabilitative model of prison is a nineteenth-century innovation. Early modern societies could not afford to keep large numbers of healthy men out of the work force for long periods, and suitable convicts were correspondingly scarce. The concept of honor extending to common soldiers may have been embryonic, but it was strong enough to focus reluctance to treat military service as an alternate form of punishment. Nor were officers exactly overjoyed at having their ranks completed by antisocial criminals. Thieves, alcoholics, and brawlers were a constant source of friction, making life far more miserable than it had to be for their better-behaved comrades, and for the officers as well. Recruiters preferred inmates whose offenses were the kind that in later centuries inspired judges to offer defendants a choice between incarceration and enlistment. In the France of Louis XIV, smugglers and debtors were particularly favored. Debtors were likely to be victims of bad luck or bad management and suitably appreciative if their creditors could be constrained to resign their claims in favor of the state. Smuggling was widely considered a victimless crime; smugglers had an image as bold adventurers, outside the law but not alienated from society. Men sentenced to the galleys were enrolled only in extreme emergencies—and then kept under heavy guard.[41]

Feudal Service and Militias

The next step in supplementing volunteers involved, logically, compulsion. This existed on two tracks, both most comprehensively developed in France. Aristocratic feudal service, the *Ban* and the *Arrière Ban*, might long have been vestigial but still remained on the books. Kings of France called out levies as late as 1689, with predictable results. The forty-day limitation on service beyond the frontiers bore no relation to the actual nature of early modern war. The men who responded personally, as opposed to paying compensation, were poorly armed and insusceptible of discipline as early modern armies understood it.

Common subjects as well were expected to serve the King of France in his wars. Partial call-ups to meet particular emergencies were a familiar last resort. In France, local levies watched roads and fords. They provided labor for sieges, 20,000 and more for a complex investment. Their carts and animals hauled supplies—sometimes even with some compensation involved.[42]

This first track of civilian service in arms involved maintaining vestiges of the feudal era: the second track created militias. Throughout Europe a variety of organizations, rural and urban, local and provincial, provided armed men for police and security purposes. Service, based on residence location or guild membership, was compulsory but also a mark of status, and the general tendency was for militias to be absorbed into social and political structures. Militias could, in emergencies, provide large numbers at limited cost. They played enough of a role in France's Wars of Religion that during the next century the revived monarchy was at pains to bring them under state control. Louis XIV summoned local militias for state service in the Dutch Wars—a process similar to federalizing state National Guards in twentieth-century America. Provinces and cities were also required to recruit and support from their own resources units for general service—though money rather than men was likely to be the true medium of compliance.

Beginning in 1688, these local organizations began giving way to a royal version initially designed to provide low-cost auxiliary troops and then to funnel replacements into line regiments. Raised by conscription, it was correspondently unpopular and rendered even more so by allowing buy-outs. It is worth noting that determining service by a lottery system, the *tirage au sort*, was widely considered unjust by the very randomness that has made draft lotteries acceptable in the twentieth century. In a society structured on the basis of privilege, the concept of privilege was universal. A man's fate should be determined by his status and his needs, not by some piece of paper drawn from an urn. The royal militias in their successive forms were generally and legitimately considered by professional soldiers and social theorists alike to do more harm than good to state-subject relations by the eighteenth century.[43]

Across the Rhine, in the lands of the Empire, militias were disproportionately attractive to the small and middle-sized territories. Their appeal persistence reflected two fundamental facts. One was economic: No German ruler was in a position to maintain operationally effective standing armies from public resources. Bavaria, which kept as many as 20,000 men under arms during the Thirty Years War, after 1648 reduced its standing force to a few companies of garrison and security troops, and with the extension of gunpowder technology, such small forces were irrelevant. The second was theological: Protestant rulers and their people shared a belief that aggressive war violated Christian principles. Militias were a reasonable compromise. They could be called up long enough to receive at least some training. They made useful garrisons for the small fortresses thickly sprinkled across the Empire. And they could be used as a recruitment/replacement pool for the paid professionals engaged for emergencies. Brandenburg and Saxony, to cite two of the best known examples, depended on militia-based systems through the Thirty Years War, despite a pattern of disappointing performance in the field.[44]

In the second half of the seventeenth century, mercenary and militia forms of warfare began merging into an auxiliary/subsidiary system. With war becoming a constant and wars lasting longer, the major combatants sought increasingly to increase their strength by going outside their borders. The first step in that process was usually an alliance *de haut en bas* in more or less traditional form, involving men for money. Such alliances were was easier to arrange since the Peace of Westphalia had recognized the sovereignty of Germany's rulers. Freshly acquired sovereignty, however, was not best served by permitting the recruitment of mercenaries in the traditional way, through contractors. Instead, the lesser states themselves assumed the responsibility of raising men and organizing regiments, whose maintenance was assumed by the larger, richer party to the alliance.

As early modern states sought advantage in diplomatic flexibility, alliance agreements tended to become fig leaves that developed into a pattern of auxiliary service. Instead of disbanding their regiments at the end of a war or campaign, the German states sought contracts for future employment—which could be as far away as North America, South Africa, or India if the terms were right. Few major campaigns—indeed, few major operations—were conducted in western Europe between 1675 and 1748, where auxiliaries did not compose up to half the forces involved. Even established states like Denmark concluded subsidy treaties with more ambitious, more affluent neighbors. Pressures soon developed to make the subsidy arrangements permanent, sustaining them in times of peace as well as war. While finance ministers, and in England, parliamentary delegates, tended to scotch such plans on grounds of cost, war ministries appreciated and acknowledged these "special relationships." These could range from the option for first refusal generally favored by Britain to the long-standing relationship France developed with the Swiss cantons that provided some of its best infantry. Hesse-Kassel, a German state, maintained a subsidy relationship with the Estates of the Netherlands from 1688 and developed it through King William into a similar one with England in 1694.

Comprehensive militarization was by no means the only middle-state response to the changing nature of war. Wuerttemberg, and to a lesser extent Baden, withdrew from the alliance/subsidy system in favor of cultivating improved relations with estates alienated by material, financial, and human demands. Standing army strength was reduced in favor of militia service; international competition was consciously shifted to cultural and intellectual contexts, with a ruler's virtue depending on the degree of his enlightenment in public contexts.[45]

States playing the subsidy game faced two problems. The relative marketability of auxiliary forces depended largely on their effectiveness, and successful participants on the supply side rapidly learned the wisdom of professionalizing their military systems. At the same time, recruiting and maintaining the numbers called for in the subsidy treaties placed unparalleled and often excessive strain on administrations not constructed for consistent effort. Addressing these issues could involve reconfiguring not only states, but societies. Again, Hesse-Kassel is a good example. Initially, its rulers sought to use subsidies to maintain an army large enough to sustain an independent foreign policy. The limits of that vision were demonstrated during the Seven Years War, when the state was repeatedly occupied and placed under contribution by the French. The resulting near-breakdown of society highlighted the worth of subsidies and the special relationships accompanying them, despite the accompanying limits on freedom of diplomatic action and the accompanying risks of being double shuffled by the stronger power.

What Charles Ingrao calls the "Hessian mercenary state" began with the Landgrave centralizing the collection and disbursement of military payments at the turn of the eighteenth century. It developed as the state encroached steadily on peasant society in search of manpower and for the funding necessary to bridge the gap between the amount of the subsidies and the actual costs of fulfilling the treaties. Military taxation and military recruitment, to be effective, required increasingly developed record-keeping—and increasingly comprehensive enforcement of the increasingly comprehensive network of laws regulating military service and its ramifications.

By the last quarter of the eighteenth century, literally the entire population of Hesse-Kassel was organized to support the state's mercenary army. All men between sixteen and thirty were listed on rolls kept by local bailiffs and were liable for service in their local regiment when that should become necessary. In practice, those owning over 250 talers in property fulfilled their obligation with money instead of blood. Craftsmen, workers in vital industries, and men essential to the prosperity of their farms or families were also exempted. Indeed, if someone in those categories enlisted, his case might be investigated to make sure he was a so-called true volunteer. On the other side of the coin the state went so far as to encourage a steady supply of marginalized have-nots by adjusting patterns of inheritance and employment. Parents were held responsible for sons who emigrated, even being imprisoned until the miscreants reported for duty.

One result was steady and profitable work for architects and construction workers, as Hesse-Kassel became a showplace of public works and public buildings. Another was the positioning of the government as a primary source of profit—not exactly through corruption, but through mutually acceptable arrangements among gentlemen. Not all the subsidy money, moreover, went for public works or private aggrandizement. Hesse-Kassel produced its own uniforms and weapons as far as possible, and the numbers of craftsmen and skilled workers correspondingly steadily increased. Given the comprehensive apparatus of control existing in Hesse-Kassel, compliance was the most reasonable behavior for commoners.[46] Government experts improved peasant agriculture, especially through encouraging potato cultivation and sheep raising. Increased wool production expanded the textile industry to a point where weavers were described as being able to eat meat and drink wine on a daily basis.

ALTERNATIVE APPROACHES TO RECRUITING SOLDIERS

In England, a military obligation of all male freeholders between sixteen and sixty, organized on a county basis, was confirmed by statute in 1558. A quarter-century later, the best of this militia were organized into "trained bands," forerunners of the American colonists' "minute companies." A mixture of government parsimony and strategic geography, however, kept the militia from seeing enough service to maintain its effectiveness—especially in the context of the growing domestic tension of the early seventeenth century.

What was most significant about England's militia system was its use to legitimate impressing individuals into service by government authority. This was something essentially different both from the communal, collective obligations of the continent and from the ad hoc practice of dragooning a community's expendables. With tongue only partially in cheek, it can be described as an early form of selective service, which individuals could compound for money, as twentieth-century Americans could through occupational and matrimonial decisions. Quite a good thing could be made of this by recruiters colluding with local authorities. Again, let Falstaff take center stage: "I pressed me none but such toasts-and-butter, with hearts in their bellies no bigger than pin's heads, and they have bought out their services. . . ." Collaborating with his companions in peculation, Justices Shallow and Silence, he exempts the stout lads Bullcalf and Mouldy in favor of Feeble, Shadow, and Wart. Shadow, he argues, is so scrawny he presents no mark to an enemy. Feeble, a woman's tailor, will be foremost in any retreat. And Wart, "little, lean, old, chopp'd, bald," is ideal for the "shot," though in his case he can manage only a caliver: light, short-ranged, roughly the sixteenth-century equivalent of the carbine used by U.S. troops in World War II and Korea—and like its successor, lightly regarded by anyone man enough to carry a real gun.

While pitched to the groundlings and played for laughs, these scenes reflected a reality in the three decades of war waged by Queen Elizabeth I. Even though most of the fighting took place outside England's boundaries, there were never enough men to meet the wastage. At the same time England's soldiers acquired a formidable skill set and a formidable reputation in continental wars, especially fighting alongside the Dutch in the Low Countries. In Ireland they simultaneously developed effective, albeit brutal, doctrines and methods of irregular warfare.

Stuart efforts, in the early seventeenth century, to overhaul militia service by establishing an "exact" or "select" force proved futile in the face of the persistent and increasing localization of a force funded by the land tax. The English Civil Wars were correspondingly waged with armies raised on the by-now historic pattern of volunteers supplemented by various forms of compulsion. The post-Restoration army of the Marlburian era and its eighteenth-century successors filled its ranks along similar lines. A percentage of the volunteers chose the uniform over prison or (occasionally) the rope. When that did not suffice, the government resorted to subsidizing foreign forces of various types. The militia was finally reformed in 1757 under the pressures of the Seven Years War and became a permanent force chosen by lot in 1769. Its service, however, amounted to only a few days annually, and its status as "the constitutional force" was so jealously guarded that it was a crime for a militiaman to enlist in the active army—until a later and more dangerous threat caused the laws to be rewritten.[47]

Army Development in Eastern Europe

The development of armies on the other side of the continent followed patterns shaped by the region's dominant military power: the Commonwealth of Poland-Lithuania. Product of a formal union in 1569 of two overextended states, the new entity claimed territory extending from the Baltic almost to the Black Sea and from the frontier of the Holy Roman Empire deep into Russia. Structurally, its army, in good part, followed what seemed contemporary Western patterns, combining local levies based on acres of land or numbers of houses with mercenary units, foreigners but often heavily Polonized, recruited on contract and raised by beat of drum.

In wartime these forces were supplemented by unpaid volunteers and peasant levies, who often proved far more effective than their Western counterparts. That effectiveness reflected the persistence of a martial spirit among the lower strata of Polish society. It reflected as well the Commonwealth's military geography: open prairies, dense forests, and a lot of mileage. Force-to-space ratios were correspondingly lower than in the West, and since no enemy could be everywhere at once, improvised formations had a chance to find their tactical feet. Terrain also contributed to preserving, and in some ways enhancing, cavalry's role as the decisive arm. Speed and shock were strategic and operational as well as tactical advantages. Indeed, they merit description as necessities. Poland-Lithuania maintained three kinds of mounted force. By the end of the seventeenth century, over three-fourths of the horsemen were titled "Cossacks." This reflected fighting style rather than heritage. Most of them were ethnic Poles or Muslim Tartars, with no cultural connection to the Zaphorozhian *seitch* beyond riding small and hardy ponies and specializing in scouting, skirmishing, and raiding. "German" heavy cavalry, again including many ethnic Poles but armed and armored along Western reiter/lancer lines, played an often-overlooked role, especially in battle. The heart of Poland's cavalry, however, and still its most familiar element, were the hussars.

Two sets of hussars armor; Polish, second half of the seventeenth century. © Erich Lessing/Art Resource, New York.

As spectacular in appearance as they were formidable in battle, these troopers attracted the attention of virtually every Western observer and of most Polish military historians. Their origins were modest: mercenary light cavalry from Serbia and Hungary, whose plundering habits earned them the nickname of *gussars*, or "bandits." During the sixteenth century they developed into a heavy cavalry depending for its effect as much on speed as weight. The hussars' armor was light—thirty pounds or so—sufficient protection on a battlefield where firearms were not predominant. Their horses were larger but still warm-blooded—the best bred in Europe. And the men were volunteers from the aristocracy and the even more numerous gentry, the *szchlachta*, skilled in horsemanship and in a spectrum of weapons and at the same time taught the value of training and discipline by generations of border war against the Cossacks and Turks. A hussar regiment began its charge in open order, closing ranks only at the last minute to minimize losses from arrows or bullets, performing the entire maneuver at the gallop.

The effect was enhanced by clothing, chosen by the individual troopers and fancier than any *Landsknecht*'s, and above all by the elaborately feathered "wings" inseparably associated with the Polish hussars.

Interpreted as everything from a defense against Tartar lassos to an effort to make their wearers look like angels, the wings are best understood as a combination of military fashion and a device for frightening enemy horses and men. A hussar charge properly delivered struck home like a pile driver. Even state-of-the-art pike and arquebus infantry was likely to be intimidated into looking side to side at how everyone else was coping, instead of facing front and doing their own jobs.[48] The best example of the result is offered in the third episode of Peter Jackson's *The Lord of the Rings* by the computer-generated charge of the Rohirrim—without the wings, but delivered at a disconcerting gallop. The heads of the orc spearmen are swiveling well before their feet take them out of range of lance and saber. It takes only a little imagination to conjure the image of old-time hussars lingering at the cavalryman's Valhalla of Fiddler's Green, shouting for another round of drinks to celebrate the show. Surely paradise incorporates modern conveniences like DVDs!

Swedish, Russian, and Prussian Army Development

The Commonwealth of Poland-Lithuania's armies were not invincible. On their own ground, however, they posed a virtually insoluble problem to enemies and prospective enemies with no hope of matching their mounted resources in numbers or effectiveness. One response of the Western states was to emphasize quality by developing an alternative, militia-based recruiting system. Beginning in the reign of Gustavus Adolphus, Sweden raised its infantry by the so-called allotment system. Groups of farms furnished a soldier, provided him with an enlistment bonus, food, clothing, and a yearly wage, and either a small plot of land or living space on one of the farms. In peacetime the soldier worked his own land and labored on the other farms in the group. In war his neighbors assisted his family. If the soldier died or was disabled, the group provided a replacement. Recruits might be younger sons of the community or outsiders, even foreigners, persuaded to participate. In either case they were able to achieve, at least in principle, a stable place in the village community, while contributing to its ongoing welfare.

The system had a number of favorable military side effects. Recruits were assigned to locally based regiments, giving them a sense of place denied the more cosmopolitan soldiers of other armies. It also facilitated a stable command system and training methods that, on an assembly-line basis, turned farm boys into soldiers at least the equal of the best professional and mercenary regiments.

Sweden's conscription system also guaranteed a steady supply of volunteers for the native Swedish cavalry regiments: service on horseback was widely preferred to being conscripted as a foot soldier. In broader terms the allotment system was so socially acceptable that it became demographically dysfunctional. As Sweden developed into a warfare state, with campaigns lasting longer and longer and occurring ever farther away, the steady drainage of men at around two percent each year led to a gradual decline in the male population. Such statistics meant land unworked, families unrenewed, and social bonds disrupted. Nevertheless, the army's connection with the people meant that it had to be used with caution. Even during the Thirty Years War, native Swedish regiments were disproportionately on home service or in garrisons. Offensive campaigns needed to be planned carefully and justified at high policy levels before being undertaken. Despite significant increases in overall population through conquest, under a warrior king and a fighting fool like Charles XII (1697–1718), Sweden essentially conquered itself to death in the first quarter of the seventeenth century.[49]

Whatever its long-term structural problems, Sweden's army demonstrated consistent and embarrassing superiority to a Russia whose military establishment was an unstable compound of irregular cavalry, Cossack and aristocratic, an uninspired mass of randomly recruited and uninspired infantry ostensibly organized on Western lines, and the once-elite corps of musketeers, or *Streltsy*, that by this time had ossified into a hereditary caste of urban craftsman and tradesmen, much as had their rough counterparts, the *Janissaries*, of the Ottoman Empire.

Czar Peter I, Russia's westernizer, replaced these vestiges and fragments by a system on the Swedish model, with every twenty "hearths" furnishing a recruit and replacing him when necessary. Initially, landowners and village councils chose among those made eligible for service as a class by the Law of 1705. Later, that role was assumed by state authorities. Recruiting and volunteering on the Western model was prohibited; landowners and officials alike feared the possible loss of control over a serf population even then called "the dark people"—a reference to their backwardness, not their color. Service was for life, discipline harsh, and conditions Spartan. Even then, life in the regiment was frequently easier than life in the village—and not necessarily that much shorter. As the regimental officer corps's initially rockbottom standard improved, the Russian soldiers developed a stoic endurance that in many ways ran counter to the military ethos of the period. Quick movement was not their forte. No one could accuse them of having imagination or initiative. But few were anxious to meet Russians face-to-face in a pitched battle—at least after the first time Frederick the Great himself was taught a few manners by the green-coated men who had to be killed twice and then knocked down before they realized they were dead.[50]

From the commencement of his reign in 1730 to his death in 1740, Prussia's king Frederick William I worked to increase the size and efficiency of the army he considered essential to Prussia's continued existence. Since the Thirty Years War, Prussia had depended for manpower on volunteers, most of them coming from Prussian territory: Local sources, however, faced unfamiliar strains as the king's demands for recruits increased. Landlords perfectly willing to see the last of a troublemaker protested at losing steady hands to crimps. By the 1720s, domestic recruiting parties increasingly resembled press-gangs. It was a common German practice for recruiters to operate across state lines, but Prussian methods so resembled manhunts that Hanover came close to declaring war in 1729. Other states made recruiting for the Prussian service a capital offence, on a par with parricide and witchcraft.

The most obvious solution to the army's appetite for men was to tap Prussia's own resources on a long-run, systematic basis.[51] Frederick William I began by conditioning his subjects to recognize their particular obligation to support the military, whether it was the aristocracy providing sons as officers, merchants and burghers paying heavy taxes, or those who had nothing else providing blood and sinew in the ranks. As early as 1713, an edict proclaimed that civilians leaving their administrative districts (*Kreise*) without permission were considered deserters.

Over the next twenty years, further declarations regularized domestic recruiting procedures. They culminated in the decrees of 1732–1733 that established the basic features of the Prussian canton recruiting/conscription system. Every regiment was assigned a specific recruiting district, further broken down into company areas. All males in the district were entered in the company recruiting rolls at age sixteen. If the companies did not fill their ranks by voluntary enlistment, then eligible cantonists were conscripted to make up the numbers.

The key word was *eligible*. While every male was registered, only those who met the height requirement of five foot seven inches (170 centimeters) or taller, were non-noble, not sons of officers, who did not directly own a farm, or whose families were worth less than 10,000 talers were eligible for induction. That reduced the number of eligibles in a company pool to about eighteen percent of the male population. As an example, in one company-sized recruiting area of 771 hearths (*Amt Bochum*), there were approximately 135 households that met the minimum requirements for conscription at any time during the cantonal era. This population filled a yearly cantonal requirement of about three soldiers—scarcely a high blood tax by any standards.

While call-ups could be increased in times of war, Prussia's state strategy in the eighteenth century emphasized using the army primarily as a deterrent force, whose effectiveness would render quick and decisive any wars it might wage. By the time of the system's abolition in 1813, fewer than half of all those registered actually found themselves in uniform—a percentage allowing ample margins for those seriously committed to avoiding service.[52]

Prussia's developed recruiting policies closely prefigured the Selective Service System practiced in the United States in the 1950s and 1960s. Prussia's economy could not spare its most vigorous element for even a few of their most productive years. Nor could the state properly train every eligible man. A process of random selection seemed as irrational to Prussia's monarchs as to America's Congress. Moreover, once the conscripted cantonist learned his new craft, he was eligible to be furloughed to civilian life and the civilian economy for an average of ten months a year, spending only two with the colors to refresh memory and reflexes. All these factors combined to produce tractable, if not enthusiastic soldiers—much like their American counterparts two centuries later.[53]

NOTES

1. John Landers, *The Field and the Forge: Population, Production, and Power in the Pre-industrial West* (New York: Oxford University Press, 2003).

2. Sydney Angelo, *The Martial Arts of Renaissance Europe* (New Haven, CT: Yale University Press, 2000).

3. Fritz Redlich, *De praeda militari: Looting and Booty, 1500–1815* (Wiesbaden, Germany: Franz Steiner, 1956).

4. M. Postan, *Essays in Medieval Agriculture* (Cambridge, UK: Cambridge University Press, 1972), 73.

5. Geoffrey Parker, *The Army of Flanders and the Spanish Road, 1567–1659: The Logistics of Spanish Victory and Defeat in the Low Countries' Wars* (Cambridge, UK: Cambridge University

Press, 1972), 180, 183. For a harsher critique of the veterans, see John R. Hale, *War and Society in Renaissance Europe, 1450–1620* (Baltimore: Johns Hopkins University Press, 1985), 115 ff.

6. For a dissenting position, see Armstrong Starkey, *War in the Age of Enlightenment, 1700–1789* (Westport, CT: Praeger, 2003), 69 ff.

7. Christopher Duffy, *The Army of Frederick the Great* (New York: Hippocrene Books, 1974), 193–194.

8. Robert C. Stacey, "The Age of Chivalry," in *The Laws of War: Constraints on Warfare in the Western World*, ed. Michael Howard, George J. Andreopoulos, and Mark R. Shulman (New Haven, CT: Yale University Press, 1994), 27–39.

9. Hale, *War and Society*, 100 ff., discusses urban demilitarization. Jan De Vries, *European Urbanization, 1500–1800* (Cambridge, MA: Harvard University Press, 1984), surveys the alternatives.

10. Gregory Hanlon, *The Twilight of a Military Tradition: Italian Aristocracy and European Conflicts, 1560–1800* (New York: Holmes and Meier, 1998), is a detailed case study.

11. J. M. W. Bean, *The Decline of English Feudalism, 1215–1540* (Manchester, UK: Manchester University Press, 1968).

12. See Ronald Asch and Adolf M. Birke, *Princes, Patronage, and the Nobility: The Court at the Beginning of the Modern Age c. 1450–1650* (New York: Oxford University Press, 1991).

13. April Harper, unpublished paper on restorative facial surgery in the late Middle Ages.

14. C. Storrs and H. S. Scott, "The Military Revolution and the European Nobility, c.1600–1800," *War in History* 3 (1996): 1–41.

15. Hale, *War and Society*, 53 ff.

16. John A. Lynn, *Giant of the Grand Siècle: The French Army, 1610–1715* (Cambridge, UK: Cambridge University Press, 1997), 248 ff.

17. Erik A. Lund, *Valor for the Every Day: Generals, Knowledge, and Warfare in Early Modern Europe, 1680–1740* (Westport, CT: Praeger, 1999).

18. Useful here is Harvey Chisick, *The Limits of Reform in the Enlightenment: Attitudes toward the Education of the Lower Classes in Eighteenth Century France* (Princeton, NJ: Princeton University Press, 1981).

19. Lynn, *Grand Siècle*, 514–515, speaks of a "culture of forbearance"; "culture of steadiness" is an alternate possibility. See William Miller, *The Mystery of Courage* (Cambridge, MA: Harvard University Press, 2000).

20. Lynn, *Grand Siècle*, 259 ff.

21. See Matthew Glozier's account of the peripatetic career of *Marshal Schomberg, 1615–1690* (Brighton, UK: Sussex Academic Press, 2005).

22. Roger B. Manning, "Prince Maurice's School of War: British Swordsmen and the Dutch," *War and Society* 23 (2006): 1–19.

23. Matthew Glozier, *The Huguenot Soldiers of William of Orange and the Glorious Revolution of 1688* (Brighton, UK: Sussex Academic Press, 2002).

24. Harman Murtaugh, "Irish Soldiers Abroad, 1600–1800," in *A Military History of Ireland*, ed. T. Bartlett and K. Jeffrey (Cambridge, UK: Cambridge University Press, 1996), 294–314.

25. William P. Guthrie, *The Later Thirty Years War: From the Battle of Wittstock to the Treaty of Westphalia* (Westport, CT: Greenwood Press, 2003).

26. Dennis E. Showalter, "Caste, Skill, and Training: The Evolution of Cohesion in European Armies from the Middle Ages to the Sixteenth Century," *Journal of Military History* 57 (1993): 407–430.

27. Quoted in C.W.C. Oman, *A History of the Art of War in the Sixteenth Century* (London: Methuen, 1937), 80.

28. Walther Schaufelberger, *Der alte Schweizer und sein Krieg: Studien zur Kriegfuehrung vornehmlich im 15. Jahrhundert*, 2nd ed. (Zurich: Europa, 1966), is good on the internal dynamics of pike war.

29. Bert S. Hall, *Weapons and Warfare in Renaissance Europe: Gunpowder, Technology, and Tactics* (Baltimore: Johns Hopkins University Press, 1997), 95–99.

30. Hall, *Weapons and Warfare*, 191–198. On the related subject of the growing importance of light cavalry, see Gervase Phillips, "'Of Nimble Service': Technology, Equestrianism, and the Cavalry Arm of Early Modern Western European Armies," *War and Society* 20 (2002): 1–22.

31. The model is adapted from that developed by Fritz Redlich, *The German Military Enterpriser and His Work Force: A Study in European Economic and Social History*, 2 vols. (Wiesbaden, Germany: Franz Steiner, 1964–1965).

32. Josef Polisensky and Josef Kollmann, *Wallenstein: Feldherr des Dreissigjaehrigen Krieges* (Cologne, Germany: Boehlau, 1997), is the best military biography.

33. Ibid., 105.

34. Richard Holmes, *Redcoat: The British Soldier in the Age of Horse and Musket* (New York: Harper Collins, 2001), 140. The poster in question dates from 1809.

35. George Farquhar, *The Recruiting Officer*, reprint ed. (Manchester, UK: Manchester University Press, 1986), 62, 98.

36. R. Chaboche, "Les soldiers francais de la guerre de trente ans," *Revue d'histoire moderne et contemporaine* 20 (1973): 10–24, presents a similar profile for the soldiers of France.

37. Parker, *Army of Flanders*, 35 ff.

38. Lynn, *Grand Siècle*, 354–356.

39. Gordon Wood, *The King's Army: Warfare, Soldiers, and Society during the Wars of Religion in France, 1561–1676* (Cambridge, UK: Cambridge University Press, 1996).

40. Parker, *Army of Flanders*, 46–47.

41. Ibid., 357–358.

42. Ibid., 369–371.

43. Gebelin Jacques, *Histoire des milices provinciales (1688–1792): Le tirage au sort sous l'ancien regime* (Paris: Hachette, 1882), remains the most detailed study.

44. Helmuth Schnitter, *Volk und Landesdefension: Volksaufgebote, Defensionswerke, Landmilizen in den deutschen Territorien von 15. Bis zum 18. Jahrhunderts* (East Berlin: Militaerverlag, 1977).

45. Peter H. Wilson, *War, State, and Society in Wuerttemberg, 1677–1793* (Cambridge, UK: Cambridge University Press, 1995).

46. The above analysis is based on Charles Ingrao, *The Hessian Mercenary State* (Cambridge, UK: Cambridge University Press, 1987); Rodney Atwood, *The Hessians* (Cambridge, UK: Cambridge University Press, 1980); and Peter K. Taylor, *Indentured to Liberty: Peasant Life and the Hessian Military State, 1688–1815* (Ithaca, NY: Cornell University Press, 1994). Generally valuable in this context is Peter Wilson, "Social Militarization in Eighteenth-Century Germany," *German History* 18 (2000): 1–39.

47. Cf. Roger B. Manning's superb *Apprenticeship in Arms: The Origins of the British Army, 1585–1702* (Oxford, UK: Oxford University Press, 2006); and J. R. Western, *The English Militia in the Eighteenth Century: The Story of a Political Issue, 1660–1802* (London: Routledge, 1965).

48. Robert L. Frost, *The Northern Wars: War, State, and Society in Northeastern Europe, 1558–1721* (London: Longmans, 2000), 16–17, 83 ff.; and Richard Brzezinski, *Polish Winged Hussar 1576–1775* (Oxford, UK: Osprey, 2006). The latter, like many of its counterparts on early modern subjects in Osprey's Warrior and Campaign series, is a neglected mine of data and analysis difficult to obtain elsewhere.

49. A. Aberg, "The Swedish Army from Luetzen to Narva," in *Sweden's Age of Greatness, 1632–1718*, ed. M. Roberts (London: Longmans, 1973), 265–287; J. Lindegren, "The Swedish 'Military State,' 1560–1720," *Scandinavian Journal of History* 10 (1985): 305–336.

50. R. Hellie, "The Petrine Army: Continuity, Change, and Impact," *Canadian-American Slavic Studies* 8 (1974): 237–253; and *Enserfment and Military Change in Muscovy* (Chicago: University of Illinois Press, 1971).

51. The long-standard rural-oriented analysis of Otto Busch, *Military System and Social Life in Old-Regime Prussia*, trans. J. Gagliardo (Atlantic Highlands, NJ: Humanities Press, 1997), is now complemented and challenged by the more urban-oriented account by Martin Winter, *Untertanengeist durch Militaerpflicht? Das preussische Kantonverfassung in Brandenburgischen Staedten im 18. Jahrhundert* (Bielefeld, Germany: Verlag für Regionalgeschichte, 2005).

52. Jürgen Kloosterhuis, ed., *Bauern, Bürger und Soldaten: Quellen zur Sozialisation des Militärsystems im preußischen Westfalen 1713–1803*, 2 vols. (Münster: Selbstverlag, 1992), I, 61, 67–68; and "Zwischen Aufruhr und Akzeptanz: Zur Ausformung und Einbettung des Kantonsystem in die Wirtschafts-und Sozialstrukturen des preussischen Westfalen," in *Krieg und Frieden: Militaer und Gesellschaft in der Fruehen Neuzeit*, ed. B. Koerner and R. Prove (Paderborn, Germany: Schoeningh, 1996), 167–190.

53. Dennis Showalter, *The Wars of Frederick the Great* (London: Longman, 1996).

Three

✵ ✵ ✵

TECHNOLOGIES, TACTICS, AND TRAINING

In *Don Quixote*, Cervantes recalled a past that did not know the terrors of gunpowder weaponry: "Blessed be those happy ages that were strangers to the dreadful fury of these devilish instruments of artillery," wrote Cervantes, "whose inventor I am satisfied is now in hell, receiving the reward of his cursed invention, which is the cause that very often a cowardly base hand takes away the life of the bravest gentleman." This chapter discusses weapons, tactics, and training. It takes the soldier from the *Landsknecht*'s pike to the flintlock musket and socket bayonet, from the mass formations of the sixteenth century to the three-rank firing lines of the eighteenth, and from imitating the veterans to the systematic training methods characteristic of all effective armies by the coming of the French Revolution. As was described in Chapter Two, gunpowder weaponry in the sixteenth century drove noble cavalrymen to abandon the lance for a brace of pistols as they wheeled and fired in the caracole maneuver. Other nobles left bands of heavily armored knights for leadership positions in an expanding and newly ascendant infantry army. Indeed, the implications of gunpowder weaponry were widespread and often profound, as shown in stunning fashion in 1453 outside the gates of the last great city of the eastern Roman Empire.

In 1453, Mahomet II, ruler of the Ottoman Empire, finally breached the walls guarding Constantinople (Istanbul), ending the Byzantine Empire, the last remnant of eastern Rome's glory. He did so with European bombards cast on the spot by Hungarian craftsmen. Constantinople's fall marked a new chapter in the history of warfare—the transition from weapons that relied on muscle power, such as the English longbow used to devastating effect against French armored knights at Agincourt in France in 1415, to weapons that relied on chemical power, such as cannons and muskets.[1] As European armies deployed smoothbore cannons and muskets in large numbers, firepower gradually became more important in battle than shock action, and thus infantry came to surpass cavalry as the combat arm of decision on European battlefields. Heavy cavalry still occasionally retained the glory of administering the coup de grâce, but only after the enemy's main infantry formations had been disrupted by concentrated infantry and artillery firepower. A new age of grunts (foot soldiers) and gunners had begun.

Tactics and training changed accordingly. Infantrymen and artillerymen now possessed weaponry that could disable the most heavily armored knights at a distance. For a time the latter attempted to adapt by adopting increasingly sophisticated combined arms tactics. In the 1470s, Charles the Bold's Ordinance of Lausanne integrated longbowmen, crossbowmen, men-at-arms, pikemen, and gunners into eight "battles" or units, each with its own carefully considered structure and with systematic provision for liaison and cooperation among the different arms. Owing to the temporary nature of these units and the lack of time spent training together, synergy was rarely attained. Nevertheless, similar attempts at combining missile with shock effectively ended the independent action of mounted men-at-arms that characterized much of medieval warfare in western Europe. Unlike their medieval counterparts, early modern battles no longer resembled aristocratic jousting tournaments writ large. Instead, they became complicated and increasingly destructive chess matches in which the carefully judged movements of stoic foot soldiers (pawns), longer-range cannons (bishops), and mounted men (knights) combined either to safeguard or threaten the positions of Europe's kings and queens.

As suggested in the previous chapter, the growing firepower of infantry and artillery generated new ideas about courage and heroism on the battlefield. In the medieval period, knights had been recognized and celebrated for individual feats of arms during a mêlée. (Indeed, they carried heraldic shields in part so that courageous deeds might be seen and recorded by chroniclers of battles.) But in the early modern period, foot soldiers as well as high-ranking officers soon became admired more for their stoicism and ability to brave the enemy's musket balls and cannon rounds without flinching, even while comrades fell around them. In an attempt to inure men to the chaos and brutality of combat and to promote cohesion on a battlefield increasingly swept by iron and lead, armies resorted to repetitive drill and rigid discipline. In the early modern period a unit's cohesiveness and ability to endure the enemy's weight of shot without breaking often proved decisive, even if cohesion had to be bought by the lash or enforced at the point of a pike or bayonet. Frederick the Great, a skilled practitioner of early modern warfare, captured the strictness of discipline required for success when he told his officers that their men had to fear them more than they feared the enemy. In this prenationalistic age, fear of punishment was an enabler, serving to keep men in line as they worked feverishly under enormous stress to maintain a high rate of fire against the enemy. Stubborn toughness shared in close quarters helped to control fear among the ordinary rank and file, caught as they were in claustrophobic formations on bloody battlefields that typified field combat in early modern Europe.

This chapter will first look at the idea of a so-called gunpowder revolution beginning in circa 1450 with the development of semimobile field cannons. These cannons made short work of medieval castles, but Renaissance engineers soon adapted and developed new fortresses that made siege warfare the most common chore and occupational hazard of soldiers in early modern armies.[2] We will then look at the infantry (foot soldiers) and their adoption of gunpowder weaponry, beginning with matchlock muskets and concluding with flintlocks—the demise of pikemen coming by circa 1680 with the invention of socket bayonets fixed to the end of smoothbore muskets. Smoothbore muskets, inherently inaccurate, put a premium on concentrated firepower delivered by well-drilled soldiers standing or kneeling nearly shoulder-to-shoulder. We will conclude with the cavalry—no longer the queen of battle, as in the Middle Ages, but still an important piece that could harass and even checkmate a suitably weakened opponent.

GUNPOWDER CANNONS, NEW FORTRESSES, AND SIEGE WARFARE

Contemporary historians have waged their own skirmishes whether changes in early modern warfare, chiefly driven by the widespread adoption of gunpowder weaponry, constituted a military revolution.[3] The concept of a revolution, attractive as it is, should be used with care, however. It tends to resolve issues before they are raised and is often insufficiently sensitive to local cultures and unique conditions. Placing the concept of a revolution momentarily to one side, one may speak with greater certainty in early modern Europe of a military reformation, the scale of whose impact on society was reminiscent of the better-known Protestant Reformation, which transformed technologies, tactics, and training among all three combat arms (infantry, artillery, and cavalry).[4]

The development of gunpowder weapons was the key event. Gunpowder was a Chinese invention that combined saltpeter, sulfur, and charcoal in combustible combination.[5] Knowledge of the formula migrated westward to Europe and, by the fourteenth century, began to shape military operations. By the fifteenth century, one may speak of an artillery revolution in Europe that quickly led to fundamental changes in warfare, most dramatically in the design and scale of military fortifications.[6]

Of course, this artillery revolution was not instantaneous. Early cannons were expensive to manufacture, difficult to move due to their bulk and weight, inaccurate, and unsafe. Spectacular and grisly accidents led early artillerists to select Barbara as their patron saint to ward off explosive failures. Despite hazards to their crews, cannons did much to drive the English out of France during the closing stages of the Hundred Years War (1337–1453). At the battle of Formigny in April 1450, the French first used cannon fire to disrupt the tight formation of English longbowmen, forcing them to flee their fortified position. Twelve hundred armored knights then galloped forward, lances at ready, skewering and scattering the English archers in their wake.

In this case the newfangled, semimobile field artillery was employed within established paradigms, temporarily revitalizing the blue-blooded heavy cavalry of France. But the renaissance of mounted knights was brief. By the mid-sixteenth century, musket-armed infantry, and especially lighter cavalry armed with wheel lock pistols, combined to make forays by the more ponderous heavy cavalry untenable.[7] As heavily armored knights enjoyed a brief resurgence, gun foundries in the Low Countries, enjoined by rulers in France and Burgundy to make efficient, semimobile siege guns, succeeded in manufacturing bronze muzzle-loading cannons, six to eight feet in length, mounted

With the transition to gunpowder, breaching tower, archers, and cannon were used in a siege during the Hundred Years War. © North Wind Picture Archives.

on wheeled carriages that enabled limited tactical mobility.[8] Firing iron cannonballs eight to ten inches in diameter, they made mincemeat of traditional castles.

In the medieval period, castles with high stone walls secured by circular towers had strong defensive qualities. Walls were both difficult to scale and nearly impossible to breech. Besiegers often resorted to expensive and time-consuming sapping and mining techniques. But these same high walls and towers became a liability when bombarded and broken up by iron cannonballs. Towers and walls shattered, then collapsed, raining boulders and shards of rock on their defenders. The defining event was Charles VIII's invasion of Italy in 1494, during which his army of 18,000 men and forty siege cannons left a trail of demolished castles and demoralized defenders in their wake on their way to conquering Naples.

Challenge and Response: *Trace Italienne* Fortresses

But defenders adapted. A new style of military fortification, known as *trace italienne*, or "Italian style," since it first arose in Italy in response to Charles VIII's invasion, replaced the castles of old.[9] The new fortresses were built around bastions: arrow-shaped artillery platforms whose low, carefully sloped, and thick walls proved impervious to cannonballs. Their careful alignment eliminated the blind spots of medieval castle, allowing defenders to sweep areas in front of the walls with enfilading fire. Attackers had to endure a withering cross fire from bastions and their outworks as they struggled to traverse dry moats. Scaling or breaching a bastion was the goal, but even a breach was no guarantee of victory when defenders were staunch. Working against attackers was the difficulty of moving up artillery, ammunition, and reinforcements while under observation and direct fire from the bastions. Frustrated attackers again resorted to sapping and mining techniques, which required Herculean and time-consuming efforts at digging tunnels and planting mines under fortress walls. Often, as many as 20,000 or more laborers had to be conscripted to advance a siege.

The appearance of *trace italienne* fortresses beginning in the 1520s ended the brief era of dominance for wall-shattering cannons. Difficult to reduce and capture, these fortresses were also treacherous to bypass. When bypassing a fortress, attackers usually had to detach a so-called masking force, both to safeguard supply lines and to counter possible forays by the enemy's garrison. In the macro scale a burgeoning system of loosely networked fortresses served to lengthen campaigns, making war even more expensive and inconclusive. In short, these beautiful yet deadly "star forts" acted as a check to the ambitions of dynastic empire builders, whether they be Habsburg or Bourbon.[10]

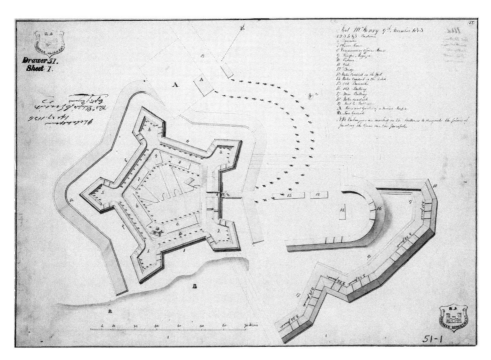

A classic *trace italienne* fortress, Fort McHenry in Baltimore. Its successful defense during the War of 1812 inspired Francis Scott Key to pen "The Star-Spangled Banner." Courtesy of the Library of Congress.

Yet, *trace italienne* fortresses had one serious drawback: They were expensive to build and garrison. Siena, an independent city-state in Tuscany, provided a cautionary tale. As Siena fought to maintain its independence against the combined forces of the Spanish Habsburgs and the Duke of Florence, Cosimo I, the city fathers modified existing medieval fortifications to the new style, adding bastions as well as outworks. The modifications worked, helping the city to withstand the initial attacks of a numerically superior enemy. But they came at an unsustainable cost. With Siena bankrupt, the city was unable to raise a field army that could break the enemy's siege and was forced to surrender after ten grueling months of resistance. Annexation by Florence, its Tuscan rival, was the price of civic pride and misplaced faith in the new fortifications.[11]

Yet as long as expenses could be controlled and garrisons supported, the new fortresses multiplied because they provided protection to urban areas and other strategically valuable points. Viewed collectively, the fortresses formed a network that provided defense in depth, cushioning the blow of enemy invasions. Even when decisively defeated by a symmetrical enemy—an occasion rare enough in early modern warfare—a vanquished army could typically retire to lick its wounds behind fortress walls.[12] *Trace italienne* fortresses, in sum, limited the decisiveness of early modern European warfare. And given the vital roles that these fortresses played, it is not surprising that sieges remained the most common form of warfare throughout most of early modern Europe.

As fortresses multiplied, a fundamental task of European armies was to garrison them, providing for external defense while also upholding internal order. Indeed, an

In contrast to medieval castles, the walls of *trace italienne* fortresses were lower and thicker. Courtesy of the Library of Congress.

essential mission of these fortresses and their garrisons was internal security. Garrisons projected power into the surrounding countryside, limiting crime and stamping out rebellion, while enforcing royal decrees and collecting taxes. Garrisons often had the unenviable, if at times profitable, chore of extracting money from recalcitrant farmers and skeptical town dwellers, none-too-pleased when the king's men darkened their doors to enforce royal decrees.

Building, stocking, and supplying these fortresses with a garrison and related equipment put a premium on a state's ability to raise funds through taxation. Helping to justify taxation to skeptical merchants and parsimonious country dwellers were the putative advantages conveyed by fortresses in securing the surrounding countryside. Here a paradox emerged. It was not always the case that more efficient finances and expanding armies facilitated the building and garrisoning of more fortresses. Instead, more detachments and fortress garrisons were needed to extract so-called contributions from ordinary citizens to support larger field armies. (Contributions, as detailed in the discussion of the fiscal-military state in Chapter One, were essentially systems of licensed extortion; means of enforcement included forced quartering of troops, hostage taking, the burning of villages, and even executions.) An army of 50,000 men was self-financing, explained the Bohemian count Albert of Wallenstein to his patron Ferdinand II, the Habsburg emperor. Its large size supported detachments that served as tentacles, gripping and extracting wealth from the countryside. A field army of 20,000 men, however, was a losing financial proposition—it lacked sufficient men to detach and form enough wealth-extracting contingents to remain on the positive size of the financial ledger.[13]

In the age of Cardinal Richelieu (chief minister to Louis XIII in France) and Wallenstein, it was the need to extort and extract wealth from the countryside, achieved in part through the building and garrisoning of additional fortresses, that spurred army growth and also the rapacity of war. Given the comparative immaturity of state finances and centralized administration, monarchs delegated to military entrepreneurs the recruitment, organization, and funding of armies. This in turn tended to reinforce the local authority of princes and the power of mercenary captains such as Wallenstein at the expense of state centralization.

This fact was not lost on the monarchs themselves. After the reign of terror inflicted by rapacious mercenary armies on Germanic territories during the Thirty Years War, powerful monarchs such as Louis XIV of France (r. 1661–1715) worked to place the army firmly under state control. Also working to spur greater central-ization and larger state bureaucracies was the expansion of *trace italienne* fortresses, which both curbed the decisiveness of field campaigns and drove up the size of armies. With their resource-intensive garrison and support needs, fortresses set a minimum size for peacetime armies. In France's case this minimum was 150,000 men by 1700.[14] Potential aggressors had to fund and field an army large enough to besiege a major fortress or city, while at the same time allowing for enough reserve forces to repel at-tempts at relief. Defenders themselves needed to raise field armies to relieve besieged fortresses or to mount diversionary attacks. This complex dynamic rewarded states that succeeded in developing centralized and reasonably efficient financial and war ministries staffed by administrators and engineers supported by intendants (com-missioners), who were attached to armies in the field. Often trained as engineers and attached to the war ministry, these men brought a more technically oriented mind-set to the military.

Indeed, the sheer scale of state resources expended to construct fortifications worked to elevate the status of engineers in military hierarchies. A young Leonardo da Vinci (1452–1519) was only the most famous among many other aspiring engineers who boasted to potential patrons of skills in military architecture and in devising new and deadly engines of war.[15] A seminal text was *The Treatise of Architecture, Engineering and Military Art* by Francesco di Giorgio Martini (1439–1502). Having witnessed Charles VIII's invasion of Italy and the obsolescence of medieval-style fortifications, Martini was instrumental in laying down the basic design of the new *trace italienne* fortresses.

This new breed of officer-warrior included not just the strong and brave, but also the literate and technically savvy. Mathematicians and engineers like Nicolas Tartaglia (1500–1575) argued that the geometrical layout of *trace italienne* fortresses was even more important to their survivability than strictly physical properties, such as thicker walls. Tartaglia also employed mathematics to describe the motion of cannonballs, or ballistics, in his *Della nova scientai* (Of the New Science), published in 1537. A can-non's maximum theoretical range, he calculated, occurred when its barrel was elevated to forty-five degrees above the horizontal.[16] France's Sébastien le Prestre de Vauban (1633–1707) was the most influential military engineer of the early modern period. His mastery of both military architecture and siege warfare earned him a marshal's baton: the highest military rank in France.[17] He built or rebuilt 133 fortresses, inte-grating them into a defensive system that lay astride traditional invasion routes used by past enemies of France. Vauban saw fortresses as focusing the burdens of war on pro-fessionals rather than civilians; the siege warfare that resulted was thus more consistent with a newly "enlightened" age seeking to restrict the social and economic impact of warfare.[18] Rarely in history have military engineers been as powerful in shaping mili-tary and sociocultural patterns as they were in early modern Europe.

In military circles, there is a saying that amateurs study tactics, while profession-als master logistics. For several reasons, fortresses proved essential to logistics. First, they acted as paymasters, centers of administration, and storehouses for war matériel. Well-stocked food, fodder, and weapon caches allowed an army to venture forth into the field sooner than the enemy and to change its lines of operation more readily. Sec-ond, border fortresses served as gateways to the resources of foreign lands. Far better to feed one's soldiers with foreign wheat, and to coerce contributions from disputed border areas, than to consume one's own limited resources. Likewise, fortresses served to deny one's own territory to enemy foraging parties, thereby solidifying support of one's own farmers and merchants. Finally, careful siting of fortresses along rivers and other choke points made movement and supply more expensive and problematic to the enemy, making potential opponents think twice before invading.[19]

Siege Warfare

Sieges themselves became regimented, rational, and predictable. Besiegers built lines of circumvallation, designed to offer protection from bombardment while serving as a fortified perimeter to defeat attempts at relief. The need to defend these lines, which often stretched for fifteen or twenty miles, established the minimum size of a besieging army. To prevail in a protracted siege, attackers often needed to outnumber defenders by twenty to one. This drove up the size of besieging armies to an average of about 27,000 men by the start of the eighteenth century.

Keeping tens of thousands of men fed and reasonably happy throughout a lengthy siege was a major challenge; the availability of forage often determined whether a siege had sufficient staying power. A serious constraint was fodder for horses. An army of 30,000 typically had 20,000 horses to feed, half for the cavalry and half for supply and transportation. Since fodder was too heavy and bulky to transport in quantity during a long siege, horses had to forage. As horses moved about, so too did the soldiers, which complicated efforts to supply them with rations. Including the extra rations needed for officers and essential noncombatants, an army of 30,000 effectives consumed 45,000 rations of bread daily. With each ration weighing two pounds, this army would consume forty-five tons of bread per day. Armies usually could not buy or extract sufficient grain from locally available sources, nor could they have processed the grain locally due to the scarcity of mills, ovens, and bakers. So they employed a shuttle system of magazines, bakeries, and wagons; although vulnerable to interdiction, this supply chain was a costly yet crucial element to the success of protracted sieges.

Foremost in the mind of skilled commanders was the need both to mobilize and safeguard one's resources for war. The positional nature of warfare that followed on the heels of the Thirty Years War reflected this. Fortresses, by dominating trading centers and strategic waterways, often became the pivot upon which campaigns turned. Many of the more famous battles of the early modern period centered on attempts to relieve besieged fortresses at strategic points. Examples included St. Quentin (1557), Nördlingen (1634), Rocroi (1643), Marston Moor (1644), the Dunes (1658), Vienna (1683), and Fontenoy (1745). For an attacker, neutralizing an enemy's fortresses was crucial to sustaining an army logistically. The powerful defensive capabilities of artillery fortresses, viewed in light of the more limited offensive abilities of armies to mask or reduce them, encouraged most generals to err on the side of caution in defining their strategic goals.

Further enhancing the staying power of fortresses was favorable geography. The Eighty Years War (1567–1648) in the Netherlands provided a prime example.[20] As the Catholic Philip II and the Spanish Habsburgs attempted to seize the Lowlands and suppress Protestantism, they confronted the Dutch strongholds of Holland and Zeeland, covered by the mouth of the Meuse, Scheldt, and Rhine rivers. From 1529 to 1572, bastioned defenses in this area proliferated. Four new citadels, twelve new circuits of walls, and eighteen circuits that were substantially new secured a formidable river line of defense. To overcome and occupy these Dutch positions, Spain had to send larger and larger armies and ever-increasing quantities of supplies along the Spanish Road from northern Italy to the Lowlands. By 1572, the Duke of Alba's Army of Flanders reached its peak size of 86,000 men.[21]

But even this huge number was not enough. Dutch fortresses and their defenders' ideological determination made the war a quagmire for the Catholic Habsburgs. Elaborate water defenses precluded mining operations and provided a sea lifeline to embattled defenders. As a tactic of last resort, the Dutch opened the sea dikes and flooded the land, thereby denying its exploitation by the Spanish, a recourse used in 1573 at Alkmaar. Rampant inflation and the loss of treasure fleets from the New World prevented Spain from paying its soldiers consistently, leading to the so-called Spanish Fury at Antwerp in 1576, where soldiers ran amuck through the streets, burning more than 1,000 homes and killing 8,000 citizens. This "hoodlums' and harlots' delight" only further inflamed Dutch passions against Spain.[22]

The emergence in 1585 of a skilled commander, Maurice of Nassau, as captain general of Holland and the Spanish field army's diversion to France in the 1590s combined to frustrate Catholic Spain's attempt to suppress Protestantism in the Netherlands. Maurice's strategy was to avoid large-scale battles, relying instead on fortresses and harassing forces to wear down the finances and will of Spain. His was a policy of protracted war, seeking to win by not losing. It worked when Spain finally conceded the independence of seven Dutch provinces (the United Provinces) in the Peace of Westphalia that ended the Thirty Years War in 1648.

What did the proliferation of fortresses and prevalence of siege warfare mean to the average soldier? To defenders, sieges meant constant vigilance; careful husbanding of ever-dwindling supplies, especially food and shot; and skilful diplomacy. Obdurate defenders faced the possibility of severe reprisals if they held out past honorable limits, a fate memorably depicted in Shakespeare's *Henry V* when King Hal warns the defenders of Harfleur that if they held out longer, his "flesh'd soldier[s], rough and hard of heart" would mow like grass "your fresh-fair virgins and your flowering infants." Yet commanders of fortresses who were too quick to accept "the honors of war" and surrender could, if repatriated, face prison or the rope. To attackers, sieges meant manual labor and drudgery. Lines of circumvallation and contravallation and parallel lines of approach trenches had to be dug and cannons manhandled into position. Rations, ammunition, and other essentials had to be lugged forward, often while under fire from the enemy's ramparts. Foraging parties provided a welcome break but brought the risk of resistance from resentful farmers and landowners. Camp life and camp followers provided companionship and sexual relief, but too much time spent in one locale spawned conditions favorable to the outbreak of the plague, venereal diseases, and "camp fever," a catch-all term that included diseases such as typhus, typhoid fever, and dysentery. (Until the twentieth century, diseases killed far more soldiers in the field than did enemy action.) Helping to sustain morale during long sieges was the promise of plunder—the tax of violence detailed in Chapter One—and of having one's way with the enemy.

Especially brutal was the break-in phase of sieges. Breaching a bastion often involved ear-shattering explosions, followed by violent and intense hand-to-hand combat. Terror-stricken before the breach, soldiers found release in a brutal catharsis afterward, notes the historian John Keegan. At times, fighting spilled into the streets and domestic areas of a fortified city, leading to acts of wanton destruction and blood-soaked revenge. At Maastricht in 1579, Spanish forces who breached the city walls first raped the women (some of whom, in fighting to defend the city, had transgressed gender roles and forfeited their right to mercy), then massacred the population, reputedly tearing people limb from limb. Sieges were prolonged emotional and physical events that often climaxed at fever pitch; frustrations built up over weeks and months were sometimes vented in unpredictable ways at orgasmic intensities commanders could do little to modulate.

More prosaically, sieges were routine and rational endeavors requiring careful planning by skilled and experienced staff officers. As outlined by Vauban, an ideal siege took seven weeks and followed a predictable course. In the first three weeks, besiegers invested the fortress, collected material, built lines of circumvallation and contravallation, and dug trenches toward the enemy's covered way. In weeks four and five, besiegers sited batteries, started mining operations, seized the covered way, and captured the *démi-lune* (an outwork protecting the curtain wall between bastions) and its defenses. Weeks six and seven were devoted to crossing the ditch, breaching a bastion, and exploiting the breach, thereby forcing the fortress to surrender. Vauban allowed an extra week or so in case of errors, damage caused by the enemy's sorties, or for exceptionally tenacious defense.

Formalized to the extreme, siege warfare led to increasing specialization within armies. Engineers were especially valuable. Lord Galway, the British commander in Portugal in 1704, complained that "good engineers are so scarce that one must bear with their humours and forgive them because we can't be without them."[23] The French army created special companies of sappers in 1673 and bombardiers in 1684. Britain in 1716 created a separate corps of military engineers, a Royal Regiment of Artillery in 1727, and in 1741 founded the Royal Military Academy at Woolwich to train engineering and artillery officers. Not to be outdone, the French founded an engineering academy at Mézières in 1749; an artillery school followed seven years later at La Fère.

Since fortresses were both defended and reduced by artillery, the results of sieges often hinged on the skills of artillerists. As early as the sixteenth century, the Spanish founded schools to teach gunnery and principles of ballistics. With the development of cheaper printing techniques, manuals and books on fortification, gunnery, and tactics proliferated. As mentioned previously, European armies in the Age of Reason founded military academies to train officers in the technical demands specific to military engineering and artillery. These military academies proved popular among the young sons of the bourgeoisie and lesser nobility, who saw military service as an honorable pursuit providing opportunities for social advance. The most famous example of an artillery officer making good was Napoleon Bonaparte.

That military effectiveness and professionalism could be enhanced through technical study was an idea whose time had come in Enlightenment Europe.[24] Within the military's technical branches, warfare was now a science as well as a profession. Besides building hundreds of elaborate fortresses, armies strove to standardize cannon types, tested field guns under controlled conditions, and encouraged arms manufacturers to develop interchangeable parts. The maturation of science-based industry in all its awful potential, however, came in the nineteenth century, after the unleashing of ideological passions associated with the French Revolution and of new energy sources associated with the Industrial Revolution.[25] Together with agricultural advancements that supported higher birth and survival rates, these twin revolutions enabled a destructive age of ecstatic industrial warfare in the nineteenth century.

DRILL, DISCIPLINE, AND MUSKETS: THE RISE OF INFANTRY

Close-order drill and strict discipline have been important ingredients in Western military success since ancient times.[26] Classical models, especially as provided by the Roman army, were much admired in Renaissance Europe, most notably by Niccolò Machiavelli. Vegetius's *De re militari*, in its 450 C.E. edition, was republished frequently and mined for its military lessons. Yet Europeans in the fifteenth century only had to look as far as Switzerland for evidence of the power of well-drilled and cohesive infantry formations. Their strength was in the coordinated push of the pike—essentially a long spear anywhere from twelve to eighteen feet in length. As discussed in Chapter Two, the pike was a relatively simple weapon in its technical demands. Any soldier possessed of reasonable strength, agility, and attitude could master it. Well into the sixteenth century, Swiss pikemen formed a major component of European armies, imparting common tactical ideas and high standards of training wherever they served.

Swiss pike tactics emphasized shock action, which placed a premium on unit commitment and cohesion. To facilitate cohesion, the Swiss formed companies of men who hailed from the same town or village. Strict requirements to maintain tight formations during battle meant that the Swiss rarely broke formation to take prisoners. Waging war for profit, they routinely looted after battle and often murdered garrisons after successful sieges. Their ferocity as well as their undeniable effectiveness made the Swiss the favorite and concomitantly the most expensive mercenaries of Europe. One exasperated French general complained that his Swiss mercenaries "ask for so much money and are so unreasonable that it is almost impossible to satisfy them."[27]

Pikemen, Swiss or otherwise, remained essential in western European armies until the end of the seventeenth century. Their collective push often proved decisive in breaking the enemy's formation; the protective hedgehog of pikes that they formed also provided cover to slow-loading, musket-armed infantry. For two centuries, pikemen and musketeers fought in concert in various infantry formations. (Halberdiers often joined pikemen, especially in Swiss formations; they used the halberd, a shortened spear with an axe head affixed for cleaving through armor.) Pike duty favored strong, brawny, physically tough men capable of handling the pushing and shoving of close-in combat; in contrast, musketeers were selected more for their ability to master loading and firing drills as well as for their coolness under fire.

Muskets

From circa 1500 to circa 1660, most musketeers were armed with matchlock muskets.[28] These took their name from the match, a length of slow-burning fuse that the musketeer fixed to the serpentine near the priming pan when he was ready to fire. Upon pulling the trigger, the match was forced into the priming pan, igniting the gunpowder and propelling the musket ball. A failed ignition might produce merely a "flash in the pan," an expression still used today to indicate a seemingly brilliant success that lacks significance or staying power. With their slow rate of fire, inherent inaccuracy, and unreliability, especially in damp or rainy weather, matchlocks were initially less effective than pikes as infantry weapons.

Indeed, matchlock muskets were decidedly inferior to the English longbow. Where a skilled longbowman could fire a dozen arrows in a minute, a musketeer in the same time was fortunate to fire once. Yet mastering the longbow took a lifetime of practice and proper technique; its physical demands led to permanent bodily deformities in the fingers, inner forearms, and backbones of archers. Muskets, in contrast, provided their own chemical energy and were considerably quicker to master, coming close to being foolproof.[29] In this context, muskets were judged the "superior" technology since the social system represented by longbowmen was no longer sustainable within English society.

English officer, musketeer, pikeman, and longbowman, Elizabethan England. © North Wind Picture Archives.

Adopted in large numbers and adapted to the conditions of warfare, smoothbore muskets and cannons radically changed the conduct and conditions of war during the late Renaissance. As the historian John Hale noted, "For the soldier they changed the equipment he wore and carried; the formations which affected his morale and practice in combat; the nature of his wounds, for they broke bones and led to the loss of limbs by gangrene; and, more conjecturally, his chances of being killed."[30] There were few places to hide on the battlefields of early modern Europe, and the very un-predictability of musketry and cannon fire led to a sense of fatalism among soldiers seeking to avoid holding a dance card with death.

Leading the way in adopting matchlock muskets were the Spanish *tercios*, infantry units that combined the arquebus with pike, sword, and buckler (a small round shield).[31] An arquebus was a shortened musket weighing ten pounds and firing a .66-caliber ball from a .72-caliber barrel. This "windage" between ball and muzzle bore helped quicken loading but led to minimal accuracy past fifty yards.[32] At six feet in length, muskets were two feet longer than arquebuses, ten pounds heavier, and somewhat more accurate if fired from a fork rest. They used a larger-caliber ball: Its key advantage was better penetrating power against the plate armor worn by knights. As armored knights became obsolete after the mid-sixteenth century, so too did these longer and heavier muskets. The term *musket* persisted, however, as a catchall for the arquebus and its variants.

Roughly analogous to a modern infantry regiment, a Spanish *tercio* consisted nominally of 3,000 men, but its usual fighting complement was half that. It was further broken down into companies, each numbering about 150 men. Arrayed in the center of the formation in ranks twenty to thirty deep were pikemen. Musketeers were stationed around the perimeter of the pike square and in smaller blocks at its corners. Until the seventeenth century, *tercios* had roughly two pikemen for each musketeer, with this ratio slowly tipping in favor of the musketeers, whose massed firepower became increasingly telling.

In essence the *tercio* was a moving fortress of men, formidable yet ponderous. Advancing toward the enemy, its arquebusiers and musketeers fired to soften up the enemy's formation, retiring within the pike hedgehog to reload. Meanwhile, pistol-armed cavalry screened the pike squares, riding forward to discharge their brace of pistols in the caracole. The shock action and death grapple of each side's pikemen often determined victor from vanquished, although artillery fire also proved important, as at the battle of Marignano in 1515, where Swiss pike formations were shattered by cannon fire and musketry.

In symmetrical battles determined by narrow margins, experience was a vital edge. Grizzled officers and noncommissioned officers (NCOs) insured that pikemen and musketeers were arrayed precisely so they did not trip, fall, or otherwise get in each other's way. Opening and closing of pike ranks to protect musketeers during reloading, straightforward in peacetime, was exceedingly difficult in wartime, especially as the smoke discharged by black powder weapons hung in the air, obscuring sight lines. Vicious hand-to-hand fighting made for a decidedly nasty battlefield, with soldiers distracted and disoriented by the screams of wounded comrades. Bearing up under these conditions was a monumental test of a soldier's discipline and willed indifference to danger. Mental and emotional endurance, not merely brute strength, became the new measure of courage.

Arguably composed of the best infantry of the sixteenth century, the Spanish *tercios* chief liability was lack of articulation. Seeking to exploit the ponderous nature of *tercios*, the Dutch in the 1570s developed smaller battalions of 550 men. Consisting of roughly equal numbers of musketeers and pikemen, they were deployed in shallower and mutually supportive formations. Under Maurice of Nassau (1567–1625), the Dutch further systematized drill and introduced coordinated volley fire by musketeers.[33] By establishing a standing army of both native sons and mercenaries, providing them with consistent pay, and instilling esprit de corps through rigorous and demanding drill, Maurice began a process of professionalization in which soldiers' loyalty rested firmly with their unit.

For the good of the unit as well as to enhance their own chances of survival, Maurice's soldiers endured repetitive drill. It conditioned them to the many pressures of the battlefield. For musketeers, loading quickly and accurately under fire was the key. Illustrated manuals appeared that depicted the proper drill steps for the *caliver* (a shortened arquebus), musket, and pike.[34] Battles were frequently decided by the combined effects of firepower by arquebusiers and of shock action by pikemen, although the coordinated volleys of the former became increasingly telling.[35]

Tactical innovations next came from Sweden and its great captain and king, Gustavus Adolphus.[36] He increased infantry firepower by reducing the depth of musketeer ranks from ten to six, by introducing standard paper cartridges (combining musket ball and powder in a single package) on a mass scale, and by emphasizing methodical drill to improve the rate of volley fire. Following Maurice's example, Gustavus used battalions consisting of 216 pikemen and 192 musketeers as his basic fighting unit, further dividing them into three or four companies for maneuverability in battle. By shortening pikes from eighteen to eleven feet, he enhanced the agility of pikemen. He also reinvigorated cavalry, arming them primarily with sabers, protecting them with breastplates and helmets, and having them charge at the gallop to administer the coup de grâce to faltering enemy infantry. And Gustavus developed battalion artillery with standardized gun calibers, although his experiment with light "leather" guns failed to live up to early promise. Overall, Gustavus's main achievement was in reinvigorating combined arms tactics. He was adept at using artillery to support infantry advances and at timing his cavalry charges to coincide with momentary breaks in the enemy's cohesion. By stressing tactical alacrity achieved through flexible formations, Gustavus often outflanked and defeated less agile opponents.[37]

Gustavus proved his tactical mettle in the Thirty Years War in Germany but died in combat in 1633. Even with his tactical innovations, however, Swedish forces could be beaten by Habsburg armies built and operated along older lines, as at the battle of Nördlingen in 1634. Interestingly, the main legacy of this war was not its tactical innovations, but the sheer devastation associated with a religious-dynastic contest that surged wildly out of control. Tens of thousands of soldiers literally went on a rampage, plundering, raping, and pillaging their way across the Germanic states. Gustavus too embraced so-called offensive logistics and the tax of violence, supporting his army through ruthless extraction of food, fodder, and wealth from the surrounding countryside, leaving in his wake swathes of exhausted land and devastated towns and villages. In these thirty years of warfare, eight million civilians died as famine, disease, and death galloped their way across Germany.[38] Taming Bellona—not seeking potentially destabilizing tactical or technical innovations—was the main concern of European states after the Peace of Westphalia.

Allowing armies to make war feed war, as they had in the Thirty Years War, led only to chaos and devastation, European monarchs concluded. After the mid-seventeenth century, these monarchs worked to prevent armies from snatching, slashing, or burning everything in sight. A consequence was that armies found themselves encumbered by logistical supply chains to obviate the need (if not perhaps the desire) to denude the countryside. More than ever, armies became like cities on the march, trailed by thousands of camp followers as well as herd animals for sustenance, including cows, sheep, and pigs. Animals' grazing needs confined large-scale military campaigns to the late spring and summer. Marking the end of major field campaigns, if not of sieges, were the rains of autumn, which turned primitive roads and dirt tracks to mud. Wholesale destruction of land and widespread famine on the scale of the Thirty Years War was largely averted, but armies on the move nevertheless continued to make huge demands on local sources for food, labor, and housing. Army requisitions, because they were more systematic than plunder, often proved especially debilitating to specific localities. Wagons and animals disappeared in large numbers. Any region unfortunate enough to be fought over or camped in for any length of time found itself impoverished by the experience.

Logistical restraints, attempts by monarchs to limit the socioeconomic impact of campaigning armies, and the constraints imposed by *trace italienne* fortresses worked collectively to thwart field commanders. Further limiting the decisiveness of field campaigns were the technical limitations imposed by weaponry. Decisive developments were few. The most notable was the bayonet, first the plug version around 1660 that was inserted into a musket's muzzle, followed by socket versions around 1690 "fixed" alongside the muzzle. An eighteen-inch serrated knife, the bayonet, provided close-in defense to musketeers and facilitated shock action during charges, eliminating the need for pikemen, who soon disappeared from European battlefields.

At roughly the same time, flintlock muskets replaced the less reliable matchlocks and more expensive wheel locks as the infantry weapon of choice. In their ignition mechanism, flint impacted steel to produce a shower of sparks, igniting the powder in the pan. Flintlocks reduced misfires by one-third and sped reloading. Further speeding reloading were incremental improvements in paper cartridges and ramrods, with iron replacing wood in the construction of the latter. A typical flintlock of the period, Britain's "Brown Bess," was a muzzle-loading, .78-caliber smoothbore. It fired a .73-caliber lead ball that weighed nearly an ounce. As with the earlier matchlocks, the "windage" or 0.05-inch space, led to questionable accuracy at ranges greater than fifty paces. Yet once volley firing commenced, aiming became impractical anyway as thousands of muskets discharging produced a fog of choking black smoke.

Through assiduous and repetitive training, highly skilled musketeers doubled their rate of fire to four shots a minute. Robotic loading and firing was the key, with no time wasted in aiming. (The standard command sequence for foot soldiers was "ready . . . level . . . fire," not "ready . . . aim . . . fire.") The famous command in the American Revolutionary War, "don't fire until you see the whites of their eyes," was not bravado but practical advice to maximize the effectiveness of inherently inaccurate musketry. The carefully sequenced firing drills, practiced under the critical eyes of eighteenth-century drillmasters, anticipated by 200 years the time-motion studies of twentieth-century Taylorism.

Musket design was a calculated mixture of practice informing technique. Barrels lacked sights since aiming was time-consuming and doctrinally unsound; they were made front-heavy to counteract soldiers' tendency to fire high in the adrenalin-driven excitement of battle. To maximize firepower, commanders worked to reduce the depth of formations; Gustavus used six ranks, with Frederick the Great cutting this to three in just over a century. And the mass fire of flintlock muskets was indeed horrifying in its killing power. A disciplined infantry platoon during the Enlightenment became the equivalent of a staccato machine gun, unleashing a fiery hail of musket balls every fifteen seconds. Slugs were so large that when they did find a human torso, the result was crippling and often fatal.

Throughout this period the design of infantry weaponry remained remarkably stable. In part this was due to the cost of changes. Since armies provided recruits with muskets from state-funded arsenals, reissuing tens of thousands of muskets for anything less than a radical improvement in gun making was simply too expensive. A decentralized arms industry that relied on artisanal shops rather than full-fledged factories responded slowly to innovation. Flintlocks were a mature technology with a well-developed doctrine that was firmly situated within the established drill routines of armies. A stable military technology, moreover, preserved a measure of predictability to military operations: a luxury that field generals and monarchs appreciated.

Soldiers armed with nearly identical models of smoothbore muskets were the main death dealers in eighteenth-century battles. But they were not unthinking automata. Even in the heat of battle, they were expected to respond to commands to take advantage of fleeting opportunities. The mind-numbing quality of drill must be understood contextually. Repetitive, precision drill fostered unit pride; better yet, it enhanced survivability in combat. Linear infantry formations had to march in step during battle, poised to shift quickly from shallow line formations to deeper squares as needed to repel cavalry charges. An unskilled soldier with two left feet in the firing line endangered his comrades as well as himself. An improperly aligned musket in the ranks could mean a burst eardrum for the man in front of it. A soldier who could not march in step was the equivalent of a butterfly flapping its wings in modern Chaos theory: the small ripple of disorder he produced compounded as it spread, dooming the disrupted battalion to annihilation by cavalry charge. Any recruit who failed to get it found himself on the receiving end of withering curses and cuffs by grizzled veterans in his unit.[39] Viewed in aggregate, an eighteenth-century infantry battalion was a killing machine, every bit as sophisticated, expensive, and capable of dealing death as the terminators of Hollywood movie making.

Infantry Training and Tactics

An important aspect of infantry training was the assimilation and acculturation of conscripts, volunteers, and impressed men into a thoroughly masculine world. A military life was not for mama's boys or milquetoasts. Most men welcomed, or at least tolerated, harsh training as the price of unit cohesiveness and effectiveness. What was not welcomed was wildly capricious or blatantly sadistic training. Even Prussian NCOs knew that the price of obedience was a willingness sometimes to look the other way, at least for minor infractions not bearing directly on combat efficiency. The rank and file returned the compliment, showing a sense of pride in being attached to units with a reputation for toughness. For men seeking adventure and a chance to prove their mettle as warriors, fighting was not necessarily an oppressive burden. When it came time to tell war stories, one could hardly boast to one's comrades or offspring of cushy assignments spent in garrison. One was not truly a veteran until one saw action in the field, where skills developed in training camp were exercised on aptly named fields of honor.

Getting to the fields of honor required marching, and the infantry column was the most practical formation to move masses of men across country, while simultaneously keeping a watchful eye out for deserters. Desertion was enough of a problem that armies avoided marching in poor light or near thick forests, favorable conditions for the disgruntled or fainthearted to melt away from the ranks. If caught, deserters received the lash or walked the gantlet while being struck dozens of times with a skin-flaying stick. Repeat cases might be sentenced to walk the same gantlet thirty-six times, a slow form of execution.

A key tactical skill was deploying quickly from column into line in preparation for battle. Moving large numbers of men across country and keeping them aligned and in step was not easy, even on a level parade field. It was infinitely more difficult and nerve-wracking while under fire from the enemy's artillery and skirmishers. Officers and NCOs carried pistols to dissuade nervous men from falling out of the ranks. Keeping the lines dressed (i.e., in order) as cannonballs bounced and scythed their way through bodies, and as musket balls whizzed past ears and slammed with gut-wrenching thuds into comrades, challenged the most poised and determined leaders. Veteran NCOs and stoic captains formed the glue that steadied green recruits who, until the battle was joined, knew only the theory of war and not its gruesome reality.

Since most European armies were doctrinally and tactically similar, battles were symmetrical and often costly. At the battle of Malplaquet (1709) during the War of Spanish Succession, 36,000 soldiers were killed or wounded in one day in ten square miles. Victory in these attritional exchanges became a thing of margins, with both contending forces so severely damaged as to make successful exploitation more exception than rule. It was possible, as suggested earlier in Chapter One, for armies to defeat their mirror image. But to do so meant taking advantage of margins and nuances. It meant moving and firing more quickly, thereby getting inside an enemy's loop of competence, converting his assets to liabilities. The unattractive alternative was bloody-minded attrition: a forever war that ended in exhaustion for all and victory for none. In short, eighteenth-century warfare was limited neither in its brutality nor in its rate of casualties. A sobering statistic is the ratio of combat deaths to the total population of Europe: the eighteenth-century ratio proving seven times higher than that recorded in the nineteenth century.

As suggested in Chapter Two, warfare in this enlightened age was both a deadly sport of kings and a form of social control. Potentially rebellious aristocrats were co-opted into the officer corps; nonproductive elements of society were conscripted into the enlisted ranks. Officers often identified more with their opposite numbers among the enemy than with conscripts or foreign adventurers in their own ranks. Money and simple survival were major concerns for the latter, not ideology or nationalism. Operational strategy, such as it was, tended to focus on avoiding pitched battles, unless victory was reasonably assured, since victory came at a high price.

For savvy eighteenth-century commanders the main tactical challenge was combining the steadiness and firepower of infantry and artillery with the mobility and shock power of cavalry to achieve decisive results.[40] England's John Churchill, First Duke of Marlborough, was especially skilled at combining the coordinated firepower of infantry platoons with bayonet assaults. Marlborough possessed *coup d'oeil*, a chess master's ability to sweep the battlefield and discern exploitable weaknesses in his opponent's deployment. A favorite tactic was to attack on a flank, forcing his opponent to commit reserves and hopefully to weaken his center. Marlborough would concentrate against this weakened center, pressing home the attack with heavy cavalry, which surged forward and exploited seams and weak spots in the enemy's ranks.

Better than winning pitched battles was winning bloodless ones. Marshal Maurice de Saxe (1696–1750) famously wrote that field generals could have successful careers without ever having to fight a pitched battle. One did this primarily through outmaneuvering one's foe. By denying resources to his army—by cutting his lines of communication—one might place him in a position where retreat, even surrender, was his only prudent option. At the very least, one might compel him to attack at a place and time largely of one's choosing. An enemy cut off from his supplies, weakened and demoralized by hunger, and forced to attack before his army dissolved into foraging parties was an enemy who was half-beaten, even before the battle was joined.

On the day of battle, traditional tactical verities such as unity of command, surprise, and initiative after contact still ruled, especially when symmetrical opponents met. Truly one-sided victories were few, although this did not mean that battles lacked importance in their effects. A sterling example of effective battlefield tactics came at Leuthen in 1757, when Frederick the Great (r. 1740–1786), King of Prussia, used his oblique maneuver to redeploy his army from the center of a formed column to a linear formation to fall unseen on his enemy's flank. Speed of maneuver was important here, but Frederick had learned too from bitter experience to emphasize fire discipline. Earlier in his reign, he spoke of a volley or two of musketry followed by the shock action of massed bayonets. After suffering punishing losses, he drilled his assault formations to deliver as many as six volleys in rapid succession before charging. As his battalions maneuvered swiftly for flanking attacks, they delivered 2,000 musket balls a minute in the direction of the enemy. Frederick's success at Leuthen was not simply a triumph of surprise through screening and rapid outflanking—it was also a triumph of infantry firepower. For the first time Prussia's musketeers took their ammunition wagons with them into battle, allowing them to fire three times their regulation allowance of sixty rounds.[41]

While line infantry remained the primary actors in eighteenth-century battles, European armies also began to experiment with skirmishers and light infantry. First used on a large scale during the War of Austrian Succession (1740–1748), skirmishers deployed irregularly ahead and along the perimeter of the line of battle. Many were sharpshooters armed with various types of rifles. Considerably more accurate than their smoothbore cousins, rifled muskets were also more expensive to produce and more difficult to reload. Skirmishers attempted to harass an enemy's deployment into line as well as to interdict his supply columns. Where formal linear tactics were impractical, such as in rough terrain or forests, auxiliary units of light infantry often took the lead. Known as *Jäger* in Prussia, *Grenzer* in Austria, and *Chasseurs à Pied* in France, soldiers selected for these units often donned uniforms that blended with their surroundings. Commanders chose these soldiers carefully since opportunities for shirking and desertion were correspondingly great. Interestingly, a few officers of noble birth considered command of these "special forces" to be beneath their dignity. But other officers, such as Britain's Thomas Gage and Lord George Howe, proved receptive, forming specialist units such as the Royal Americans and the Eightieth Foot, Gage's Light Infantry.

By the mid-eighteenth century, a typical European infantry battalion consisted of 800 men. It was further subdivided into eight companies: six companies of the line and two flanking companies. Grenadiers formed one flank company; they were usually the burliest men, specializing in shock action and employing hand-to-hand weapons such as swords and axes. Special miter caps—designed so as not to interfere with the grenadiers' use of hand-thrown bombs (grenades)—distinguished them from men of the line. The other flank company consisted of light infantry. Composed of nimble and reliable men, light infantry units skirmished and performed other "detached" duties as needed.

Deployed on the battlefield in three ranks, an infantry battalion fronted 200 yards to a depth of 10 yards. Secondary and tertiary lines were often deployed behind the first; these lines added resilience in case the first line broke and also provided depth to counter enemy flanking attacks. A typical eighteenth-century battlefield was often no more than five square miles in area. A commanding general wielding a spyglass (field telescope) on high ground could often watch an entire battle unfold before him. Commanders controlled movements on the battlefield via shouted commands, drums, and trumpets. Signal flags conveyed orders by line-of-sight, but once battle was joined and the smoke and dust rose, commanders resorted to verbal or written orders dispatched by couriers on horseback. Since mounted couriers often drew fire and became casualties, commanders such as Marlborough employed more innocuous "running footmen" to convey orders. These men carried special gold-, silver-, and bronze-tipped staffs and wore unique jockey caps so that unit commanders might recognize them more readily in the chaos of battle.

Command structure was strictly hierarchical. Broadly speaking, generals or field marshals led armies in the name of the monarch; major generals led divisions; brigadier generals led brigades; colonels led regiments; lieutenant colonels or majors led battalions; captains led companies; and lieutenants or subalterns led platoons. Although officer ranks were standardized, aristocrats could also purchase them, skipping several subordinate ranks in the process. A rich nobleman of independent means could raise and fund his own regiment, selling company captaincies to other aristocrats of a military and entrepreneurial bent. This "purchase system," discussed further in Chapter Four, led occasionally to rank amateurism but kept the military firmly in the grasp of wealthy aristocrats and thus of men who had already invested in the goals of the polity.

Artillery's Importance

Countering the occasional amateurism of infantry commanders was the educated professionalism of artillery officers. As the century wore on, artillery emerged as a battlefield arm that rivaled infantry in its importance. Essential to this process were theoretical developments in ballistics, notably by Benjamin Robins (1707–1751) of England and Leonhard Euler (1707–1783) of Germany. Aspiring artillery officers began taking classes in calculus, ballistics, and engineering. A combination of controlled experiment, battlefield experience, and increasingly sophisticated theory led to the production of accurate artillery firing tables.[42] Also important were improved manufacturing techniques, such as the use of early machine tools for consistent center boring of muzzles, which made artillery pieces lighter and therefore more mobile.

Leading the way was Frederick the Great, who used mobile six-pound guns at the battalion level to supplement infantry musketry. These guns also served as rally points during battle, their ability to belch forth hundreds of antipersonnel rounds (case shot and canister) often proving instrumental in stabilizing wavering portions of the line. Also instrumental in close quarters were short-barreled, high-trajectory howitzers, which lobbed both explosive shells and large quantities of antipersonnel shot.

In 1759, Frederick further enhanced the mobility of his guns by developing horse artillery. These guns could be shifted to trouble spots on the battlefield or massed to support an attempt at breakthrough. Prior to Frederick's initiative, most battlefield artillery remained fixed in place once the battle was joined. Along with greater tactical mobility of guns came improvements in their strategic mobility as European nation-states invested in better roads and more accurate maps with standardized measures.[43]

The Seven Years War and French Military Reformers

Artillery was one area in which the army's effectiveness at the operating level could be improved. Frederick's innovations with artillery had not been lost on his French rivals. Under Jean-Baptiste Vaquette de Gribeauval (1715–1789), who served as France's first inspector general of artillery, the French rationalized their production of artillery. They developed a mechanized factory system to support a product line of standardized gun calibers and carriages with interchangeable parts. New machines for consistent gun boring meant that barrel walls could be made thinner, lowering the overall weight of the guns and reducing the weight of powder needed for consistent muzzle velocities. Substituting wood for iron in gun carriages (with iron remaining as needed at stress points), the French developed light yet powerful artillery pieces that two horses could pull about the battlefield.[44] Greater maneuverability allowed for more rapid concentration. Chevalier Jean du Teil, a French artillery specialist, advised his fellow commanders in 1778 to "collect the greatest number of troops and a greater quantity of artillery" at the point where they wished to break the enemy; "artillery, thus intelligently sustained and multiplied, brings decisive results." An avid student of Du Teil's was a young Corsican artillerist, Napoleon Bonaparte.

Infantry flexibility was addressed with the divisional system. Eighteenth-century armies possessed no articulation, or interconnection, above brigade level. Under the auspices of the duc de Broglie, France introduced the division: a grouping of several brigades, plus cavalry and artillery. The direct impact of that innovation to the army must not be exaggerated. French divisions under the ancien régime still tended to be administrative or ad hoc formations, whose operational possibilities remained largely theoretical. It was, however, clear that an army organized in divisions could expand its marching areas and rates of movement. Administratively, divisions would be able to carry a higher proportion of their requirements with them and could make up the rest locally, without devastating an entire zone of operations.

While reaffirming the line as the basic infantry formation because it allowed for maximum development of firepower, Compte Jacues de Guibert advocated the increased use of columns both for battlefield maneuver and for attack. Known as *l'ordre mixte*, or "mixed order," this complex synthesis of column and line formations stressed maneuverability and shock power at the company and battalion levels. He further stressed the use of skirmishers, specially trained light infantry, both to screen French movements and to disrupt the enemy's tactical order. Insightful too was his prescription for army movements. An army of 40,000, he concluded, needed to march in separate divisions of 10,000. Strong enough to fight alone if separated from the army, these divisions were easier to supply and more tractable on the march. They could also disperse and live off the countryside, cutting the army free from its cumbrous supply chain.

Guibert went even further when he issued calls for a citizen army, one that would be "vigorous in spirit, in government, in the means at its disposal," one whose aggressive designs and ideological fervor would lead it to "subjugate its neighbors." He reversed this call, however, when he realized his ideal of a citizen army fired by ideology could conceivably threaten the social order of the ancien régime. Events following on the heels of the French Revolution in 1789 proved Guibert a prophet, but not even he had predicted the emergence of a power-hungry genius unconstrained by enlightenment limits on warfare—a man who would use France's standardized artillery and newly articulated battalions and divisions within a paradigm favoring maneuver, shock, and decision. He came to France by way of Corsica.[45]

THE POOR BLOODY CAVALRY

Except in eastern countries, such as Russia and Poland, where the topography and large open spaces favored mounted action by Cossacks and Polish hussars, cavalry was largely a subsidiary combat arm in the early modern period. This represented a fundamental change from the medieval period and reflected the vulnerability of armored knights and their horses to gunfire and disciplined infantry formations employing either pikes or muskets fitted with bayonets. Cavalry could not close against unbroken infantry without suffering crippling losses. Horses could not be made to charge into an infantry square, especially one bristling with sharp pikes or serrated bayonets. Unless or until infantry formations wavered or broke, cavalrymen could not wield their lances or swords to any great purpose. In early modern battles, cavalry units were often reduced to jousting with the enemy's cavalry in a sideshow equivalent in importance to the exchange of knights in a game of chess.

Early in the game, some European elites proved reluctant to adopt firearms precisely because they eroded the traditional supremacy of aristocratic heavy cavalry. In the early 1500s, the French persisted in using pikes, halberds, and crossbows as their main infantry weapons, until they suffered a major defeat at Pavia in 1525. Chastened by this, they quickly fielded arquebusiers in larger numbers. The French cavalry also were slow in adopting pistols, in part because of their disdain for this "unchivalrous" as well as unreliable weapon. Arguably, the leading reason for the French nobility's preference for lance and sword was that these shock weapons upheld both class identity and powerful codes of honor and manliness: the concept of *gloire* as defined in Chapter One. Indeed, a preference for cold steel and the arme blanche remained a feature of French military thought well into the 1700s.[46]

As noted previously, the large-scale manufacture of wheel lock pistols and their employment by light cavalry in the caracole during the sixteenth century marked the end of knights as well as the nadir of shock action by cavalry. There was neither glory nor honor to be had in riding forward to discharge a brace of pistols, then quickly wheeling about and retiring to the rear to reload and repeat the same maneuver. Restoring the shattering kinetic energy of the mass cavalry charge to the battlefield was the goal of cavalry-minded officers throughout the seventeenth century.

The solution involved synergy achieved through effective combined arms action. The renaissance of heavy cavalry came with Gustavus Adolphus, who emphasized anew the cold, hard steel of the saber. Protected by armored helmets and the cuirass (body armor consisting of linked metal breast- and backplates that buckled beneath the arms), squadrons of cuirassiers (heavy cavalry) marked the return of effective cavalry shock action in western Europe.

Napoleon once observed that in warfare the moral is to the physical as three is to one. The sound and fury of a mass cavalry charge—the thunder of hooves followed by the clash of steel—had a tremendous moral impact, especially against fatigued or inexperienced foot soldiers. Nevertheless, its ultimate success depended on timing. When used properly, however, no combat arm other than cavalry had the potential to rout large numbers of enemy infantry and drive them in disorder from the field.

Together with the revival of heavy cavalry, mounted units continued to be used for traditional roles like reconnaissance, screening, ambush, and communication. Cavalry were the fastest units on the early modern battlefield. They were the eyes and ears of a commander. In the early modern period, inaccurate maps, poor roads, and inadequate intelligence made it difficult even to find the enemy's army. Indeed, it was not always easy for separate columns in the same army to stay in contact when crossing broken terrain or in rough weather. A commander who dispersed his army to forage or maneuver on the march had to guard against the possibility that these units could then be ambushed and defeated in detail before reinforcements could arrive. Preventing such nasty surprises was an essential mission of light cavalry screens, small detachments that were extended like feelers ahead of and on the flanks of an advancing army.

Cavalry Specialization

The many roles of cavalry led to specialization of types. Dragoons were basically mounted infantry. Armed with carbines, they were deployed to shore up weak areas of the line and were involved in smaller actions, such as ambushes, that characterized much of day-to-day fighting during the campaigning season. Hussars were based on Hungarian light cavalry units; experts at skirmishing, they also screened armies and relied primarily on the saber. Lancers, as the name suggests, relied primarily on the lance to attack infantry, although they also carried secondary armament like swords and pistols. They were especially effective in open country against wavering or fleeing infantry and sometimes joined cuirassiers in the charge. Dragoons and hussars also joined the cavalry pursuit once enemy infantry formations were broken.

Cavalry action could prove decisive to victory, but only under the proper conditions. Creating these conditions was a goal of skilled commanders. Assuming one had superior numbers of cavalry, once could attempt to drive off or destroy the enemy's cavalry without oneself suffering debilitating losses. One could then redeploy the remaining cavalry for unbridled assaults on unprotected areas of the enemy's line, especially on a vulnerable flank or in the rear. A potentially lucrative target was the enemy's artillery batteries as these were normally fixed in place. Denying the enemy his artillery could change battlefield odds quickly. Artillery protected itself with grape shot and canister but was vulnerable to flank attacks since cannons were difficult to swing about. Cavalry units that succeeded in neutralizing the enemy's artillery, in cutting the enemy off from his magazines or line of retreat, and in maintaining harassing fire from the flanks often provided the preconditions for a decisive volley and charge by the line infantry.

Cavalry, in short, was of secondary but nonetheless vital importance to warfare in the seventeenth and eighteenth centuries. Highlighting its secondary nature was the decline in the proportion of cavalrymen to foot soldiers, which decreased from one to four in 1700 to one to seven in 1750. Cavalry was expensive to create, train, and field, and as artillery grew in importance, the logistical demands of the latter resulted in increased competition for fodder for draft animals. Commanders sacrificed cavalry horses for draft animals, placing firepower ahead of shock action.

The technologies, tactics, and training of early modern armies reflected the variegated nature of warfare in Europe. The largely mercenary armies of the early sixteenth century gave way to the dynastic armies of the seventeenth and early eighteenth centuries and the nascent national armies of the late eighteenth century. Armies grew in size from 20,000 or 30,000 men in 1500 to 400,000 men (at least on paper) 200 years later, during the age of Louis XIV. Private entrepreneurs and contractors gave way to state bureaucracies and an increasingly professional officer corps. Highly localized control of the military, which reached its chaotic peak during the Thirty Years War, spurred a strong reaction from monarchs and the assertion of rigid state control over the tools and techniques of war. Armies were soon subjected firmly to *raison d'état* (reason of the state), becoming in the process the ultima ratio regum.

It was arguably in the realm of training, rather than in technologies or tactics, where the most important changes came to early modern warfare. States largely succeeded in making war into a regularized and predictable instrument of policy that also reinforced monarchical control and existing social hierarchies. Rebellious aristocrats were brought to heel, becoming rule-bound officers who sought *gloire* in serving rather than opposing the state. Marginal or unproductive elements within society joined or were co-opted into the enlisted ranks of armies. Some of these men found death, but many found purpose and an honorable, if harsh, life. Ultimately, rigorous training and harsh indoctrination converted warrior-mercenaries, who fought when they willed, into soldier-citizens, who fought when they were told. This dramatic change in mind-set constituted perhaps the clearest military transformation of the early modern period.

NOTES

1. Two general surveys of technology and warfare that address the early modern period are William H. McNeill, *The Pursuit of Power: Technology, Armed Force, and Society Since* A.D. *1000* (Chicago: University of Chicago Press, 1982); and Martin Van Creveld, *Technology and War: From 2000* B.C. *to the Present* (New York: Free Press, 1989).

2. Michael Howard has noted that siege warfare was the most common form of warfare in the early modern period, with the exception of a brief period from 1480 to 1530, when the new cannons dominated the old-style medieval castles. See his *War in European History* (Oxford, UK: Oxford University Press, 1976).

3. Originally proposed by Michael Roberts, *The Military Revolution, 1560–1660* (Belfast: Queen's University Press, 1956), and reprinted in *Essays in Swedish History* (London: Weidenfeld and Nicolson, 1967), 195–225; substantially modified and extended by Geoffrey Parker, *The Military Revolution: Military Innovation and the Rise of the West, 1500–1800* (Cambridge, UK: Cambridge University Press, 1988). Critiqued by Jeremy M. Black, *A Military Revolution? Military Change and European Society, 1550–1800* (London: Macmillan, 1991); David A. Parrott, "The Military Revolution in Early Modern Europe," *History Today* 42 (1992): 21–27; and Clifford J. Rogers, ed., *The Military Revolution Debate: Readings on the Transformation of Early Modern Europe* (Boulder, CO: Westview, 1995). For related case studies, see Mark Charles Fissel, *English Warfare, 1511–1642* (London: Routledge, 2001); John Stone, "Technology, Society, and the Infantry Revolution of the Fourteenth Century," *Journal of Military History* 68 (2004): 361–380; and Simon Adams, "Tactics or Politics? 'The Military Revolution' and the Hapsburg Hegemony, 1525–1648," in *Tools of War: Instruments, Ideas, and Institutions of Warfare, 1445–1871*, ed. John A. Lynn (Urbana: University of Illinois Press, 1990), 28–52.

4. John R. Hale, "The Military Reformations," in *War and Society in Renaissance Europe, 1450–1620* (Baltimore: Johns Hopkins University Press, 1985).

5. Saltpeter was initially difficult to obtain in quantity in western Europe. Formulae for gunpowder varied as well, and much experimentation was required to develop the optimum mixture of ingredients. See Bert S. Hall, *Weapons and Warfare in Renaissance Europe: Gunpowder, Technology, and Tactics* (Baltimore: Johns Hopkins University Press, 1997), chap. 3; and Thomas Kaiserfeld, "Chemistry in the War Machine: Saltpeter Production in Eighteenth-Century Sweden," in *The Heirs of Archimedes: Science and the Art of War through the Age of Enlightenment*, ed. Brett D. Steele and Tamera Dorland (Cambridge, MA: MIT Press, 2005), 275–292. See also articles on gunpowder production in this same volume by Brenda Buchanan and Seymour Mauskopf.

6. Clifford J. Rogers, "The Military Revolutions of the Hundred Years' War," *Journal of Military History* 57 (1993): 241–278.

7. Hall, *Weapons and Warfare*, 190–200.

8. Because cast iron had a tendency to crystallize, becoming hard and brittle and often fracturing under the pressure of an explosion, all large-caliber cannons were bronze and brass until the 1560s. They were therefore expensive to produce.

9. Earlier adaptations to the new cannons are addressed by Kelly DeVries, "Facing the New Technology: Gunpowder Defenses in Military Architecture before the *Trace Italienne*, 1350–1500," in Steele and Dorland, *Heirs of Archimedes*, 37–71.

10. See the works of Christopher Duffy, including *Siege Warfare: The Fortress in the Early Modern World, 1494–1660* (London: Routledge/Kegan Paul, 1979); and *The Fortress in the Age of Vauban and Frederick the Great, 1660–1789* (London: Routledge/Kegan Paul, 1985).

11. For details, see Simon Pepper and Nicholas Adams, *Firearms and Fortifications: Military Architecture and Siege Warfare in Sixteenth-Century Siena* (Chicago: University of Chicago Press, 1986).

12. Highlighting the indecisiveness of early modern European warfare is Russell F. Weigley, *The Age of Battles: The Quest for Decisive Warfare from Breitenfeld to Waterloo* (Bloomington: Indiana University Press, 1991).

13. David A. Parrott, "Strategy and Tactics in the Thirty Years' War: The 'Military Revolution,'" *Militärgeschichtliche Mitteilungen* 18 (1985): 7–25. For further details on France, see David A. Parrott, *Richelieu's Army: War, Government and Society in France, 1624–1642* (Cambridge, UK: Cambridge University Press, 2001). On the complexities of state building in general, see Thomas Ertman, *Birth of the Leviathan: Building States and Regimes in Medieval and Early Modern Europe* (Cambridge, UK: Cambridge University Press, 1997).

14. John A. Lynn, "The *Trace Italienne* and the Growth of Armies: The French Case," *Journal of Military History* 55 (1991): 297–330.

15. Da Vinci wrote his boastful letter in 1480 to Ludovico Sforza, Duke of Milan. As an afterthought to this letter, he added that he could also sculpt and paint!

16. See Mary Henninger-Voss, "Between the Cannon and the Book" (Ph.D. diss., Johns Hopkins University, 1995). On a cautionary note, A. Rupert Hall noted that "existing military art was incapable of adopting a mathematical theory of projectile flight and applying it to practice, nor (so far as one can tell) did it ever attempt to do so, at least before the death of [Isaac] Newton." See his "Gunnery, Science, and the Royal Society," in *The Uses of Science in the Age of Newton,* ed. John G. Burke (Berkeley: University of California Press, 1983), 111–141: 116.

17. John A. Lynn, "Vauban," *Military History Quarterly* 1 (1989): 50–61; Henry Guerlac, "Vauban: The Impact of Science on War," in *Makers of Modern Strategy: Military Thought from Machiavelli to Hitler,* ed. Edward Mead Earle (Princeton, NJ: Princeton University Press, 1986), 26–48.

18. See Janis Langins, *Conserving the Enlightenment: French Military Engineering from Vauban to the Revolution* (Cambridge, MA: MIT Press, 2003).

19. See John A. Lynn, ed., *Feeding Mars: Logistics in Western Warfare from the Middle Ages to the Present* (Boulder, CO: Westview, 1993).

20. Mahinder S. Kingra, "The *Trace Italienne* and the Military Revolution during the Eighty Years' War, 1567–1648," *Journal of Military History* 57 (1993): 431–446.

21. Geoffrey Parker, *The Army of Flanders and the Spanish Road, 1567–1659: The Logistics of Spanish Victory and Defeat in the Low Countries' Wars* (Cambridge, UK: Cambridge University Press, 1972).

22. John J. Murray, *Antwerp in the Age of Plantin and Brueghel* (Norman: University of Oklahoma Press, 1970), 14, 40.

23. Quoted in Matthew S. Anderson, *War and Society in Europe of the Old Regime, 1618–1789* (New York: St. Martin's Press, 1988), 89.

24. On connections among science, the Enlightenment, and military practice, see the essays by Janis Langins and Brett Steele in Steele and Dorland, *Heirs of Archimedes.*

25. These points are fully developed by Michael S. Neiberg in *The Nineteenth Century* volume in the Soldiers' Lives through History series.

26. William H. McNeill, *Keeping Together in Time: Dance and Drill in Human History* (Cambridge, MA: Harvard University Press, 1995).

27. Quoted in Steven Gunn, "War, Religion, and the State," in *Early Modern Europe*, ed. Euan Cameron (Oxford, UK: Oxford University Press, 1999), 102–133: 112.

28. The ignition mechanism of wheel lock muskets (a spring-loaded grinding wheel that used iron pyrite to produce sparks) was more complex and expensive than that of matchlocks and only slightly more reliable. It was employed mainly in pistols carried by the cavalry.

29. As late as the 1770s, Benjamin Franklin seriously recommended during the American Revolutionary War returning to longbows in place of muskets. But longbows were weapons mastered over decades of archery practice; already by the time of Henry VIII, archery in England had declined to a point where proficient longbowmen were scarce. See Thomas Esper, "The Replacement of the Longbow by Firearms in the English Army," in *Technology and the West*, ed. Terry S. Reynolds and Stephen H. Cutcliffe (Chicago: University of Chicago Press, 1997), 107–118.

30. Hale, *War and Society*, 46.

31. See René Quatrefages, *Los Tercios*, trans. E. Jarnes Bergua (Madrid: Colección Ediciones Ejército, 1983).

32. On the unpredictable and complex ballistics of round shot fired from smoothbore muskets, see Hall, *Weapons and Warfare*, chap. 5.

33. See Gunther E. Rothenberg, "Maurice of Nassau, Gustavus Adolphus, Raimondo Montecuccoli, and the 'Military Revolution' of the Seventeenth Century," in *Makers of Modern Strategy: From Machiavelli to the Nuclear Age*, ed. Peter Paret (Princeton, NJ: Princeton University Press, 1986), 32–63.

34. Its illustrations allowed illiterate soldiers to practice and master weapons drill. A German edition appeared in 1614 and a Russian edition in 1649. A recent edition in English, originally published in 1607, is Jacob de Gheyn, *The Exercise of Armes* (London: Greenhill Books, 1986).

35. For contemporary accounts of early modern battles, see Roger Williams, *The Actions of the Low Countries*, ed. D. W. Davies (Ithaca, NY: Cornell University Press, 1964) (original published 1618); John Smythe, *Certain Discourses Military*, ed. John Hale (Ithaca, NY: Cornell University Press, 1964) (original published 1590).

36. An excellent short introduction is Michael Roberts, *Gustavus Adolphus*, 2nd ed. (London: Longman, 1992). For a well-illustrated and concise treatment of Gustavus's tactical innovations, see Philip J. Haythornthwaite, *Invincible Generals* (New York: Da Capo Press, 1994), 17–22.

37. For details on battles, see William P. Guthrie, *Battles of the Thirty Years War: From White Mountain to Nordlingen, 1618–1635* (Westport, CT: Greenwood Press, 2002).

38. For the cultural and demographic impact of this war, see Herbert Langer, *The Thirty Years' War* (London: Dorset Press, 1990).

39. See Dennis E. Showalter, *The Wars of Frederick the Great* (London: Longman, 1996).

40. For further details on tactics, see Brent Nosworthy, *The Anatomy of Victory: Battle Tactics, 1689–1763* (New York: Hippocrene Books, 1990); David Chandler, *The Art of War in the Age of Marlborough* (New York: Hippocrene Books, 1976); and Robert S. Quimby, *The Background of Napoleonic Warfare: The Theory of Military Tactics in Eighteenth-Century France* (New York: Columbia University Press, 1957).

41. Dennis E. Showalter, "Weapons and Ideas in the Prussian Army from Frederick the Great to Moltke the Elder," in Lynn, *Tools of War*, 177–210.

42. See Brett D. Steele, "Muskets and Pendulums: Benjamin Robins, Leonhard Euler, and the Ballistics Revolution," in Reynolds and Cutcliffe, *Technology and the West*, 145–179.

43. France had roughly a quarter of a million different units of measurement in use in the eighteenth century, notes Ken Alder. Measures even varied from parish to parish and village to village. See his *The Measure of the World: Dibner Library Lecture, 5 November 2003* (Washington, DC: Smithsonian Institution Libraries, 2004), 14.

44. See Ken Alder, *Engineering the Revolution: Arms and Enlightenment in France, 1763–1815* (Princeton, NJ: Princeton University Press, 1997).

45. For a concise summary of the system Napoleon inherited and his mastery of it, see Gunther E. Rothenberg, *The Art of Warfare in the Age of Napoleon* (Bloomington: Indiana University Press, 1978), chap. 1. Also useful is Rory Muir, *Tactics and the Experience of Battle in the Age of Napoleon* (New Haven, CT: Yale University Press, 2000).

46. Frederic J. Baumgartner, "The French Reluctance to Adopt Firearms Technology in the Early Modern Period," in Steele and Dorland, *Heirs of Archimedes*, 73–85.

Four

✳ ✳ ✳

COMMAND AND LEADERSHIP

In the prenationalistic armies of the early modern period, ordinary foot soldiers often hailed from several countries. Some were volunteers seeking adventure or opportunity for plunder, some were mercenaries-for-hire, some were desperate men seeking relief from poverty, and some were simply impressed and compelled to serve against their will. Keeping these soldiers in line often required oppressive discipline and harsh punishment, a situation reminiscent of Niccolò Machiavelli's advice in *The Prince*. On the question "whether it is better to be loved more than feared, or feared more than loved," Machiavelli replied that a prince "ought to be both feared and loved, but as it is difficult for the two to go together, it is much safer to be feared than loved."[1]

Apt advice, yet soldiers were something more than "the dregs of society" who needed to be flogged or beaten into line. They were men of multiple motivations, many of whom took pride in embracing what they considered to be an honorable and thoroughly masculine way of life. Experienced mercenaries knew their business and sought to sign on with competent units, well knowing that their survival depended on the steadiness of their fellow rank and filers and the skill of their commanders.

Thus we come to the critical importance of command and leadership.[2] While there are many definitions of leadership, a pithy one that captures a vital aspect of command is "the ability to make good things happen." War, as the Prussian military theorist Carl von Clausewitz reminded us, is the realm of fog and friction, a realm of great resistance in which the easiest things to achieve in peacetime prove almost impossibly difficult in wartime.[3] A competent commander steeled his men for combat, held his units together during long campaigns or sieges, and made smart and timely decisions while under stress. Commanders able to make good things happen won the confidence of superiors as well as peers and subordinates.

Throughout the early modern period, officers drawn from the ranks of the nobility often saw command as a privilege that went with their social position, rather than as a responsibility that they had to earn. Within their social matrix, nobles both expected and demanded respect from social inferiors. In turn, their social inferiors looked to them to lead. Younger sons of the aristocracy, left out of the family inheritance due to primogeniture, sought to make names for themselves through honorable military service. They often began their careers by purchasing officer commissions. Well-heeled aristocrats bought regimental colonelcies, using their own personal funds to recruit and equip the regiment, augmented by the sale of captaincies to aspiring company commanders. Regiments returned the compliment by assuming the name of their colonel-proprietor or his region.

The prenationalistic and preprofessional officer corps of the early modern period upheld fundamentally different social values and structures than their modern American and European equivalents. Nevertheless, then as today, certain attributes separated successful commanders from failures. A short list would include ambition, doggedness, intestinal fortitude, personal magnetism or charisma, and taking pains to insure that one's soldiers were ready to fight and, if need be, to die. In an age when military technology, tactics, and techniques were fairly stable and consistent across opposing European armies, the spark provided by inspirational commanders often proved decisive in igniting the torch of victory.[4]

THE AGE OF ENTREPRENEURS, 1494–1648

Lacking well-developed administrative structures and reliable streams of revenue, European states from the time of the Italian Wars, from 1494 to 1559, to the Thirty Years War in 1618–1648 had great difficulty raising, equipping, feeding, and paying for large armies over the long term. Thus they turned to military entrepreneurs and resorted to borrowing or floating loans, with periodic defaults often ending in unpaid armies rioting out of control, as did Spanish forces at Antwerp in 1576. Because early modern European armies lacked strong institutional underpinnings, they often operated more like joint stock companies, with the rank and file motivated by profit and with officers serving as contractors with a vested interest both in turning a profit and in securing their own *gloire* as warrior-captains. Ideological factors, with the notable exception of confessional beliefs, played little role. Even theological disputes between Protestants and Catholics flared intensely but then died out: Ordinary foot soldiers' concerns were usually more present-minded and pedestrian.

Throughout this period, mercenary soldiers remained vital to militaries, whether they were Italian *condottiere*, Swiss pikemen, German *Landsknechte*, or Scottish adventurers. They and their commanders went to war for profit. Fighting was their mutual vocation. Since the most important cause to a mercenary was his own fortune, a commander's overriding priority was to insure that he could compensate his men. To this end, mercenary captains had to be tough—the alpha male in a pack of wolves. They had to be shrewd as well: following Machiavelli's advice, both lion and fox. Much profit could be had from capturing and ransoming enemy nobles, but none from killing them outright. A population cowed made contributions grudgingly, but they nevertheless made them. A population whose women were raped, whose taverns were smashed during drunken brawls, and whose possessions were stolen was a population ripe for revenge. Controlling a company of boisterous soldiers sometimes hinged on a commander's willingness to execute renegade or criminal elements within it, a harsh reality captured in Shakespeare's *Henry V*, where young King Hal upholds the execution of Bardolph, an old comrade and drinking buddy, for indiscipline.

A depiction of a commander in Erhard Schön's *A Column of Mercenaries* (c. 1532) captured the mercenary captain's essence. Riding at the head of the column, flanked by two halberd-toting guards, the captain cut a fine figure in splendid armor and luxuriant clothing, a flamboyant plumed hat completing the martial picture. His outfit and bearing bespoke confidence and gallantry. In the caption accompanying the image the captain boasted of his war chest (said to contain 100 gold pieces), enabling him to hire soldiers who passed muster and to provide them with decent pay and provisions. He further boasted of his ability to provide weaponry and equipment to new recruits and of his confidence that he would lead them in noble and mutually profitable feats of arms.[5]

Confidence was one thing, but since mercenary captains led packs of opportunists, not bands of brothers, a certain measure of controlled ruthlessness was vital. A sense of the nasty reputation of ordinary foot soldiers may be gained from Johann Eberlin von Günzburg, a Lutheran propagandist writing during the Protestant Reformation. For Günzburg, German mercenaries were "soulless people" typified by "whoring, adultery, rape, gluttony, drunkenness, and [other] beastly things, such as stealing, robbing and murder." Mercenaries, he railed, were "entirely in the power of the devil."[6] A harsh description, perhaps, but it rang true. Many, if not most, mercenaries were escaping hardscrabble lives, and some were hardened criminals. Their relationship to peers and commanders was initially instrumental, with comradeship and group loyalty emerging slowly during successful campaigning. To control these men, commanders applied both carrot and stick: regular rations and wages to maintain morale, together with fines, flogging, imprisonment, and even execution for rogues, rebels, and runaways. War was a bloody-minded business—one that necessitated firm and consistent discipline exercised by tough-minded captains.

Equally as tough and unforgiving was the nature of combat at close quarters—physically intense, brutal, and often lethal. Casualty rates were high, approaching thirty percent for pitched infantry battles. As musket balls whizzed, halberdiers hacked, and pike phalanxes pushed, commanders had to keep demoralized or fearful men in line and battle-crazed men under control, all the while mastering their own emotions. Signs of panic had to be countered immediately, as panicky men quickly disintegrated, with rout soon following. Panic spread rapidly among the rank and file partly because little social penalty was attached to it. For officers the social penalty was more dear—shame to one's own sense of self and one's family's honor, even in cases where the latter was merely posture and pretense.

The Commander

To exert the necessary moral force, a commander had to be a man apart. Thus he rode into battle; ordinary foot soldiers, as their name indicates, walked. A commander's weapons were intended mainly for close-in defense; his essential weapon, his sword, remained a mark of nobility throughout this period. He usually donned a breastplate and ancillary armor, which provided limited protection but served also as a sign of class-based authority. Long after armor had lost any practical function on the battle-field, seasoned commanders such as John Churchill, First Duke of Marlborough, and Marshal Maurice de Saxe were still depicted wearing armor in eighteenth-century paintings.

A breed apart, commanders took special care to preserve their dignity and authority. Slights and insults from rank and file could not and were not tolerated. Officers may have shared the hazards of war with their men, but they rarely fraternized with them. In the British army, for example, fraternization was a punishable offense. Nevertheless, aspiring officers often learned their craft and established credibility by trailing a pike as young men. Then, as now, there was no substitute for leading by example and showing a (calculated) willingness to risk death. A few campaign scars did much to establish credibility, and so too did expressions of confidence before battle, haughty insouciance toward the enemy, and willed indifference to enemy fire. As John Keegan rightly noted, leaders donned a mask of command. In the tragic theater of war they had to act their part, even if, on the day of battle, they struggled to control their nerves and bowels as much as their men did.

Capitalistic Entrepreneurs in the Military

Along with these military and personal qualities, it should be recalled that merce-nary captains were contractors—they sought to turn a profit. Like carrion birds, they flocked to the fighting, especially to Germany during the Thirty Years War, where 1,500 military contractors gathered. They fought and clawed each other for limited resources, seeking thereby to gain a competitive advantage. But this struggle for subsis-tence and profit was neither evolutionary nor inherently progressive. Widespread re-course to entrepreneurs worked against standardization and professionalization within officer corps.

But to raise regimental- or larger-sized units, restless monarchs like the Habsburg emperor Ferdinand II had little choice but to turn to a handful of prominent and well-connected military entrepreneurs. These men then subcontracted to lesser captains. In exceptional cases, powerful entrepreneurs like Albert von Wallenstein (1583–1634) and Duke Bernhard of Weimar (1604–1639) raised armies consisting of tens of thou-sands of men.[7] As we have seen, Wallenstein in particular gained enormous influence and wealth through his ability to raise and field large armies—with Ferdinand reward-ing him with the Duchy of Mecklenburg in 1628.

Yet the short-term profit motives of entrepreneurs like Wallenstein led to practices that contributed to the fragmentation of state authority and the pillaging of dynastic treasuries. Wallenstein's chief concern was to grab and hold territory so that he could extract money and supplies from it. His mercenary warriors waged war more intensely against the German citizenry than the enemy. They became leeches, multiplying and spreading across the body politic while bleeding wealth and vitality from the people, with whom they had little sympathy and scarcely less affection. As his army conducted its reign of terror in Germany and Bohemia, Wallenstein's power and vaulting ambition made him a threat to rival captains and even to the emperor. Taking no chances, the emperor ordered his assassination in 1634.

The soaring trajectory of Wallenstein's career achieved at state expense highlighted the fact that the practice of absolute monarchy had yet to catch up to the theory. Even the ruthless and imperious Cardinal Richelieu failed in his efforts to control France. The revolt of the French nobles in the Fronde (1648–1653) witnessed French generals fighting against each other as well as the king, calling into question the *gloire* and thus the viability of the monarchy. After the Fronde was crushed, Louis XIV ushered in the age that bears his name, an age that witnessed the coalescence of state power through centralization and monopolization of the means of violence. To this end, Louis XIV connived and succeeded at bringing his noble officers to heel or, more accurately, to court. There they served his whims rather than their own agendas.

New Models: Maurice of Nassau and Gustavus Adolphus

If Wallenstein was the ultimate example of the great captain as independent capitalist-entrepreneur, Maurice of Nassau provided a different vector that at first glance seemed to point toward the future. Yet like many intellectuals and reformers of the early modern period, Maurice looked backward to Classical models for inspiration. For him this was the Roman army and its strong discipline, regularized structure, and tactical flexibility.[8] Maurice recognized that his units, which incorporated healthy numbers of mercenaries, would resist stricter discipline and rigorous training unless it produced results. Important too was regular pay to prevent reoccurrences of riots like the Spanish Fury. By joining reliable pay to demanding drill that produced victories over Spanish forces in the field, Maurice won the trust and respect of his men. By awarding extra pay and recognition to soldiers who took on unpopular or high-risk positions, he also won their affection.

Recognizing too the importance of steady pay and tight unit cohesion attained through demanding drill and discipline was Gustavus Adolphus (r. 1611–1632).[9] Whenever possible, he recruited and formed units from specific regions in Sweden. He also insured equitable burden sharing of military service. All Swedish males aged fifteen to sixty who lacked a settled dwelling owed service. Ten percent of the remaining male population was chosen by lot to serve, although exemptions were possible for critical occupational specialties. Gustavus still used mercenaries, but he incorporated them wherever possible in Swedish territorial formations, insuring closer integration with his command. As both captain and king, he granted tax breaks to nobles who signed on as officers. These incentives, combined with demanding training and shared sacrifices, worked to strengthen esprit de corps within his army.

An element to Gustavus's success as a commander was his mix of ideology with state aggrandizement: his self-styled mission of rescuing Protestantism from Catholic Habsburg suppression, while simultaneously seeking to expand Swedish hegemony. Image was important too. The paradigmatic warrior-king, Gustavus was seen in some quarters as the fulfillment of a fifteenth-century prophecy that spoke of a golden-maned lion emerging from the north. By showing inestimable courage on the battle-field, Gustavus did indeed earn the title "Lion of the North." Yet he was more than a courageous commander; he was also a prudent administrator and an educated man

The Warrior-King: Gustavus Adolphus of Sweden. Courtesy of the Library of Congress.

who spoke eight languages, composed hymns, and designed buildings. At a time when commanders were still measured by their *virtù*, a complex mélange of qualities that included breeding, courage, sagacity, and moral virtue, Gustavus was the standard-bearer.

His military masterpiece was the battle of Breitenfeld in September 1631, where he defeated an Imperial Catholic force under Count Tilly. But the next year, Gustavus fell at the battle of Lützen when he became separated from the army while leading reinforcements to a wavering sector. Ironically, a key element of his success—his willingness to lead from the front—also proved to be a fatal flaw, as rashness and valor got the better of coolness and discretion. His death did much to prolong the Thirty Years War. As this war galloped wildly out of control, European monarchs realized that they needed to tighten the reins on their mercenary and aristocratic war horses. Naturally, their efforts did not go uncontested.

THE AGE OF NOBLEMEN, 1648–1740

The enormity of Germany's devastation in the 1630s and 1640s shocked Europe. The first priority of Europe's heads of state was to limit the destructiveness of future wars; no king or queen wished to rule over a blasted landscape strewn with corpses. To this end, Hugo Grotius's *The Law of War and Peace* (1625) was the first serious attempt to control war through the definition and promulgation of international law. But in this case the lawyer's pen was not mightier than the warrior's sword. Rather, it was the bureaucrat's pen and his control over state finances, backed by the authority of the monarchy, that translated into tighter control over the means of waging war. For members of the nobility, submitting to intrusive controls enforced by a Hobbesian Leviathan, led by a more or less enlightened monarch, was arguably better than enduring decades of sectional strife and yet another round of deadly and inconclusive internecine struggles.

Both to put down rebellious nobles acting from within and to expand state power, monarchs such as Louis XIV sought to raise standing armies organized around a permanent body of professional infantry. Armies and their commanders were thus subordinated to the political interests of monarchs. They became yet another means to compete for power and *gloire* in a European dynamic in which favorable dynastic marriages, profitable trade agreements, and political coalitions all played crucial roles. Within this dynamic, any aristocratic commander worth his salt preferred a boots-in-the-stirrups life in the field to a boot-licking life at court, with those officers who excelled both in the field and at court often achieving the highest rank.

A New Breed of Aristocratic Professional: Montecuccoli and Marlborough

A sterling example of an emerging breed of aristocratic military professional was Raimondo Montecuccoli (1609–1680). While fighting for the Habsburg cause at Breitenfeld, Lützen, and elsewhere during the Thirty Years War, he became a prisoner of war, which gave him time to think and write about warfare. In the service of Emperor Ferdinand III, he became a field marshal. After expelling Swedish forces from Pomerania and Denmark (1658–1660), he defended Austria against a resurgent Ottoman Empire, earning the title "the savior of Christendom" for his decisive victory at Saint Gotthard in 1664. Recalled to active duty at the age of sixty-three, he stymied a French offensive led by Marshal Henri de Turenne until poor health and old age forced him to retire for good in 1675.

Known for his coolness under fire, Montecuccoli was a master of so-called limited warfare fought for dynastic ends. Skilled at using fortresses as a base for maneuver, he sought patiently to wear down opponents through attritional campaigns, although he also recognized the importance of battles. In an age when the financial sinews of war were of uncertain strength, he famously stated that a commander needed three things to wage war: money, money, and money. Echoing this sentiment was Charles D'Avenant, who wrote in *An Essay upon Ways and Means of Supplying the War* (1695) that "the whole art of war is in a manner reduced to money; and nowadays, that prince who can best find money to feed, clothe and pay his army, not he that has the most valiant troops, is surest of success and conquest."

On the basis of a study of previous military theorists and his own battlefield experience, Montecuccoli penned *Dell'arte militare* (Of Military Art) and *Sulle battaglie* (On Battle).[10] He argued that states had to build and field their own standing armies rather than rely on mercenaries or militia. A standing army, he argued, was both more skilled and more responsive to crises than militias, better disciplined than mercenaries, and less prone than both to panic under pressure. By its nature a standing army would also be more loyal to the state, a vital consideration for his nervous Habsburg patrons. In highlighting the advantages of permanent armies and touting their political reliability, Montecuccoli also vigorously affirmed the importance of strong leadership. A passage from *Sulle battaglie* demonstrated the vigor of his pen:

> The captain must get up in front of those who are fleeing, stimulate them with good counsel and arouse them with his gestures and the tone of his voice. He must carry out his role as leader resolutely like the sturdy champion he is supposed to be. In one case certain legions of an army had turned about, but the general made the soldiers ashamed of flight. Jumping in front of them, sword in hand, he cried, "If anyone should ask you, 'Where is your captain,' say 'We have left him where he was fighting.'" . . . There have also been occasions when a legion was going too slowly and its commander cut down the standard-bearer. The warriors, terrified by this example, pressed forward bravely against the enemy.

Even the savviest political general, Montecuccoli advised, had sometimes to draw his sword and brave the maelstrom.

An educated man who was intrigued by the ideas of Paracelsus and other natural philosophers, Montecuccoli was emblematic of a new breed of military professional who sought to approach war as a science that could be analyzed and mastered. Their efforts were consistent with an enormous expansion in knowledge among European elites that judged themselves more enlightened than their predecessors. European expeditions to the New World discovered previously unknown peoples, animals, and plants. New instruments such as the telescope, microscope, and precision clocks extended the range of human senses. As an ambitious and literate landed class attempted to master and manipulate this clockwork universe, a protoscientific mentalité began to take hold that fostered a meshing of gears within nascent state military machines. Armies themselves became somewhat akin to highly articulated and complex clocks. Operating within a rule-bound system that relied on precision movements for success, commanders became the equivalent of clock makers who integrated all the pieces to insure that the machine ran smoothly.[11] In an emerging Newtonian paradigm predicated upon order and predictability, astute commanders nonetheless recognized that war stubbornly remained a realm of chance, one in which the volatility of human emotions and the vagaries of weather and other imponderables continued to intrude and shape outcomes.

The officer as rational expert was an emerging trend, but it remained just that. Newly organized scientific societies, such as the Royal Society of London, founded in 1660, may have attempted to rationalize and improve gunpowder recipes, saltpeter production, techniques in metal and smelting industries, and related areas of what is today referred to as applied science. But they were often thwarted in their efforts by a craft tradition jealous of its trade secrets and also by the complexity of the problems they tackled.[12] Nevertheless, ambitious men like Robert Moray, first president of the Royal Society and a lieutenant colonel of the Scottish guards, pursued diverse and technical subjects—coal mining, salt making, the determination of longitude, and the preservation of herring—both for military and economic advantage.

Military commanders like Montecuccoli and Moray were harbingers of an emerging technocratic and military elite. A few of the more effective military commanders of this period were self-educated polymaths whose peacetime responsibilities as landowners placed a premium on educated judgment. Running a large agricultural concern was sound preparation for keeping an army supplied and healthy in the field. Pitched battles may have gained historical notice, but what consumed the day-to-day energies of commanders were the demands of recruiting, equipping, moving, and supplying an army in the field and working out details such as the layout of temporary camps and cantonments. Here commanders tapped into an "economy of knowledge" from which they "incurred relative advantage by collecting more forage, digging drainage ditches more quickly, and building better bridges" than the enemy. Such seemingly mundane activities "often determined whether battles would be won, or even whether they were fought at all," notes Erik Lund in his insightful study of command and war.[13]

Yet logistical prowess and technical expertise only got one to the battlefield. A commander still had to command in combat. Here, as ever, qualities such as resolution, energy, and decisiveness often carried the day. Important too was a commander's personal relationship to his men. While some officers treated the rank and file with disdain or even disgust, others recognized the motivating effects of a few well-chosen words or gestures. Sir Robert Harley, an officer in the English army in the 1600s, argued that "a Captaine's good look, or good word (some times) does infinitely winne [the men] and oblige them . . . 'twas to admiration how Souldiers will venture their Lives for an obligeing Officer." A shining example of an obliging officer was Colonel Charles Cavendish, who "used the same familiaritie and frankness amongst the meanest of his Souldiers, the poorest miner, and amongst his equalls; and by stooping so low, he rose the higher in the common account, and was valued accordingly as a Prince, and a Great one."[14] This dashing Royalist cavalry officer was both loved and feared—that rare combination so admired by Machiavelli.

The most famous example of an aristocratic officer who possessed the common touch was "Corporal" John Churchill, First Duke of Marlborough (1650–1722). Marlborough took pains to care for the

The Noble Captain-General: John Churchill, First Duke of Marlborough, shown wearing the ceremonial armor appropriate to his rank and station. Courtesy of the Library of Congress.

welfare of his men. A reputation for fairness preceded him into the field, helping him to win soldiers to his standard. A popular recruiting song included the refrain, "who'll come a-soldiering with Marlborough and me?" sung to the melody later adopted for *Waltzing Matilda*.[15] Soldiers eagerly repeated stories of the young Jack Churchill, who allegedly bounded from the window of the chamber of the Duchess of Cleveland, one of King Charles II's favored mistresses, to avoid being caught in an indelicate position. Marlborough also fought and survived several duels; in this he was typical of his class, quick to take offense at perceived insults to his honor and quicker still to demand satisfaction, whether by apology or the sword. A reputation as a hot-blooded rake only enhanced his legend, but it was his performance in battle that cemented his reputation as a winning captain-general.

Marlborough combined political acumen with battlefield bravado and near-limitless ambition.[16] An acknowledged master of early modern warfare, he fought audacious and exciting campaigns. Perhaps Macaulay caught him best when he described Marlborough as having "the firmness of . . . mind which, in the midst of confusion, uproar, and slaughter, examined and disposed every thing with the serene wisdom of a higher intelligence."[17] His 1704 campaign in Bavaria that ended at Blenheim on August 13 was a logistic and strategic masterstroke. This and subsequent victories at Ramillies (May 23, 1706), Oudenarde (July 11, 1708), and Malplaquet (September 11, 1709) proved decisive in limiting Bourbon expansion in Europe.

Throughout these years, Marlborough's most impressive feat was keeping the "grand alliance" of England, Holland, and Austria together against France during the War of Spanish Succession. Here he willingly partnered with Prince Eugène of Savoy, known affectionately among the rank and file as "Ye Olde Italian Prince." Eugène was thirteen years younger than Marlborough and arguably a more brilliant tactician. Marlborough took full advantage of Eugène's skills, yet he was even more astute in leading a coalition army composed of Dutch, Germans, Danes, Scots, and other nationalities, with a few regiments of English soldiers tossed as leavening into the mix. For his successes he was richly rewarded, gaining a principality in Bavaria (which he later lost) and the magnificent palace of Blenheim in Oxfordshire, to which the English government eventually contributed the princely sum of £240,000 toward its construction and furnishings.

Marlborough was the apotheosis of the age of noble commanders. As the eighteenth century unfolded, states placed new emphasis on creating truly national armies led by officers trained as specialists in the profession of arms. Ironically, the state that pointed the way, Prussia, was led by one of the last of the great warrior-kings, Frederick the Great. He was nonetheless a man who was thoroughly a product of his age, one that styled itself more enlightened than ages past—and one that sought a thoroughly rationalized military that upheld the social structure as well as the values of the ancien régime.

THE AGE OF THE OFFICER, 1740–1789

Historians have termed the period from 1688 to 1788 the "Second Hundred Years War" since European nations were at war for 53 of these 100 years.[18] This period also witnessed the beginnings of professional officer and noncommissioned officer corps within armies, although mercenaries still appeared in significant percentages. For example, fifty-four percent of the British army was composed of foreigners in 1701, and thirty-eight percent in the 1760s. During the reign of Frederick the Great, the Prussian army had the highest percentage of foreigners, peaking at sixty-six percent in 1743.[19] Officers were still drawn primarily from the nobility, although the definition of *nobility* was labile, judged in part by performance on the battlefield. Especially valorous behavior while under fire was thought to ennoble an officer, even if his social origins were not quite top-drawer. Put differently, if an officer displayed tremendous courage consistent with *gloire*, it was assumed he had to have the flame of nobility burning inside of him, even if its source was of questionable or indeterminable origin.[20]

Noble officers possessed the formal authority that came with their lineage and social position, although a fancy pedigree was no guarantee of a commander's fitness to lead. Recognizing this, militaries began increasingly to stress education and technical training of officers, with career progression tied to merit as measured by results attained in combat rather than by purely social and personal connections. While patronage and money remained important to officer advancement throughout this period, an emerging process of professionalization was also taking root, especially in technically oriented branches, such as artillery and military engineering, that stressed expertise and a shared sense of belonging. Here an officer from the middle classes, possessed of a technical education as well as military talent and a modicum of social grace, could well and truly make a name for himself.

Attributes of successful commanders depended in part on the rank and function of those officers within the army. Regimental colonels were primarily entrepreneurs. They received the king's warrant to raise and outfit a regiment and were reimbursed by the head. They were also granted concessions for feeding, clothing, and equipping their soldiers. Responsible colonels provided reliable equipment and decent food while turning a respectable profit; irresponsible colonels scheming for high returns on their investment provided poor-quality clothes, unreliable equipment, and atrocious food. Unscrupulous officers inflated regimental rolls to wring more money from the monarchy; if not taken to an extreme, such "paper strengths" largely went unchallenged by state bureaucrats. Colonels also oversaw the selection of contractors, many of whom were ex-officers. These private contractors supplied food, fodder, and other necessities to the regiment.

Saddled with responsibilities to the crown as well as pressing financial and managerial demands, proprietary colonels often delegated day-to-day operational command to a lieutenant colonel or sergeant major (later simplified as "major," and not to be confused with the senior NCO rank of sergeant major). This lieutenant colonel or major often hailed from the lesser nobility and was selected for his skill at training and forming the regimental line for battle. Captains were subordinate to him and commanded companies within the regiment. Lieutenants served as seconds and replaced the captain if he was killed in battle or otherwise indisposed. Because regimental lieutenants and captains jockeyed for opportunities to advance, often purchasing commissions at equal or greater ranks in more prestigious regiments, they had a high rate of turnover, which militated against regimental continuity.

As late as 1750, no European army possessed a permanent formation larger than the regiment. Regiments consisted of roughly 1,600 men grouped in two battalions. Battalions were normally subdivided into eight companies, each consisting of approximately 100 men commanded by a captain. In the Seven Years War (1757–1763) the first formalized army divisions appeared, consisting of six or eight regiments grouped in two brigades. Field armies of 30,000 or 40,000 men remained ad hoc conglomerations; commanders had no opportunity in peacetime to prepare for the demands of leading such large formations. Experience therefore came on the march and in combat. A lieutenant general typically commanded a field army; this rank was often temporary, with the officer reverting to his regimental rank of colonel or lieutenant colonel at the close of hostilities. In essence he served as a "lieutenant" to the sovereign, unless the sovereign himself took to the field, as did Russia's Charles XII or Prussia's Frederick the Great. A sergeant major general was often appointed to prepare and deploy the army for battle; later this rank was simplified to major general.

As field armies approached 50,000 effectives, command grew too complex for any one man. A standardized staff soon emerged to support the commanding general. Its primary purpose was to keep the army running smoothly. Provision and wagon masters took care of logistics and supply. A provost marshal and judge advocate administered court-martials and punishments. An adjutant general administered officer assignments. Also serving on commanders' staffs were captains of specialized troops, such as artillery, engineers, and sometimes cavalry. Another important position was the commander's secretary, usually filled by a civilian assisted by a few clerks. The most important staff officer was the quartermaster. He prepared each day's marching orders and rode ahead of the main force to select suitable places to halt and encamp. He needed to have a discerning eye for terrain as well as considerable guile in dealing with local, frequently hostile, populations. He also led efforts at gathering local intelligence, including the employment of spies.

What personal qualities characterized a successful field general in this period? First, he recognized that he served at the discretion of his monarch. Serving the monarch meant recognizing that battles were fought for dynastic purposes and not solely for the glory of the commander. Second, skilled commanders recognized the limits of warfare and possessed a firm grasp of the art of the possible. They conserved resources and were wary of seeking battles of annihilation since pitched battles in the field between symmetrical armies often became debilitating exercises in attrition. Armies were highly sophisticated and expensive machines for waging war; smart commanders were chary of battle, even at short odds, since a few hours of combat at close range could prove devastating, marking the destruction of thousands of highly trained soldiers and the end of a season of campaigning.

Commanders of this period have often been compared to chess masters, coolly surveying the field of battle and pushing units forward like so many pawns. But they often more closely resembled players of the Japanese game of Gō. Through careful maneuvers and placement of forces, they sought to constrain the enemy's options until he had little choice but to attack at long odds, retreat along poor lines, or surrender. One did this by cutting lines of communications to depots and magazines, by denying suitable fields and agricultural resources for food and fodder, and by besieging strategic points at which one's opponent would be forced to give battle at a time and place of one's choosing. Diversion and deception, march and countermarch, were among the most commonly reached for tools in a commander's tool kit.

The very best commanders possessed *coup d'oeil*, defined by Frederick the Great as the ability to judge the number of soldiers that could operate effectively within a given area and to grasp fully the military advantages of terrain. One might further define *coup d'oeil* as the penetrating and educated sweep of the eye (often extended by the spyglass) that enabled commanders to deploy units effectively and to recognize the shifting patterns and sounds of battle. Recognition implied action: the temerity and boldness to take full advantage of fleeting opportunities, even when information was incomplete or seemingly contradictory. Timing was everything, especially when making quick decisions under stress to deploy from column to line, to commit reserves to shore up a faltering position, or to order a cavalry charge as an attempt at a killing stroke.

Effective commanders also had an eye for selecting and developing trustworthy subordinates. In the long shadow cast by successful commanders like Marlborough often stood a loyal second like William Cadogan: a quartermaster general and chief of staff who sweated the details so his commander could fight the army. Besides Cadogan, Marlborough also counted on the highly efficient services of Adam Cardonnel as military secretary, the spectacularly named Colonel Holcroft Blood as commander of the artillery train, and Colonel John Armstrong as engineer officer and senior aide-de-camp. Staff service was essential, but it was no safe haven: The Duke's equerry, Lieutenant Colonel James Bingham, was beheaded by a cannonball at the battle of Ramillies.

Prussian mythology to the contrary, it was not Frederick alone who took Silesia and who then withstood the combined efforts of Austria, France, and Russia, but also stout-hearted officers like General Friedrich von Seydlitz, his audacious commander of heavy cavalry. Confident and far-seeing commanders created processes and institutions in which success reinforced success. They encouraged strong-willed subordinates to speak their minds, knowing full well that men of valor seldom hold tepid views. And they recognized that even awkward or unpromising material deserved a chance. His mother may have thought him "food for powder and nothing more," but the young Arthur Wellesley (later Lord Wellington) proved her appraisal to be unduly pessimistic.

Despite the creation of effective staffs, field generals knew that on occasion they themselves had to take direct charge of events. Sword in hand, Marlborough led a cavalry charge at the battle of Ramillies. During the Seven Years War, Frederick toured the Prussian lines within range of enemy musketry. (A French general refused as ignoble a sharpshooter's request to target the king.) No one campaigned harder than Old Fritz, a fact that earned him the respect of his men and legendary status within German military history. In the words of one admirer,

> Even the private soldier in Frederick's army felt a personal acquaintanceship with the King through hardships and dangers shared together. The sternness with which the King continually demanded more and more sacrifices was feared; but every man knew that Frederick was even more stern with himself—that he did his own duty in spite of the torments of fever and gout, and that he exposed himself unhesitatingly to the enemy's bullets, whose whistling never caused the slightest change in his countenance.[21]

Even a warrior-king as brave and skilled as Frederick, however, rarely escaped the devastating calculus of symmetrical battles. At Zorndorf (1758) he suffered thirty-eight percent casualties while fighting Russia; at Kunersdorf (1759) he lost a staggering forty-eight percent of his army at the hands of the Russians. Indeed, Frederick lost roughly half the battles he fought, but he never lost his grip on Prussia. Nevertheless, Frederick and his army were nearing exhaustion and defeat when a deus ex machina appeared in the guise of the death of Empress Elizabeth of Russia in 1762, which led Russia to withdraw from the war. Frederick's career thus revealed the last secret of successful commanders: luck.

Ultimately, the exercise of command was broadly consistent with, and served to reinforce, Enlightenment mores and social hierarchies. As state hirelings and functionaries, officers were expected to uphold

The Warrior-Statesman: Frederick the Great of Prussia after the Battle of Kolin. Courtesy of the Library of Congress.

dynastic structures. While one began to perceive a shift in attitude toward Voltaire's idea that "whoever serves his country well has no need of ancestors," bourgeois officers rarely attained high rank. Low-born officers found paths to promotion blocked by nobles having more money and better court connections. The social rigidity of France's army during the ancien régime—and the alienation and sense of outrage shared by many French officers of humble stock—contributed to antiaristocratic sentiment and the destabilization of France after 1789. In Prussia as well, officers of high talent but of lower social status rarely rose above the company-grade level. In 1789, only 2 of 379 majors, lieutenant colonels, and colonels in the Prussian army were not members of the nobility.[22] Non-nobles were also the first to be relieved of duty and discharged from the Prussian officer corps at the end of both the War of Spanish Succession (1713) and the Seven Years War (1763). Such an abrupt end to promising military careers could be emotionally devastating, especially within a society that attached high status to officer rank.

Whether of noble or non-noble origins, officers sought to embrace and exhibit a martial and personal code of behavior that stressed honor. Notions of honor harkened back to chivalric codes of the Middle Ages; noble deeds of arms were thought to confirm one's worthiness and identity as a man of honor.[23] Honor implied devotion to duty, a certain sense of noblesse oblige or paternalistic concern for one's men, and dignified grace in one's day-to-day behavior. Officers were quick to respond to perceived slights against their honor; duels were frequent occurrences, and an officer who refused to defend his honor was often disgraced. Aspirants to the French officer corps, for example, were expected to prove themselves by dueling with an expert swordsman, with the latter inflicting a few flesh wounds as a rite of passage. Some regiments preserved hereditary feuds with rival regiments, with officers being honor bound to fight if their regimental opposites were posted in close proximity.[24] Concepts of masculinity, of a warrior's ethos, and of the liberating effects of violence all interacted in a physically straightforward yet emotionally complex code of behavior. Most of all, honor was judged by one's behavior in combat. Junior officers were expected to expose themselves to fire, displaying not merely bravery in battle, which could perhaps be a momentary byproduct of adrenalin and the ecstasy of battle, but courage as well—a sustained exhibition of steady nerves and stoical resolve for hours at a time. Honor, once lost, could rarely be regained.[25]

Related to honor was gentility, a more subtle quality that was thought to be a product of proper breeding and upbringing. Proper decorum meant that an officer did not condescend to join his men at undignified manual labor. Officers remained a breed apart, with those at the highest levels putting on conspicuous displays of consumption. To sustain a regal lifestyle, a gentleman officer might take a dozen or more wagons filled with personal baggage into the field. Along with the baggage came a retinue of personal servants. The Duke of Northumberland, admittedly richer than most officers, took with him to Flanders three gentleman attendants, a page, two footmen, a wagoner, a sumpterman, and three grooms.[26]

By placing the sale, purchase, and administration of military commissions into the hands of the upper classes, the state insured that nearly all officers had a financial as well as personal stake in upholding established hierarchies. Indeed, the army's rank gradations and social structure were broadly consistent with Enlightenment notions of a great chain of being within nature.[27] Abuses in the sale and purchase of commissions, however, led at times to absurdly top-heavy officer corps. In 1775, the French army had 60,000 officers on the rolls in an army mustering 170,000 men. Reforms like the Ségur ordinance reduced the number of officers through stricter enforcement of aristocratic lineage for officer candidates, with the latter required to trace their family's aristocratic line back four generations. Unfortunately, "right born" did not always translate easily to military effectiveness, and officers stripped of their rank for no other reason than their social origin bore grudges that festered.

Noncommissioned Officers: Backbone of Armies

Equally as important as officers to the smooth running of armies and their performance on the day of battle were seasoned NCOs. For the historian these men are somewhat more difficult than officers to examine since many were illiterate. As a group, they left far fewer records of their actions and attitudes than did officers. Unlike junior officers, NCOs typically did not seek transfers to other regiments. Their long-term service within the regiment conveyed the important advantage of stability and continuity; within British regiments, NCOs "demonstrated greater corporate spirit as the regimental 'backbone' than did their officers."[28] NCOs took charge of day-to-day training and the nitty-gritty details of soldiering. An ordinary soldier's life, one must remember, was one of drudgery and mind-numbing routine, especially from November to March, when most units wintered in garrison or barracks (or in alehouses in England). Sieges entailed backbreaking work and constant vigilance and could persist for two or even three seasons. NCOs had the unenviable task of maintaining the fighting spirit of fatigued and often desperately hungry men, who despite their privations, had nevertheless to perform all the normal duties common to soldiers. Pulling guard duty in teeth-chattering cold or serving on burial details in sweltering heat was part of a soldier's lot. Effective NCOs rewarded promising soldiers who obeyed the rules, while punishing the deviant, the cowardly, and the criminal.

Thus a tall order for any NCO was motivating soldiers under the normal conditions of military service in the field. Men who were cold, wet, footsore, famished, and fearful could not be kept together solely by flogging or even by the so-called courage of habit instilled by regular drill. Inspirational leaders who willingly shared the hardships of military service with their men performed wonders in maintaining fighting spirit. A dictum applied in a different context by Frederick the Great—"Cunning succeeds where force fails"—equally applied to the day-to-day running of an army. Long-serving conscripts and battle-hardened veterans who had little tolerance for sadists and fools often paid commanders of any rank or stripe whose first recourse was to the lash back in kind. Soldiers occasionally killed their own officers if the latter were especially craven and callous. These cases, though rare, were nonetheless telling. The historian David Chandler quotes a ranker who declaimed against officers "who instead of treating their men with GOOD NATURE, use them with CONTEMPT and CRUELTY; by which those gentlemen often meet their FATE in the day of battle from their own men." Chandler further cites the case of a pusillanimous major who was shot down by his own men after the battle of Blenheim.[29]

This violent case of battlefield justice returns us to the attributes of successful commanders. Then, as now, styles of command varied greatly, but there was no substitute for taking pains. Officers and NCOs who took pains made sure that their tactics matched local topography; that they took full advantage of cover and concealment to limit casualties; that they coordinated logistics support to maintain combat readiness and fighting power; that they watched the enemy closely and therefore were rarely surprised or caught in untenable positions; and that they were decisive, and even ruthless, when the conditions called for it. The road to victory was paved by good commanders.

THE RELATIONSHIP BETWEEN THE LEADER AND THE LED

All soldiering requires some manner of contractual relationship between leaders and led, whether monetary, behavioral, or formal in the sense of oaths taken and contracts signed and witnessed. Mercenary captains hired men, supplied them with a semblance of equipment, and gave them opportunities for plunder as well as a sense of identity and purpose. In dynastic armies, officers from the upper classes led soldiers who were often dragooned or recruited from the lower orders of society within a hierarchical military structure that reflected and reinforced the established order. Some of these officers were most concerned with their own career advancement and self-identity, particularly their status as honorable gentlemen within aristocratic and dynastic structures. But the most successful officers treated their men humanely and reaped the awards of allegiance justly and honorably gained.

It represents no whitewash of severe disciplinary practices to note that many of the more vivid horror stories were reported either by officers advocating a discipline based on mutual honor and respect or by soldiers whose military service proved unhappy or unfortunate. As in any army, a disproportionate amount of punishment fell to a disproportionately small number: the dull-witted and the loud-mouthed, the sullen, the vicious, those too smart for their own britches, and those unfortunate enough to be made scapegoats by their superiors and fellow soldiers. Soldiers who were tractable and showed good will were usually dealt with patiently, if not always gently, by NCOs and officers.

Ultimately, the exercise of command depended on authority. But authority was not conveyed merely by fear or repetitive drill. Nor was it achieved simply through fair and humane treatment. Rather, command had a mystique to it. A commander was and had to remain a man apart. His social origin and behavior, his weaponry and prowess, his demeanor and swagger, marked him as a man of authority who was worthy of being obeyed and even admired. The best commanders nevertheless tapped into and activated the communal spirit within the rank and file. In the absence of unifying ideologies such as nationalism, and in an age that still discouraged ideologically charged citizen-soldiery, effective commanders relied on their own mystique and charisma to inspire belief and camaraderie among the men. The result was men who truly believed that their best chance at survival, and even self-fulfillment and glory, resided within their unit.

The final arbiter of effectiveness for commanders was the clash of arms. As Clausewitz noted in the early nineteenth century, warfare perhaps most resembles a game of cards. It rewarded the skilled gambler who knew the odds and who was willing to take calculated risks. But it also punished ruthlessly both the foolhardy and the timid. Even during the "rational" Enlightenment, war remained a thoroughly human endeavor, a realm of entropy and disorder that unleashed primal emotions that were ungovernable by reason alone. In this chaos, effective commanders imposed their will on events. They chose the right time to raise the stakes, the right time to check or call, and the right time to fold and wait for a new hand to be dealt. Those who were able consistently to impose their will on the battlefield, those who were consistently "lucky" in choosing the most opportune time to act, were those who combined talent informed by hard-won experience. The most effective commanders knew the odds, kept their cool and a hole card in reserve, and dared to win.

NOTES

1. Machiavelli, *The Prince* (New York: Random House, 1950), 61.

2. Two insightful studies of command are Martin van Creveld, *Command in War* (Cambridge, MA: Harvard University Press, 1985); and John Keegan, *The Mask of Command* (New York: Viking Penguin, 1987).

3. The best modern edition is Carl von Clausewitz, *On War*, ed. and trans. Michael Howard and Peter Paret (Princeton, NJ: Princeton University Press, 1989).

4. After studying 625 battles from 1600 to 1973, Ralph Rotte and Christoph Schmidt concluded that leadership was the most important factor in determining the outcome of battles, with a marginal impact of nearly fifty percent. Superior intelligence conveyed an advantage of about twenty-five percent, with surprise conveying an advantage of fifteen percent. Of course, the best commanders set up processes to gather and exploit intelligence while insuring that they themselves were not taken by surprise. See The Institute for the Study of Labor, "On the Production of Victory: Empirical Determinants of Battlefield Success in Modern War," cited in "The Wellington Effect," *Atlantic Monthly*, May 2003, 46–49.

5. See Keith Moxey, *Peasants, Warriors, and Wives: Popular Imagery in the Reformation* (Chicago: University of Chicago Press, 1989), 69. Other illustrations of commanders and soldiers in the fifteenth and sixteenth centuries, together with critical commentary, are provided by John R. Hale, *Artists and Warfare in the Renaissance* (New Haven, CT: Yale University Press, 1990); and Peter Paret, *Imagined Battles: Reflections of War in European Art* (Chapel Hill: University of North Carolina Press, 1997).

6. Cited in Moxey, *Peasants*, 96.

7. On the "age of the entrepreneur," see Matthew S. Anderson, *War and Society in Europe of the Old Regime, 1618–1789* (New York: St. Martin's Press, 1988); Peter H. Wilson, "The German 'Soldier Trade' of the Seventeenth and Eighteenth Centuries: A Reassessment," *International History Review* 18 (1996): 757–792; and Fritz Redlich, *The German Military Enterpriser and His Work Force: A Study in European Economic and Social History*, 2 vols. (Wiesbaden, Germany: Franz Steiner, 1964–1965).

8. For example, Maurice read Aelian's *Tactics* (c. 100 c.e.), which highlighted the coordination of slingshot and javelin throwers in the Roman army. Apparently inspired by this, Maurice trained his musketeers in coordinated volley fire.

9. Michael Roberts, *Gustavus Adolphus: A History of Sweden, 1611–1632*, 2 vols. (London: Longmans Green, 1953–1958); Nils Ahnlund, *Gustavus Adolphus the Great*, trans. Michael Roberts, Foreword by Dennis E. Showalter (New York: History Book Club, 1999). Portraits of Gustavus show a rather placid man. Better capturing Gustavus's immense force of will was a monumental bronze bust completed by Hans von der Putt.

10. Thomas Mack Barker, *The Military Intellectual and Battle: Raimondo Montecuccoli and the Thirty Years' War* (Albany: State University of New York Press, 1975). Barker's study includes a translated text of Montecuccoli's *Sulle battaglie*. See also Azar Gat, "Montecuccoli,"

chap. 1 in *The Origins of Military Thought: From the Enlightenment to Clausewitz* (Oxford, UK: Clarendon Press, 1989).

11. Mechanical clocks were arguably Europe's most intellectually demanding mechanism, notes Otto Mayr in *Authority, Liberty, and Automatic Machinery in Early Modern Europe* (Baltimore: Johns Hopkins University Press, 1986), 27; Carlo M. Cipolla in *Clocks and Culture 1300–1700* (New York: W. W. Norton, 1978) notes that towns and villages took enormous pride in their clocks, spending large sums of money to build them. Clockwork analogies reached their peak of popularity during the Scientific Revolution. For many deists of this period, God was compared to a great clock maker who created the universe (the clock) and set its pendulum into motion.

12. See Kathleen H. Ochs, "The Failed Revolution in Applied Science: Studies of Industry by Members of the Royal Society of London, 1660–1688" (Ph.D. diss., University of Toronto, 1981). On the attempt to compile a "history of trades," see Walter E. Houghton Jr., "The History of Trades: Its Relation to Seventeenth-Century Thought," *Journal of the History of Ideas* 2 (1941): 33–60. Other countries also founded societies to pursue and advance "applied" science, including France in 1666 (the Royal Academy of Science) and Prussia in 1700 (the Berlin Academy).

13. Erik A. Lund, *War for the Every Day: Generals, Knowledge, and Warfare in Early Modern Europe, 1680–1740* (Westport, CT: Greenwood Press, 1999), 66 passim.

14. John Aubrey, *Aubrey's Brief Lives* (London: Penguin Classics, 1987), 157. Aubrey wrote in the seventeenth century; his original spelling is retained.

15. David Chandler, "The Great Captain-General 1702–1714," in *The Oxford History of the British Army*, ed. Chandler Beckett and Ian Beckett (Oxford, UK: Oxford University Press, 1996), 67–91: 75.

16. Correlli Barnett, *The First Churchill: Marlborough, Soldier and Statesman* (New York: Putnam, 1974); David Chandler, *Marlborough as Military Commander*, 2nd ed. (London: Batsford, 1979); Winston Churchill, *Marlborough: His Life and Times*, 4 vols. (London: Harrap, 1933–1938); John B. Hattendorf, "Churchill, John, first duke of Marlborough (1650–1722)," in *Oxford Dictionary of National Biography*, ed. H.C.G. Matthew and Brian Harrison (Oxford, UK: Oxford University Press, 2004). In the words of Jonathan Swift, Marlborough was "as covetous as hell, and as ambitious as the prince of it."

17. T. B. Macaulay, *Critical and Historical Essays*, vol. 2 (London: Longmans, Green, 1890), 723.

18. Overviews that address this period include John C. R. Childs, *Armies and Warfare in Europe, 1648–1789* (New York: Holmes and Meier, 1982); Christopher Duffy, *The Military Experience in the Age of Reason, 1715–1789* (New York: Atheneum, 1988); André Corvisier, *Armies and Societies in Europe, 1494–1789* (Bloomington: Indiana University Press, 1979); and Jeremy M. Black, *European Warfare, 1660–1815* (New Haven, CT: Yale University Press, 1994).

19. See the useful statistical chart in Janice E. Thomson, *Mercenaries, Pirates, and Sovereigns: State-Building and Extraterritorial Violence in Early Modern Europe* (Princeton, NJ: Princeton University Press, 1994), 29.

20. Lund, *War for the Every Day*, 24.

21. Hugo von Freytag-Loringhoven, *The Power of Personality in War* (Harrisburg, PA: Military Service, 1955), 20–21.

22. Cited in Larry H. Addington, *The Patterns of War through the Eighteenth Century* (Bloomington: Indiana University Press, 1990), 118.

23. On the importance of honor to an officer's identity, see Yuval Noah Harari, *Renaissance Military Memoirs: War, History, and Identity, 1450–1600* (Woodbridge, UK: Boydell Press,

2004); and Malcolm Vale, *War and Chivalry: Warfare and Aristocratic Culture in England, France, and Burgundy at the End of the Middle Ages* (London: Duckworth, 1981).

24. See Victor G. Kiernan, *The Duel in European History: Honour and the Reign of Aristocracy* (Oxford, UK: Oxford University Press, 1989), 114, 124.

25. On the "culture of honor," see Armstrong Starkey, *War in the Age of Enlightenment, 1700–1789* (Westport, CT: Praeger, 2003), chap. 3.

26. Richard A. Preston, Sydney F. Wise, and Herman O. Werner, *Men in Arms: A History of Warfare and Its Interrelationships with Western Society* (New York: Praeger, 1956), 139.

27. The idea of a rationally ordered and hierarchical "chain of being" that applied to human affairs as well as nature is given its classic explication in Arthur O. Lovejoy, *The Great Chain of Being: A Study of the History of an Idea* (New York: Harper and Brothers, 1936).

28. G. W. Stephen Brodsky in *Gentlemen of the Blade: A Social and Literary History of the British Army Since 1660* (Westport, CT: Greenwood Press, 1988), xviii.

29. David Chandler, "The Great Captain General 1702–1714," in *The Oxford History of the British Army*, ed. David Chandler (Oxford, UK: Oxford University Press, 1996), 79.

Five

✳ ✳ ✳

MORALE AND MOTIVATION

In *Candide, or Optimism* (1759), a famous satire of Enlightenment culture, François-Marie Arouet de Voltaire offered a scathing critique of "rational" warfare that captured the hellish nature of close-in combat in the age of gunpowder weaponry:

> Nothing could be so beautiful, so smart, so brilliant, so well drilled as the two armies. Trumpets, fifes, oboes, drums, cannons formed a harmony such as was never heard even in hell. First the cannons felled about six thousand men on each side; then the musketry removed from the best of worlds some nine or ten thousand scoundrels who infected its surface. The bayonet also was the sufficient reason for the death of some thousands of men. The whole might well amount to about thirty thousand souls. Candide, trembling like a philosopher, hid himself as best he could during this heroic butchery.[1]

Aiming his critique at his erstwhile friend and admirer, Frederick the Great, Voltaire simultaneously poked fun at himself as a "trembling" philosopher who preferred to hide from battle, rather than seek posthumous honors as a hero. Yet, given the sheer scale and nastiness of the "heroic butchery" of early modern warfare, one might well ask why any man chose to expose himself to withering fire rather than hiding or fleeing. What motivated men to endure extreme conditions of combat? How did military units sustain morale and remain steadfast?

Throughout the early modern period, nationalism—defined here as the belief in the inherent superiority and even sanctity of one's own nation and people when compared to other, "foreign" nations and peoples—was virtually nonexistent as a motivating and unifying force. In its absence, other ideologies, belief systems, and interests interacted to sustain morale. The previous chapter looked at commanders and leaders and their influence on morale. This chapter examines other wellsprings of morale and motivation. These included religious belief; naked self-interest, such as the desire for plunder, adventure, and opportunity as well as self-preservation; and personal and collective notions of honor, *gloire*, and masculinity forged within contexts of group loyalty, class identity, and unit camaraderie.

With the obvious exception of self-defense or the immediate defense of one's kith and kin, soldiers in early modern Europe often lacked a single clear and emotionally compelling reason to serve and fight. Ordinary foot soldiers were mostly illiterate or barely literate. Units in which they served often lacked a common language or shared sense of tradition. Strong devotion to a single ideological cause was unusual, assuming there was an identifiable "cause." For many men, military service was either a last resort or a means of escape, or both. Young men reaching maturity in deferential and patriarchal societies found a soldier's career attractive precisely because it promised release from the restraints or ennui of the familiar. Pregnant girlfriends, legal wrangles, and domestic quarrels drove young men from parental firesides in the early modern period, just as they continue to do in modern times.[2] Military service also promised starving men food and poor men avenues for enriching themselves. For an ambitious young man possessed of martial interests, military service offered an opportunity to make a name for himself—a chance to win a measure of independence and even glory, which could, in rare instances, lead to ennoblement, even for base commoners.

As we examine morale and motivation, we should keep in mind young men like Georg Behaim. Son of a wealthy Tyrolean copper mine developer in the early sixteenth century, Behaim attempted, through military service, to make his own mark on the world, while gaining a measure of freedom from parental constraints. Instead, he succumbed, in his early twenties, to one of the many diseases endemic to densely populated areas through which campaigning armies passed.[3] Behaim's early death reminds us of the fragility and unpredictability of life in the early modern period. Short life expectancies of both men and women (due in part to the hazards of childbirth) worked to shape aspirations. As the English philosopher Thomas Hobbes famously noted in *Leviathan* (1651), life in an unmitigated state of nature was "solitary, poore, nasty, brutish, and short." The onset of illness was unpredictable, its course was often poorly understood, and death often followed with shocking suddenness. The transitory and sometimes solitary nature of life made it even more pressing to impetuous youth—in whose arteries blood pulsed red-hot—to establish, through collective military service, their reputation and standing among contemporaries and seniors.

RELIGIOUS BELIEF AS MOTIVATION FOR WAR

Since ancient times, religious beliefs have often spurred men to fight and kill, even though mainstream religions, such as Christianity and Islam, enjoin against killing. During the Crusades of the Middle Ages, Catholic soldiers marched in large armies to the Levantine to cross blades with the Muslim "infidel," seeking, among other goals, to regain the Holy Land for the Roman Catholic Church. Under Ferdinand and Isabella in the late fifteenth century, Spain expelled Muslim believers as well as Jews and unified the country under Catholicism (although significant regional and cultural differences remained in place in Spain). Many of the Jews expelled found new homes in the Muslim Ottoman Empire (present-day Turkey); this empire's formidable corps of Janissaries continued to pose a serious threat to Vienna and the Catholic Habsburgs until the eighteenth century. But the confessional earthquake that shook Christian Europe at its foundation was the Protestant Reformation. Soon after Martin Luther nailed his Ninety-five Theses to the church door in Wittenberg in October 1517, Europe found itself wracked by bitter internecine struggles over Christian doctrine and practices.

Confessional disputes between Catholics and Protestants were rarely the sole or even the proximate cause of most wars in the 1500s and 1600s. Struggles for power and authority among the ruling dynasties of Europe often intervened and overrode strictly denominational concerns. For example, in the 1520s and 1530s, the Catholic Valois dynasty of France made common cause with the Muslim Ottoman Empire in an attempt to frustrate the Habsburg emperor Charles V's attempt both to subjugate German Protestant princes and to dominate central Europe. A century later, French Catholic forces again fought bitterly against their Catholic Habsburg rivals during the Thirty Years War, joining with Protestant forces in an attempt to curb Habsburg power. These and similar cases notwithstanding, confessional and doctrinal disputes dividing Catholics and Protestants often gave local outbreaks of violence unprecedented staying power, scorching the landscape of Europe from the start of the Protestant Reformation well into the Enlightenment.

Examining the extent to which religious beliefs motivated individual soldiers to serve and fight requires a degree of speculation, however. The sincerity of an individual's religious professions is difficult to judge, especially from a distance. As we attempt to do so, we need to examine past actors on their terms, based on their belief systems, even though the latter may never be fully recoverable. With this as a caution we can with confidence highlight cases where religious belief gave succor to morale and served as a unifying force for early modern armies.

As detailed in Chapter One, Dutch Calvinist soldiers of the Eighty Years War made common cause in resisting what they viewed as religious oppression and domination exerted by Spain's Philip II and the Catholic Counter-Reformation. A few outspoken Calvinists saw the Pope himself as the anti-Christ and believed themselves to be embroiled in a struggle that possessed eschatological significance. At the same time, other Christian sects often found it necessary to take active measures for self-defense if they wished to preserve unique or heterodox denominational practices and doctrinal teachings. In the early modern period, choices about denominational allegiances often became literally a matter of life or death for many Christians—as well as a matter of concern whether salvation or perdition awaited them in an eternal afterlife.

Through religious belief and practice, individuals actively sought to forge an identity for themselves as well as a sense of their own importance within a demanding and seemingly uncaring world. Few people wished to think of themselves as expendable pawns in a meaningless game—their religion taught them differently. Christianity, especially in newly minted Protestant strains, emphasized a God who took an intensely personal interest in individual souls and their salvation. Indeed, under Calvinism, some individuals believed themselves to be predestined as members of God's elect—literally a chosen people from birth. Within this and other highly emotive and spiritually complex worldviews, individuals believed that their behavior, acts, and even their unspoken thoughts mattered. They mattered because God knew all and judged all, both here and in the hereafter. And if God did not, people residing in close-knit villages and towns knew their neighbors and respected elders were doubtless watching and sitting in judgment.

Certainly, the Peasants' Revolt (1524–1526) within Germany was inspired in part by an emerging Lutheran idea that each man was capable of interpreting the word of God for himself—and that each man was accountable ultimately to God rather than to a mediatory and possibly manipulative priesthood. The social disorder that resulted from this revolt soon drove Luther to condemn roving bands of peasants as unrighteous, murderous, and thieving hordes who deserved to be smited, stabbed, and slayed by their social betters. Efforts at brutal repression, however, did not stamp out religious enthusiasm and heterodox views. Although conflicts between German peasants and more wellborn elements possessed class as well as religious dimensions, in most cases it was religious imperatives that acted as the primary ideological driver.

As the Bible as well as innumerable religious tracts were printed in vernacular tongues by the millions and distributed in cartloads by zealous prophets and missionaries seeking to mobilize the faithful and win converts, new and sometimes schismatic interpretations of Scripture emerged. During the 1530s, Anabaptists who denied the sacramental validity of infant baptism were hunted down and killed as heretics by Catholics and Protestants alike in Germany and the Low Countries. The barbarity exhibited during these purges bred apocalyptic fears. Many self-styled seers saw these and similar massacres as presaging the end of days as foretold in prophetic books like Daniel and Revelation. Existing within a grand biblical scheme that threatened to overwhelm and obliterate them, even halfhearted Christians grew interested in interpreting the "signs of the time." Apocalyptic fears reached a peak during the Thirty Years War and only abated as states succeeded in limiting the wider impact of military conflict on societies—in part by extending a measure of religious tolerance within Trinitarian Christianity.

Throughout the sixteenth and early seventeenth centuries, violent religious conflict and purges waxed and waned as rulers and political fortunes changed. Thwarted in his decades-long attempt militarily to suppress Protestantism, the Habsburg emperor Charles V relented with the Peace of Augsburg (1555), granting German princes the right to choose either Catholicism or Lutheranism for their subjects. Four years later, the Treaty of Câteau-Cambrésis (1559) marked a momentary pause in Habsburg-Valois dynastic struggles for hegemony.

Yet the treaty also marked the opening of a new phase in Europe's religious wars. France itself was soon wracked by internal dynastic and confessional disputes that culminated in the infamous Saint Bartholomew massacre (August 23–24, 1572), during which Catholic soldiers dragged Huguenots (Protestants) from their homes and churches and slaughtered them by the thousands in the streets of Paris. "Sadistic violence was the order of the day," notes Jean Delumeau, and not just in Paris. "The people of Luderon were smoked inside caves, monks were buried alive by the Gueux, English Catholics were disemboweled, some alive, with their hearts and viscera already torn out, children were roasted on the spit (in the Vivarais, ca. 1579) in the presence of their parents, and so on."[4] These and other ostensibly religious struggles devolved into a Grand Guignol of violence whose bloodthirsty and brutal nature was later echoed in a harrowing series of etchings by Jacques Callot, *Misères de la Guerre* (Miseries of War). Atrocities in these wars demonstrated how Christian teachings could be manipulated to support literally the demonization of the enemy, thereby facilitating torture and other acts committed ostensibly in the name of greater righteousness. As suggested in Chapter One, developing theologies often proved malleable, so much so that they were used to justify further repression and atrocity.

Massacre of Saint Bartholomew, August 23, 1572, detail. By François Dubois. © Erich Lessing/Art Resource, New York.

To the people who suffered through them, these religious wars (c. 1559–1689)[5] literally turned their world upside down. Burned over by religious fervor and blasted by war, the resulting damaged mindscapes and landscapes supported apocalyptic fears that were further heightened by virulent outbreaks of plague and other deadly diseases. Believers as well as some skeptics in turn interpreted these as divine retribution for humanity's sins. With humanity's very survival uncertain, and with passions inflamed by cycles of atrocity and revenge, mercenaries found both motivation as well as opportunities for exploitation. In his *Tragiques*, Agrippa d'Aubigné condemned the beastly excesses of mercenaries who fanned the flames of war:

> I saw the dark mercenary crashing through
> The cottages of France, and like a storm,
> Carrying off what he could, raping the rest . . .
> There in a thousand homes one finds only flames,
> Carrion, dead bodies, or fearful faces.[6]

This and similar manifestations of war's barbarity reinforced a biblical sense that the four horsemen of the apocalypse galloped across the land, with War wielding a blood-drenched sword on a blood red steed.[7] Religious and dynastic conflict finally abated in France only in 1593, when Henry IV converted to Catholicism. ("Paris is worth a Mass," he famously quipped.) Instrumental though it may have been, his conversion helped to end a vicious cycle of sectarian violence, bringing a peace of exhaustion to France. In 1598, the Edict of Nantes (rescinded in 1685 by Louis XIV) formally extended religious toleration to Huguenots.

Religious toleration between Catholics and Protestants in France was one thing, toleration across Europe another. Philip II of Spain, son of Charles V, was devoutly and aggressively Catholic. Unfortunately for Philip, the Dutch were equally as committed to Protestantism and a way of life untrammeled by Habsburg imperial agendas. Their confessional allegiance and resistance to Spanish power were both instrumental in attracting support from Protestant England. Moral support was one thing; England sent money and mercenaries too. Philip's attempt to invade England and dethrone the intransigent Protestant Queen Elizabeth I met its demise with the catastrophe that befell the Spanish Armada in 1588. He was, however, able to recatholicize southern portions of the Low Countries, which formed the nucleus of modern-day Belgium. Micromanaging his vast empire from the stark splendor of the Escorial, Philip believed it was his holy mission both to spread Catholicism and suppress Protestantism, while expanding his own empire. Simultaneously, he sought to limit the Muslim Ottoman Empire's power in the Mediterranean. He was more successful with the latter, but the sheer extent of his religiously motivated military campaigns ended up bankrupting the Spanish Empire, opening the door to future challenges by Catholic France as well as Protestant England.[8]

Philip's Catholic fervor and sense of mission blinded him to the cost his empire was paying in trying to suppress Protestantism among his Dutch and English opponents. Both Lutheranism and various strains of Calvinism emphasized the sanctity of individual conscience and personal witnessing. Salvation, whether predestined or otherwise, they viewed as a referendum on the worthiness of an individual's soul before his God, unqualified by a hegemonic church and unsullied by Inquisitional heavy-handedness. Many found these ideas to be powerful, sacred, and worth defending until death, or so the determined military resistance of Holland, England, and other Protestant countries and regions showed.

The sheer power of religious ideas was amply demonstrated in an explosion of eschatological excitement during the Thirty Years War. In its opening stages Ferdinand II, the Holy Roman Emperor, boasted it would be "better to rule over a desert than a country of [Protestant] heretics." But as the war dragged on and devastation spread, so too did disillusionment. By the 1630s, apocalyptic fervor waned. Protestants still seeking a messianic Germanic leader, whose proselytizing armies would espouse Lutheranism, slay or convert the infidel Turks, and conquer and convert Asia and Africa, settled instead for a Swede: Gustavus Adolphus. Some even believed that his arrival in Pomerania in 1630 fulfilled a prophecy about a *Löwen aus Mitternacht*, a Lion of the North, appearing. But Gustavus's meteoric rise had an equally spectacular fall at the battle of Lützen in 1632. After his death at this battle, prophesies about the end of the world and cries for repentance died down. More sober sermons were now heard in the pews, calling for a return to an orthodox eschatology that avoided rash apocalyptic claims and speculative divination. Instead of looking without for heaven-sent signs presaging earth-shattering changes, Protestants began looking within, seeking to cultivate spirituality through devotional practices consistent with more private and heartfelt expressions of faith. This quest for an "inner light" led to Pietism, a movement in which personal salvation was thought to be gained best through reflection, prayer, and devotional acts, rather than through battle and militant efforts at proselytizing.[9]

As the flames of religious excitement burnt themselves out on the continent, they jumped the channel to inflame a civil war in England. Indeed, the clearest example of a religiously motivated army in early modern Europe was the New Model Army captained by Oliver Cromwell during the English Civil War.[10] The Puritan Cromwell and his fellow officers referred unironically to themselves and their regiment as a "gathered church." Cromwell's famed cavalry, known as the Ironsides, consisted of "honest, godly men" who sang psalms as they rode down and skewered the fleeing Cavalier (Royalist) forces of Charles I.[11] The Ironsides' unbroken string of victories was in large measure due to their fervid belief that they were literally instruments of God.

A strongly shared sense of millenarian purpose made the New Model Army unique in early modern Europe. To understand England's descent into civil war and barbarity, ordinary soldiers "searched their Bibles and their consciences" to identify the guilty party, believing that identifying and subsequently punishing the evildoer would efface the "defilement . . . upon the whole land."[12] They settled on the king as the biblical "man of blood" who needed to die, with his death cleansing England of its sins and paving the way for Christ's return and the rule of the saints. Charles I's execution in 1649 was viewed by many soldiers as a ritual cleansing of millennial import.

Of course, scattered among the ranks of true believers in the New Model Army were nonbelievers, joined by the usual assortment of opportunists and wastrels.[13] In an army consisting of 22,000 men, soldiers came and went for multiple causes. Often, those who chose to stay did so in part to insure that Royalist retribution would not be visited upon them. Recognizing this diversity of motives, Cromwell's army was nevertheless remarkable for the consistency of its ideological fervor. With this fervor rode devastation. Two hundred thousand men and women died in the English Civil War, 80,000 of them soldiers. Both sides committed atrocities; looting, pillaging, raping, and other forms of savagery were routine. Cathedrals were a special target. In Worcester, soldiers desecrated the cathedral, smashing its organ, windows, and images and burning its sacred books. Indeed, to these men, nothing was sacred if it was viewed as contravening their faith. Nave and cloisters became horse stalls; choir and aisles became latrines. These and similar acts of desecration were consistent with *The Souldiers Catechisme* (1644), wherein it was stated, "God hath put the sword of reformation into the soldiers' hand, [and] I think it not amiss that they should cancel and demolish those monuments of superstition and idolatry, especially seeing the magistrate and the minister that should have done it formerly neglected it."[14] Rampant iconoclasm thus became a sacred duty; none too rarely has pillaging, looting, and just plain bestial behavior been justified so uncritically by calls to greater holiness.

Ideological purpose pitched at high levels ran to extremes. Levelers emerged who sought more radical changes to traditional class and social hierarchies within England. Rogue armies appeared, including one led by the lowborn "Tinker" Fox of Walsall, a Birmingham blacksmith and self-appointed "colonel" who briefly gained control over the Midlands of England until suppressed by Cromwell's New Model Army. In the New Model Army itself, Levelers within the ranks used a dispute over wages left in arrears to justify demands for a "citizen-army" that would represent the views of common soldiers rather than social elites. In the Army's declaration of June 14, 1647, spokesmen drawn primarily from the middling and lower social orders spoke confidently of a new army, neither mercenary nor beholden to state caprice, but rather one "called forth and conjured by the several declarations of Parliament, to the defence of our own and the people's just rights and liberties . . . resolved . . . to assert and vindicate the just power and rights of this kingdom in Parliament, for those common ends premised, against all arbitrary power and violence and oppression."[15] Several of Cromwell's officers even spoke of confiscating landed estates from royalist gentry, effectively reducing them to landless peasants. More outspoken Levelers sought a return to a state of nature, in which the power of the sword would rule—a sword wielded ostensibly by common people and yeomen against the propertied and landed gentry. For two years these democratic soldiers' councils debated a radical model for a citizen army in which officers were to be elected based on merit rather than social caste. When they dared to mutiny for their beliefs in May 1649, Cromwell ruthlessly suppressed them.

Levelers and other schismatic elements within the New Model Army failed to overthrow existing social hierarchies to prepare the way for the Second Coming of Christ. But they did succeed in creating an army that was firmly controlled by Parliament rather than by the autocratic power of a monarch. Even after Charles II was restored to the throne in 1660, the English army remained a parliamentary instrument. However imperfectly, the New Model Army had cleared a new path of leadership to be walked by "plain men" rather than one reserved exclusively for the moneyed or privileged orders. Cromwell himself declared, "I had rather have a plain russet-coated captain that knows what he fights for and loves what he knows than that which you call a 'gentleman' and is nothing else."[16] "Peers were now little more than rich citizens," the historian Christopher Hill noted. "The civil war had shown that they had no special military abilities. Generals no longer commanded armies because they were peers; they became peers because they successfully commanded armies. If they were very successful they became dukes."[17] In England John Churchill embodied this new reality, becoming the first Duke of Marlborough on the strength of his military victories.

With the restoration of Charles II, religious tensions died down in England, only to flare briefly again in the events leading up to the Glorious Revolution (1688). While England largely managed to avoid major bloodshed in the 1680s (Ireland was another story), across the channel, the French again embroiled themselves in denominational conflict. In revoking the Edict of Nantes, thereby ending Henry IV's policy of state toleration of Protestantism, Louis XIV precipitated a wholesale flight from the country by Huguenots. The Camisards of France (a Huguenot sect whose name came from their practice of wearing shirts over armor) first revolted, then sought sanctuary in Holland, England, and Switzerland. In this confessional struggle French army officers became prophetic religious resisters, one example being Elie Marion, a former captain in "Colonel" Jean Cavalier's army. The latter's army seized Aubais in France, burned the local Catholic church, and sacked the presbytery, leaving the sacramental vessels broken and desecrated. Cavalier's men then tore down ten rural crosses. Believing themselves to be engaged in a "Fight of Faith," they showed religious fervor by singing psalms as they marched forth to battle. A favorite was Psalm 51: "Then I will teach transgressors thy ways, and sinners will return to thee. Deliver me from bloodguiltiness, O God, thou God of my salvation, and my tongue will sing aloud of thy deliverance."[18] Ultimately suppressed, the Camisard revolt provides a salutary reminder to modern readers that the so-called Age of Reason still witnessed outbreaks of intense religious warfare.

Indeed, as late as the American War for Independence in the 1770s and 1780s, one witnessed religious enthusiasm as a motivator within the nascent colonial army in America.[19] The sheer variety and sustained tradition of outspokenness exhibited by religious sects and denominations that settled in North America forged compelling precedents for dissent from, and resistance to, established authority. Dissenters from England's Anglican Church were heavily represented among American colonists, with Massachusetts Puritans and Pennsylvania Quakers being only the better-known examples. In 1775, the year the colonial rebellion began at Lexington and Concord, seventy-five percent of English colonists dissented from Anglicanism. (Dissenters in England proper represented a mere ten percent of the population.) In the American colonies, dissenters extended the concept of religious liberty (however imperfectly defined and put into practice) to the realm of politics to convey a right—even a compelling duty— to resist oppressive exercises of royal power, especially when sanctioned by England's established church. The "frenzied" rhetoric and "paranoia, mass hysteria, [and] virulent hostility" of these formerly loyal English colonists, most notably expressed by elements in New England, was ultimately attributable, the historian J.C.D. Clark concludes, to deep-seated denominational divisions within Christianity and concomitantly deep-rooted animosities. One does not have to agree completely with Clark's conclusion that the American Revolutionary War was the last great war of religion in the Western world to affirm the rightness of his observation that religious motives were often central to this war.[20]

Political discourse too can be framed in providential terms. The American Revolutionary War was not only a harbinger of a new age of people's wars motivated by nationalism; it was also a vestige of providential religious wars. America's founders conceived and defined the war in eschatological terms as producing "a new order for the ages."[21] The famous clause in the U.S. Bill of Rights calling for a "separation" of church and state reflected deep-seated fears of arbitrary state interference in the free exercise of Christianity. It was not an expression of freely exercised deistic or secular values associated with an emerging Age of Reason.

By way of contrast, the French Revolution did inaugurate a secular ideology of liberty, equality, and fraternity that was embraced by an inflamed citizen army. The ideological and class-based intensity of the French Revolution saw political and military leaders like Lazare Carnot tap new emotional and ideological wellsprings, enabling nearly universal conscription of unmarried male citizenry (known as the *levée en masse*). Widespread democratization of the officer corps within France's revolutionary armies saw the redefinition of French officers as model citizens. Even common foot soldiers, traditionally seen as the dregs of society, emerged as more or less respectable defenders of the sacred soil of France. Following France's lead, other European nation-states soon insisted that healthy male citizens bore a duty to report to the colors and serve as soldiers, especially during national crises. In a concert of Europe that increasingly favored military marches, it became a matter of adapt or die. Yet, tragically for Europe, nationalistic propaganda and mass armies coincided with industrialization and the emergence of the new ideology of militarism, a coalescence of forces that, in the nineteenth and early twentieth centuries, proved even more destructive to Europe than older forms of religious faith.

MORALE AND MOTIVATION OF OFFICERS

Armies are composed of individuals but operate as organisms. Indeed, an atomistic army is an oxymoron; it is also little better than an armed mob. Thus an officer's primary goal was to ensure that his men worked collectively as a disciplined team. Instilling and maintaining high morale was crucial in stimulating and sustaining the high level of disciplined effort required from men engaged in the decidedly nasty business of killing other men at close range. Analyzing the wellsprings of morale and motivation is therefore complex for many reasons: These wellsprings have collective as well as individual qualities, they vary across cultures and over time, and they deal in changeable mind-sets and fleeting moments. A battle fought by 10,000 men is not one battle but 10,000 battles endured and processed by 10,000 minds. This being so, soldiers do, of course, share feelings, experiences, and attitudes with their comrades in arms, which effective officers tapped into and exploited for larger goals that were often poorly understood by the soldiers they led.

For mercenary captains in the sixteenth and seventeenth centuries, morale was maintained among the rank and file by fairly steady wages, adequate provisions, and promising prospects for plunder. Yet one may ask what motivated the captain himself. Answers varied, of course, but profit was one motive shared in common. In wartime, mercenary captains sold their services dearly, with the cleverest parlaying a skill in attracting men to their standard into greater wealth and power (here the singular success of a Wallenstein was simultaneously seductive to prospective imitators and terrifying to prospective patrons). A further motivator was codes of masculinity operating within early modern culture. Men who were by temperament poorly fit to manage estates or to compose sermons for wealthy parishioners could enhance their social position and self-worth by proving their toughness in the cut and slash of swordplay. Military service was, in addition, a uniquely male rite of passage that also won the favorable attention of available females. Condotierre wore elaborately and individually colored "uniforms" in unconscious imitation of strutting peacocks.[22] Codpieces emphasized male sexual organs in ways that Charles Darwin would have understood in his writings on sexual selection in the nineteenth century.

Money, manliness, and getting the girl are perhaps timeless as motivators for military men. Important too were class pretensions and ambitions. After the looting, drinking, and whoring was over, what next? Officers who aspired to the nobility, and who wanted to lead something more than brigands and braggarts, paid homage to chivalry and related codes of martial honor, which had concomitant benefits of tightening discipline and of garnering respect from both rivals and potential patrons.[23] For mercenary captains, warfare was often much more than an economic transaction: It was a way of life that evoked ancient martial codes whose respectability was deeply rooted within and nourished by Western culture.

Despite their pretensions to honor, however, mercenary captains earned the opprobrium of military reformers like Machiavelli, who denounced them as expensive and untrustworthy turncoats, which many in fact were. Machiavelli saved his worst criticism for the Sforzas, who betrayed the city of Milan and deprived the Milanese of their liberty. Such mercenaries, he noted, lacked "sufficient *virtù* to suffer honorably in poverty and obscurity," instead choosing a dishonorable life of brigandage and petty tyranny under the guise of military expediency.[24] Mercenary captains nevertheless served vital roles into the 1700s, especially for European states that lacked large standing armies or effective militias.

But the heyday of mercenary captains had passed by the end of the Thirty Years War. In a complex process that still requires further elaboration by historians, armies and their officer corps slowly professionalized during the seventeenth and eighteenth centuries.[25] Certainly, monarchs encouraged this process of professionalization and state bureaucracies who sought to gain control over both the means of violence and a fractious and potentially rebellious nobility. Important too in this process was the gradual emergence of a bourgeoisie or middle class, some of who had military aspirations of their own. At the same time, the emergence of technical branches within armies, especially artillery and engineers, involved as they were in the intricacies of siege warfare and city planning, placed a premium on systematic study in dedicated military academies. This process of professionalization was also given impetus by, and further strengthened within, a socio-cultural matrix that recognized and rewarded able men who demonstrated mastery of command in war in the service of state and monarchical ambitions.

Again, much depended on local conditions and context. In Brandenburg-Prussia, for example, commanding men in war while in the service of the king was the raison d'être of *Junkers* (the landed nobility). Their social contract enforced a willingness to lead men in harm's way, which further served to justify their privileged position in Prussian society. By way of contrast, in the constrictive and highly stylized court of Louis XIV, an ambitious young noble lacking a gift for gab or a taste for palace intrigue might turn instead to martial pursuits to establish his reputation. Indeed, the soaring social trajectories achieved by England's Marlborough or France's Vauban, exceptional though they were, nonetheless suggested that the sky was the limit to those able to bring victory to the monarch.

In the mid-eighteenth century, warfare among nation-states in Europe exhibited certain modalities summed up by the notion of war as "the sport of kings." As potentially trivializing as this phrase may be, it reminds us that war provided a (somewhat controlled) outlet for male aggression that was otherwise limited or lacking in early modern culture. Men of this day could not give vent to their aggression in organized field sports like football, rugby, and other mass events of the coming industrial age. The pageantry and jousts of the medieval period were passé. Combat was thus not just the sport of kings, but also a realm of fanfare for the common man, a place where men could belong to something larger than themselves, where they could submerge their own identities while simultaneously forging and expressing them within a male-dominated world. Put in anachronistic terms, combat was the ultimate reality show, played out in full view of a mass audience of one's subjects, peers, and betters for perhaps the only prize that truly mattered to these men: recognition of their courage and the feelings of pride and satisfaction that came when they earned the esteem of friends and rivals on unforgiving fields of battle.[26]

In fact, the persistence of warfare throughout this period (and throughout European history) lies in part in the high value Western societies invest in military heroes and the rewards they gain (financial, emotional, spiritual) through honorable service. Such service was even supranational since officers drawn from the aristocracy had social identities that transcended national borders. A common rite of passage for young men reaching maturity in early modern Europe was the so-called grand tour, a leisurely but nevertheless well-considered journey through Europe to forge social connections; to develop a taste for learning, music, and other refinements appropriate to one's station in society; and often to learn something of military value, such as fencing. As cadets and subalterns, young men often served as unpaid observers or combatants attached to the staff of foreign armies; here one recalls John Churchill's service at the age of twenty-three on the staff of Marshal Turenne of France.

Aristocratic allegiances and social identities were not just flexible laterally across national borders, but also vertically within emerging nation-states. A social gulf may have separated nobility from commoners, but it proved bridgeable within carefully defined settings. These were the days, the historian G. M. Trevelyan reminds us, "when the ensign fresh from Eton was handed over to the respectful care and tuition of the color-sergeant, [and] the relation of the two closely resembled that to which the younger man had been accustomed at home, when the old gamekeeper took him out afield to teach him the management of his fowling-piece and the arts of approaching game."[27] The military provided such settings in which normally rigid class and social boundaries proved surprisingly labile. Commoners might openly praise an officer's generosity or his sangfroid under fire, while the officer returned the favor, celebrating the courage and rewarding the manly deeds of ordinary rankers.

This being said, motivations for officers had their darker sides. Some officers essentially saw regiments as economic investments, profiting both from the sale of commissions, especially in Guards and other elite units, and from government stipends for food and equipment. Spoiled rations, threadbare uniforms, and shoddy boots may have favored the financial bottom line, but they also compromised military effectiveness and contributed to moral rot within a unit. Other officers allowed sangfroid to harden into callousness or a reckless disregard for the lives of their men. In other cases, warfare became ritualized to a degree that seems absurd to modern sensibilities. Perhaps the most famous example came during the opening stage of the battle of Fontenoy (1745), when Britain's Lord Charles Hay bowed and toasted to the health of his French opponents just before the day's death-dealing volleys commenced. Such outlandishly romantic courtesies should not blind us to the horrors of the eighteenth-century battlefield, horrors to which the French king, Louis XV, was not immune. Crossing Fontenoy's corpse-strewn battlefield later that day, Louis reflected to his son that "the blood of our enemies is still human blood. True glory consists in sparing it." The sentiment was Louis XV's best moment, but it was not one commonly shared by his fellow monarchs.[28]

The increasingly stylized and formalized nature of major battles in the eighteenth century was not solely a product of romantic gestures or rational calculations. It served simultaneously to limit disorder and to inhibit erosion of military elites. A slow pace of change in the art and scale of warfare, moreover, enabled even aristocratic amateurs to fancy that they could contribute to it, even if their contributions proved unsound. Aristocratic commissions and pretensions were especially common in prerevolutionary France. In the aftermath of humiliating defeats suffered in the Seven Years War, however, French military reformers called for a reinvigoration of morale via a motivated citizen-army supported by a professionalized officer corps wielding artillery and other technical weaponry to greater purpose. This nascent military machine awaited a genius willing to embrace and master it in all its dimensions, one who, in the process, would establish new paradigms and potentialities of Western warfare. Provided an opening by the French Revolution, an ambitious artillery officer grabbed the reins to show that he could both wield and master the new, ideologically motivated, mass armies of his age. Napoleon Bonaparte was his name.

MORALE AND MOTIVATION OF ORDINARY SOLDIERS

Negative images of early modern soldiers as the drunken dregs of society are common. Their pervasiveness highlights the fact that rank and filers were not choirboys but also that their military service did not carry with it the social cachet afforded to officers. It also rarely conveyed financial success, although it did afford an alternative to debtors' prisons. Military recruiters enjoyed fat pickings during lean times, when men contemplating financial ruin or patting empty stomachs turned to the army as the only respectable option left open to them. Capturing this sentiment was Miguel Cervantes in *Don Quixote*, in which a man fallen on hard times ruefully says, "My purse is lean, so to war I go / If I had money, more sense I'd show." Recruiters sought out the gullible, the desperate, and the naïve, using whatever blandishments and deceptions they had at hand. As Marshal Maurice de Saxe admitted, soldiers of the early modern period were "raised by enlistment with a fixed term, without a fixed term, by compulsion sometimes, and most frequently by tricky devices."

Young men caught in the path of war often faced the stark choice of being windshield or bug, of joining a fighting unit or becoming a victim of it. If not sold into slavery or exchanged after battle, prisoners of war were often impressed into the ranks of their adversary, a practice that was not considered a violation of prevailing codes governing military conduct. In short, a military life was a hard lot whose end was unforeseeable and often unfortunate, especially for men stuck at the low end of society's totem pole. The latter's understandably disagreeable temperament drew fire from their own leaders, most famously Arthur Wellesley, Lord Wellington, who, in a high-minded mood, declared that England's rankers were "the scum of the earth" who enlisted for love of rum rather than for country.

Yet not all men who marched to the colors did so for drink or out of desperation. Individual motivations for joining and fighting proved diverse. They varied with age, family background, geographic location, previous exposure (or lack thereof) to military realities; the list could be multiplied. Noncommissioned officers (NCOs) who more or less chose to make the army their life naturally had a stronger commitment to military service than recently dragooned privates. But the latter learned a lot from the former about reciprocity and implied rights owed to the rank and file by the state. Soldiers may have enlisted under what amounted to absolute terms of service. In practice, they insisted on fair, if still rough and ready, treatment. Soldiers fed poorly enough to perceive their short rations as a breach of contract might not risk deserting, but they could and did develop a spectrum of maladies ranging from incapacitating boils to debilitating homesickness: the *nostalgie du pays* dreaded by all armies.[29] Keeping unit morale high and rankers relatively content was in the best interest of officers, especially when well-trained and disciplined replacements were not readily at hand.

Armies throughout history have mixed praise and punishment, carrots and sticks, to motivate men. At the close of the early modern period, Private William Wheeler recounted his service with the Fifty-first Light Infantry Regiment of the British Army and the behavior of its commander, Lieutenant Colonel Mainwaring. To raise morale before a forthcoming battle, Mainwaring reminded his men of the courage their predecessors had shown during the battle of Minden (1759).[30] In Wheeler's words the colonel

shewed us the word *Minden* on our Colours, and reminded us it was inscribed on our breast plates. He said it was probable we should fall in with the enemy that day, and if we did not give them a good drubbing, how could we ever return home to our Fathers, Mothers etc. Our country expected much from us, the Regiment in its infant state had performed prodigies of valour on that day, and now that we had grown grey (some of us) in the service, would it not be expected we should eclips them in glory.

Speeches that recalled valorous exploits and honors won by the regiment, with reference to the agreeable prospect of adding to this roll of honor and thus of being able to hold one's head high before one's peers and family, resonated with military men. The compelling military necessity of maintaining honor as well as fighting spirit justified harsh punishment in the eyes of rankers. Again, let Private Wheeling speak of his colonel's treatment of a deserter. Despite the colonel's distaste for flogging, Wheeling noted, he ordered 500 lashes, with the sentence being commuted to 75. The deserter "was then taken down," Wheeling recounted, "our ranks opened, and the poltroon, as the Colonel justly called him, was ordered to march between the ranks. At the same time Colonel M[ainwaring] kept shouting 'soldiers spit on the cowardly poltroon, you should all p[iss] over him if it were not too indecent.'"[31] Rare is the man who can endure the humiliation of one's peers and social betters without conforming, and rare are the men who would not risk death to avoid such ritual humiliation.

For the vast majority of more or less praiseworthy soldiers, a mixture of motives, to include compulsion, survival, the desire for plunder and adventure (to include sexual), a steady salary and decent rations, combined to shape their terms of service. Many young men soon found a home within the ranks, thriving on the sense of purpose and urgency military service provided them, the exhilaration of battle, and opportunities to travel beyond the limited horizons of local villages and to experience life outside the restrictions of local custom. Helping to relieve the tedium was the fact that military service was not commonly a full-time profession. Campaigning seasons typically began in late spring (as mud dried from winter thaws and spring rains) and ended with harvest season in the fall and the onset of colder temperatures. Soldiers in garrison often fell out to plant or harvest crops, to work on civil engineering projects, such as irrigation, and to train in the field. In these circumstances, military service provided opportunities to young men to learn new skills, such as handling and riding horses, fixing wagons, proper storage and transportation of supplies, and carpentry (soldiers in such units were known as pioneers).[32] Valuable trade skills could often be acquired more quickly within military settings than in strictly civilian ones as the former were not constrained by guild rules and mandatory apprenticeships.

Together with transferable skills, armies also provided a sense of identity for the rootless as well as companionship and pride. Well-led regiments promoted esprit de corps and the notion of the regiment as an extended family. Senior NCOs served as surrogate fathers, administering tough love to turn callow youths into seasoned soldiers and respectable men. Armies promoted camaraderie not just for instrumental reasons, but for emotional ones as well. Men found a sense of belonging within the ranks that made the tedium, the petty regulations, the harsh punishments, and the hard marching and fighting tolerable. This sense of belonging sometimes extended to encompass the fighting man's family. Soldiers' wives might supplement their husbands' pay by selling alcohol to men[33] but also by performing such innocuous yet indispensable chores as mending uniforms or providing fresh produce to supplement standard rations.

Ultimately, military life provided an identity and defined a way of life that was equal measures good and bad. Smart uniforms, opportunities to cavort with the opposite sex, and chances to supplement pay with plunder were balanced by boredom, isolation, and the all-too-real hazards of death in battle or in camp (the latter due mainly to disease). State hospitals to support wounded, old, and infirm soldiers only began appearing in the mid-eighteenth century; before this, veterans went begging or sought Christian charity at monasteries. Faced with grim prospects, soldiers nevertheless served, at times heroically. They did so based upon the strength of an unwritten moral contract, negotiated within a military culture that stressed competence and camaraderie and that incorporated a calculated willingness to risk death. The remarkable consistency of their valor, expressed largely within prenationalistic settings and with little fanfare, raises important questions about the persistence of warfare both as a constructive and destructive force within Western culture.

NOTES

1. Voltaire, *Candide* (1759), chap. 3, as translated by Donald M. Frame in *Voltaire: Candide, Zadig and Other Stories* (New York: New American Library of World Literature, 1961).

2. Dennis E. Showalter, "Caste, Skill, and Training: The Evolution of Cohesion in European Armies from the Middle Ages to the Sixteenth Century," *Journal of Military History* 57 (1993): 407–430.

3. Steven Ozment, *Flesh and Spirit: Private Life in Early Modern Germany* (New York: Viking, 1999), 11–12.

4. Jean Delumeau, *Sin and Fear*, trans. Eric Nicholson (New York: St. Martin's Press, 1990), 104.

5. Richard S. Dunn, *The Age of Religious Wars, 1559–1689* (New York: W. W. Norton, 1970). Cf. Henry Kamen, *The Rise of Toleration* (New York: McGraw-Hill, 1967).

6. Delumeau, *Sin and Fear*, 105.

7. See Andrew Cunningham and Ole Peter Grell, *The Four Horsemen of the Apocalypse: Religion, War, Famine, and Death in Reformation Europe* (Cambridge, UK: Cambridge University Press, 2001); and John Aberth, *From the Brink of the Apocalypse: Confronting Famine, War, Plague, and Death in the Later Middle Ages* (London: Routledge, 2001).

8. On the enigmatic Philip, see Henry Kamen, *Philip of Spain* (New Haven, CT: Yale University Press, 1997); and Geoffrey Parker, *The Grand Strategy of Philip II* (New Haven, CT: Yale University Press, 1998).

9. Robin Bruce Barnes, *Prophecy and Gnosis: Apocalypticism in the Wake of the Lutheran Reformation* (Stanford, CA: Stanford University Press, 1988), 249–260.

10. Christopher Hibbert, *Cavaliers and Roundheads: The English Civil War, 1642–1649* (London: Harper Collins, 1993).

11. Christopher Hill, "Agitators and Officers," chap. 4 in *The World Turned Upside Down: Radical Ideas during the English Revolution* (New York: Viking Press, 1972).

12. Christopher Hill, "The Man of Blood," chap. 15 in *The English Bible and the Seventeenth-Century Revolution* (New York: Penguin, 1993).

13. On the multiplicity of motivations within Cromwell's army, see Ian Gentles, *The New Model Army in England, Ireland and Scotland, 1645–1653* (Oxford, UK: Blackwell, 1991).

14. Hill, *World Turned Upside Down*, 30.

15. Christopher Hill, *The Century of Revolution, 1603–1714* (Edinburgh: Thomas Nelson, 1961), 130.

16. Hill, *Century of Revolution*, 127.

17. Christopher Hill, *The Experience of Defeat: Milton and Some Contemporaries* (New York: Penguin, 1984), 197.

18. Clarke Garrett, *Spirit Possession and Popular Religion: From the Camisards to the Shakers* (Baltimore: Johns Hopkins University Press, 1987), 30–41.

19. David S. Lovejoy, *Religious Enthusiasm in the New World: Heresy to Revolution* (Cambridge, MA: Harvard University Press, 1985); Stephen A. Marini, *Radical Sects of Revolutionary New England* (Harvard, MA: Harvard University Press, 1982).

20. On the religion of British regulars, see Michael Snape, *The Redcoat and Religion: The Forgotten History of the British Soldier from the Age of Marlborough to the Eve of the First World War* (New York: Routledge, 2005).

21. See J.C.D. Clark, *The Language of Liberty, 1660–1832: Political Discourse and Social Dynamics in the Anglo-American World* (Cambridge, UK: Cambridge University Press, 1994). Also insightful are Forrest McDonald, *Novus Ordo Seclorum: The Intellectual Origins of the Constitution* (Lawrence: University Press of Kansas, 1985); and Gordon S. Wood, *The Radicalism of the American Revolution* (New York: Vintage Books, 1991).

22. Richly illustrated on the front- and endpapers of John R. Hale's *Artists and Warfare in the Renaissance* (New Haven, CT: Yale University Press, 1990).

23. On mercenaries, see in particular Michael E. Mallett, *Mercenaries and Their Masters: Warfare in Renaissance Italy* (London: Bodley Head, 1974).

24. Niccolò Machiavelli, *The Art of War* (New York: Bobbs-Merrill, 1965), 16 (original published 1521). See also John R. Hale, *War and Society in Renaissance Europe, 1450–1620* (Baltimore: Johns Hopkins University Press, 1985).

25. See the classic study by Samuel P. Huntington, *The Soldier and the State: The Theory and Politics of Civil-Military Relations* (New York: Random House, 1957), chap. 2, as well as Hale, *War and Society*, chap. 5, and André Corvisier, "The State and the Army," part II of *Armies and Societies in Europe, 1494–1789* (Bloomington: Indiana University Press, 1979).

26. See the suggestive comments of John Keegan, "Why Do Men Fight," in *A History of Warfare* (New York: Alfred A. Knopf, 1994), 79–94. Suggestive too is Barbara Ehrenreich, "A Rough Male Sport," chap. 7 in *Blood Rites: Origins and History of the Passions of War* (New York: Henry Holt, 1997).

27. G. M. Trevelyan, *English Social History: A Survey of Six Centuries, Chaucer to Queen Victoria* (Harmondsworth, UK: Penguin, 1967), 514.

28. See Armstrong Starkey, "Field of Honor: Fontenoy, 1745," chap. 4 in *War in the Age of Enlightenment, 1700–1789* (Westport, CT: Praeger, 2003).

29. Marcel Reinhard, "Nostalgie et service militaire pendant la Révolution," *Annales historiques de la Révolution française* 30 (1958): 1–15. See also Gervase Phillips, "To Cry 'Home! Home!': Mutiny, Morale, and Indiscipline in Tudor Armies," *Journal of Military History* 65 (2001): 313–332.

30. At Minden the British infantry first withstood and defeated a French cavalry charge (taking nearly thirty percent casualties), then turned and charged the French infantry with the bayonet.

31. William Wheeler, *The Letters of Private Wheeler, 1809–1828*, ed. with a foreword by B. H. Liddell Hart (Gloucestershire, UK: Windrush Press, 1998), 21, 28. Original spelling retained.

32. On pioneers and the skill-based nature of military service, see Erik A. Lund, *War for the Every Day: Generals, Knowledge, and Warfare in Early Modern Europe, 1680–1740* (Westport, CT: Greenwood Press, 1999), 10–12, 88–90 passim.

33. Paul E. Kopperman, "'The Cheapest Pay': Alcohol Abuse in the Eighteenth-Century British Army," *Journal of Military History* 60 (1996): 445–470.

Six

✴ ✴ ✴

STRUCTURE AND ROUTINES

So fall in lads behind the drum
With colors blazing like the sun
Along the road to come what may
Over the hills and far away.[1]

EARLY DAYS FOR THE SOLDIER

Once the token coin was accepted, the bounty paid, and the toasts drunk, the new-fledged recruit found himself in a different world—not entirely an alien one, at least to peasants and workmen, but certainly one with its own rules, written and unwritten, and its own household deities, rational and otherwise. It even offered opportunities for do-overs. For example, a recruit to the *Landsknechte*, the formidable south German mercenary pikemen of the fifteenth century, usually enlisted for a period of six months or less. Once attested, he was on his own until the time fixed for mustering, when the regiment assembled for the first time. The recruits fell in more or less, depending on the number of old soldiers, with the company they had joined. Then the mustering officer appeared, along with the regiment's clerk and legal officers. Each recruit, when his name was called, passed before the colonel and the officers and through a gate in front of the mustering officer, who described his equipment and the pay scale accompanying it as the clerk noted the information. Then the recruit moved to the paymaster's station and received the first recompense for his service.

This elaborate public and ritualistic process was designed in part to avert corruption: recruits, sometimes with the connivance of their officers, passing through twice to inflate the rolls and thus the pay or borrowing armor and weapons from each other and claiming higher pay for better equipment. But it was also a public occasion: probably the first such occasion since his christening at which the recruit was, however briefly, the center of attention. As much to the point, should he have failed to appear, nothing was likely to happen to him—except remaining in the life he was living. Whatever came afterward, the new *Landsknecht* had committed himself to service in arms as a self-respecting man.

Promoting Collegiality

The second step in the soldier's transformation was collective and collegial. The regiment would assemble in a circle around its colonel to hear read the "articles of war" under which it served. The circle was not merely a concession to an as yet underdeveloped ability to form ranks. It was also a conscious throwback to an earlier time when war bands enjoyed the self-image of "Free Companions" voluntarily deciding their own laws. The *Landsknecht* articles were a good deal more rigid. They listed the senior officers and described the requirements for being paid. They spelled out behavior in the field and in camp. A man who fled in battle should be immediately struck down by his comrades. Looting in any form from an enemy was forbidden, except by direct order; anything taken in friendly territory should be paid for. "Civilians," women and children, the elderly, priests, churches, and convents were to be protected. Delay of pay for any reason did not release the soldier from his service—recognition of a post–Black Death pattern among urban unskilled laborers of "cash as agreed upon or no work today." The always-delicate subject of pay was the major reason no unit meetings could be held without the colonel's permission.

Discipline and Morality

When it came to discipline in the ranks, anyone who saw a fight but failed to try to stop it was himself considered guilty of fighting. On the other hand, anyone who flattened a troublemaker after warning him would not be punished. Regimental authority attempted to keep in check the most common causes of fighting: gambling and drinking. As a further incentive to moral behavior, recruits were encouraged to avoid swearing and to attend church regularly. Having heard the articles of war, the regiment then took a collective oath to observe them.

Whenever possible, armies sought to recruit subjects of the realm. Sixteenth-century Spain, for example, drew the bulk of its non-Spanish recruits from Habsburg lands elsewhere in Europe. Next best was to make subjects of soldiers, at least for their term of service. In both cases the oath was an important part of the process of providing more than a straight cash connection among the man, his unit, and the government employing him. It was a statement of personal honor. A common man's version of the oath of fealty taken by medieval noblemen, once sworn, it was not lightly broken. Not until the Thirty Years War did soldiers change allegiances as casually—and at times more frequently—than their shirts, becoming only swords for hire whose words could prove as empty as their purses.[2]

The pattern described was roughly standard for units recruited at the beginning of the early modern period. It varied, depending on the place and type of unit recruited.

The practice in Scottish units was more strongly religious, usually featuring pious exhortations culminating in a sermon. Mounted units devoted more attention to such matters as condition of horses and responsibility for their replacement. Artillery trains were more likely than the other combat arms to have their essential cadres in place. Good gunners were as valuable in the sixteenth century as trained missile technicians are in the twenty-first. States were correspondingly likely to keep on retainer as many as could be afforded: Of the 340 artillerymen in French service in 1566, 211 were listed as "cannoneers."[3] Artillery matériel, difficult to secure on an ad hoc basis, was kept in storage in central locations. What remained to be done involved filling out the ranks with recruits considered more as laborers than real soldiers, much less true artillerymen. On the whole, however, the rituals and their purposes remained consistent. They tended indeed to become increasingly homogenized as recruitment cast nets outside a particular region. Soldiers appreciated familiarity.

MOVING INTO WAR, PHYSICALLY AND PSYCHOLOGICALLY

The next step in a new soldier's career involved getting him from his place of enlistment to the theater of war. Initially this was a fairly simple process: a few days' march through reasonably familiar territory. The English and Scottish armies that met at Flodden, Solway Moss, and Pinkie were virtually next-door neighbors, each drawing the bulk of its men from their respective frontier zones.[4] But as states grew larger and expanded into empires, the story became a different one. The standing armies that developed during the sixteenth century, relatively small in any case, were, for logistic and administrative reasons, widely and thinly distributed. Their men as well often lived and worked away from the garrisons. Returning absentees to the colors and filling out ranks were, however, only first steps in taking the field. Bringing together newly organized native regiments and the foreign contingents necessary to create viable war-strength field forces would have daunted the organizing skills of the vaunted nineteenth-century German General Staff.[5]

A big part of the challenge was logistical. Feeding soldiers on the march was literally the least of the problems accompanying concentration. Europe's road network was not only thin; most of it was unsuited to the kind of use imposed by the passage of even relatively small bodies of troops. Surfaces, once damaged, rapidly collapsed, turning the roadbeds into a sea of rock fragments embedded in either dust or mud, depending on the season and the weather, and setting march schedules at defiance. The diplomatic and financial considerations involved in recruiting foreign troops made their arrivals even less predictable. More than administrative factors were involved. Even with good will on all sides, the technical problems of moving a large body of men unaccustomed to moving together is arguably war's most demanding task, except for combat itself. Though the exact origins of cadenced marching—or marching in step—remain debatable, one of its taproots was arguably the introduction of marching in ranks at what would later be called "route step." This was as much a matter of comfort for the men as discipline for the officers. It seldom took more than a few days moving in "column of flocks" to convince new soldiers that organized movement was less tiring in the long run.[6]

Physical Condition of the Soldiers

Fatigue was generally an important problem for early modern armies. By twentieth-century standards, most males were not particularly robust. Limited diets and rudimentary health care produced men who could work steadily enough, but at a pace that would be considered slow today. Diet was more of a complex consideration than is generally understood. The image of early modern Europeans as able to live on coarse fare must be tempered by the effect of such food on digestive systems. Here, again, surface robustness was accompanied by subterranean frailty. Even unaccustomed food could occasion devastating outbreaks of digestive ailments—to say nothing of the impact of unfamiliar water on stomachs accustomed only to local bacteria. Immunities were also highly localized. As late as the American Civil War (1861–1865), what today are considered childhood diseases like mumps and measles devastated regiments recruited from the relatively isolated environment of farms and small towns. With most of its baggage carried in carts and wagons, a seasoned regiment could be pushed too hard for too long. A green regiment on the march, even one that took extreme care, could expect to have increasing numbers to carry—and more than a few to bury.[7]

Psychological Condition of the Soldiers

Early modern armies faced a more insidious medical problem as well, variously called *mal du pays*, homesickness, or nostalgia. Sometimes described as resembling clinical depression, it is better understood as a dissociative reaction to finding oneself completely isolated or removed from an entire environment supportive and reassuring by its familiarity. More common in recruits, it developed in old soldiers as well. The sufferer protected himself by withdrawing: shutting down emotionally. Heavy drinking was perhaps the most common initial coping mechanism. As alcohol's deadening effect diminished over time, physical symptoms emerged, such as loss of short-term memory, impaired speech, and sleep disturbances. That the condition long went unremarked reflects in part the lack of interest shown by officers in the emotional lives of their rank and file. Until the late Enlightenment, the common soldier was expected to be an uncommunicative drunk. The relative invisibility of *mal du pays* reflected as well the large amount of off-duty time in most armies until the development of barracks and their accompanying structure of routine controls made it easier to notice quietly deviant behavior. A soldier unable, or simply not caring, to respond to an order or otherwise to account for himself quickly found himself in a web of difficulty his predecessors had been better placed to avoid—but he was also living in an age that encouraged seeking remedies other than condign punishment.

The disorder's roots seem closely connected to the long-term separations increasingly characteristic of military service since the sixteenth century. In the Revolutionary, Napoleonic, and American Civil wars, it persisted despite exponentially higher levels of literacy that facilitated regular contact with home and loved ones. The real problem of *mal du pays*, however, was its indirect consequences. Victims were disproportionately susceptible to negatives. Minor illnesses and slight wounds could become disabling, even mortal. Hunger and fatigue could collapse bodily functions, with men dying of heart failure without any previous symptoms. While impossible to calculate exactly, *mal du pays* certainly increased the death rates in early modern armies. And at the outer limits of speculation, perhaps it increased as well the indiscipline characteristic of the period's early years. Certainly a plethora of contemporary literature urged taking all possible measures to keep soldiers from lapsing into sullenness and inanition.[8]

"Seasoning" Soldiers

One way of addressing the problem of *mal du pays* was to "season" soldiers in the way ships' timbers were seasoned. Spain was the most systematic and the most successful at this, taking advantage of its far-flung empire to send recruits from Spain to the Italian provinces of Lombardy, Sicily, and Naples. Italian service was always popular, having some of the reputation that service in Indochina had for the French Foreign Legion until 1945: mild climate, strong wine, and available women. From there, task forces could be sent to less attractive theaters like the Low Countries.

Only Spain had the geography and the wealth to implement seasoning in full. Whenever possible, early modern generals sought to achieve similar results. Most, however, had to accomplish that task on the march. Here as well Spain established the parameters. Its major theaters of operation were separated on land by hundreds of miles and some of western Europe's most difficult terrain. Dispatching troops by sea, especially to the Low Countries, became an unacceptably high risk as relations with France and England worsened. As its second choice, Spain established, by conquest and negotiation, a land route from northern Italy to the Low Countries.

This so-called Spanish Road was an early version of the Ho Chi Minh trail (associated with the Vietnam Conflict from 1964 to 1975), consisting of a number of parallel routes. Keeping it going generated a comprehensive set of records describing how long-distance troop movements were organized and supported under optimal conditions in early modern Europe. Each route was systematically mapped to show the tracks available, the fords and bridges (the latter being relatively easy to install and maintain), and the nearby population centers. Whenever possible, Spain avoided requisitioning supplies on the spot as expensive, wasteful, and bad for discipline. The preferred alternative was a chain of permanent supply centers, restocked from local sources. In the middle was the *etape*, a place where merchants delivered supplies for bulk sale. Lodging was compensated by certificates that could be used to fulfill tax liabilities.[9]

This system hardly prevented looting, as shown by the common response of regional authorities when apprised of an approaching column: the issuance of warnings to communities to break out their weapons and display armed men prominently. Nor did the Spanish Road secure every trooper food and lodging at the end of every march. What the Spanish Road and any other well-organized march did was to contribute to a culture of competence: the sense that the individual soldier was part of a system that understood its business enough of the time to make tolerance an appropriate response when things did not work as they should.

CAMP LIFE

At the end of its march the regiment set up camp. That could be a network of billets or an open-air enterprise, built—albeit without the walls—more or less along lines developed as far back as the Roman Empire, by the soldiers themselves or, more commonly, by whatever labor force traveled with the regiment or could be contracted and compelled from the local population. In both friendly and hostile territory, prudent commanders sought to make general arrangements with the business community regarding the amount and nature of provisions to be made available for sale. Making the men responsible for buying their own supplies worked far better when the supplies were on hand in bulk than when they sought their meals on their own accounts.

Keeping Order[10]

The provost-marshal was by far the most influential officer the soldier encountered on a daily basis. He and his assistants were responsible for maintaining collective order and regulating individual behavior. That in turn involved keeping in touch with the men's attitudes. Like his successors to the present day, a good provost-marshal understood what to see and when to see it, when to crack down and when to turn a blind eye. One could scarcely speak of routine formal discipline in a *Landsknecht* regiment, for example. Control beyond the necessary minimum to sustain order was considered risky and even counterproductive, in part because physical aggression and violence were exactly the qualities that generals sought in their soldiers. *Landsknechte* and their comrades were free men—spirited men in the sense of Plato's Guardians—who fought because they chose to. They were not pawns to be ordered here and there at the whim of higher powers.

Uniforms were correspondingly beyond the pale. Even drab clothing was considered to put the warrior spirit at risk; soldiers' finery was, for example, specifically exempted from the strict sumptuary laws, which had been enacted to control extravagance of dress in seventeenth-century Spain. Sleeves puffed and slashed, hose with legs striped in rainbow colors, floppy hats with plumes and feathers, codpieces so large that they could store a purse, the whole made of the richest cloth the wearer could afford and incorporating as many fabrics and colors as ingenuity might contrive—that was a *Landsknecht* in full regalia.

Landsknecht cleaning a musket. © Foto Marburg/Art Resource, New York.

The Camp Market

The provost-marshal's chief domain was the camp market. Early modern armies attracted followers naturally and inevitably. Even the wealthiest and best-administered states were barely able to provide essentials, and those no more than part of the time. The rest was a matter of free enterprise. Soldiers with money in their pockets or loot in their packs were good business prospects. Not every supplier was a victim of war on the model of Bertold Brecht's Mother Courage, who follows the armies because she has no alternative and winds up pulling her cart herself. Particularly in the first half of this period, vendors offered everything from jewelry to decorated cartridge boxes to exotic pets. Markets were usually located on the outskirts of camp. Goods, services, and pleasures of all kinds could be had at prices set by the provost-marshal. Liquor, gambling, and women were also available, how openly depending on the regiment's articles of war, the colonel's disposition, and the uprightness of the provost, who collected a percentage of every transaction conducted. Since the regiment was constantly on the move, it was correspondingly in his long-term interest to look after the men, seeing that the wares offered were reasonably priced, the whores reasonably accommodating, and the dice reasonably honest, even when he might be financially encouraged to turn a blind eye.

Camp Followers and Soldier Support

An early modern regiment's train of camp followers did far more than participate in the camp market. Soldiers at the beginning of that period tended to keep their property portable. Veterans and senior soldiers like the so-called double-pay men of the *Landsknechte* might take the field with tents, beds, wall hangings, and cooking gear, enabling them to match the domestic comfort of the most prosperous villagers. All of that required observation and supervision. Even the less affluent soldier needed as well a personal support system—at the minimum, someone to prepare his food, maintain his clothes and gear, and provide basic care should he be wounded or fall sick. His regiment provided none of these essential services. It is a reasonable assumption that the average seventeenth-century male did not know how to cook or sew competently. Among peasants and town laborers alike, domestic roles were sharply divided—less from patriarchal sexism than because they were sufficiently demanding that no one could perform all of them well. Besides, two in a cloak were warmer than one, on those rainy nights when the *etape* failed and there were no villages close to hand.

WOMEN AND CHILDREN WITH THE REGIMENT

At the top of the train's unofficial female hierarchy stood the wives of the senior men. Though precise distinctions between officers and what are now called senior warrant officers may not have existed at staff levels, the women seem to have established their own, often reflecting civilian social status. A captain's wife was likely to be from the lesser aristocracy, and a warrant officer's spouse may have begun much lower down in the hierarchy. On the other hand, a woman who lost her husband faced a sufficiently daunting trek back to a home to which she may not have wanted to return that remarrying slightly downward to remain with the regiment was often preferable. The ladies, in short, mostly got along, despite their social differences.

Many camp women had been whores, and might well be again if Fortune was un-kind. The difference in role was often a matter of being asked by a man or wanting one enough to accept or encourage an offer. By comparison with camp followers of later centuries, a woman seems to have lost relatively little status by periodically earning her living commercially, as long as she met the criteria of comradeship: even-tempered in hard times, generous when purse and kettle were full, and above all, able to produce food and liquor under any circumstances. The old soldiers' axiom that "whores make the best wives" neither originated nor ended in the armies of early modern Europe but was certainly illustrated in their tents and billets.

Most companies also had a few unattached women who "did for" unpartnered men. These soldiers usually formed informal bonding groups, whose Spanish name of *cama-rada* best describes their nature. They lived together, looked out for each other in brawl or battle, shared whatever plunder came their way, and often became each others' heirs. Many such groups preferred to negotiate with a woman or two to cook and clean, with individuals seeking their sexual outlets elsewhere. For the women this collective house-keeping was usually a step toward the next level of camp precedence: as wives, both unofficial and legal.

Particularly in the sixteenth century, a fair number of women were officially married. It was a more pious time, and the exigencies of a soldier's life meant the bonds were unlikely to endure long enough to become restraints. The most common pairings, how-ever, were common law, sustained by mutual consent. Most of the wives seem to have been reasonably faithful, if for no better reason than the fact that even brief encoun-ters were difficult to arrange discreetly in the highly public environment of camp and march. In a community where honor was enforced with steel, getting caught too often meant one man dead, another sentenced to execution, and the woman thrown out of the regiment with no more than the clothes on her back.

To outsiders, military camps seemed overrun with children of all ages. Most of them were cared for in what might be called blended families: the couple's biological children, those from previous relationships, and three or four orphan or abandoned children as well. That could pose problems for a new widow seeking a replacement husband, but soldiers seemed on the whole to have been decent enough about extending protection to fairly large broods—though waifs were expected to "bring their own bread" some-how, as opposed to depending on their quasi-stepfather.

That was easier than might have been expected. A regiment's women and its half-grown children had more than domestic duties to perform. Among other things, they cleaned latrines and they groomed animals. Boys—sometimes men as well—acted as servants to officers. There was always work in an artillery park for "sons of guns"—boys fathered by artillerymen and therefore under the gunners' protection—who might themselves someday learn the craft. Sixteenth-century armies knew the value of entrenchment, but that did not mean that the soldiers were willing to do the construction work themselves. Escaping such labor was one of the reasons they became soldiers in the first place. So digging became women's work, and boys' and girls' work as well, until they were old enough to take a place in the regiment or to go off on their own.

Women were far less likely than men to follow the drum by choice. At the same time it is an error to assume as typical the conditions in the worst years in the most devastated locations of the Thirty Years War, where becoming soldiers' chattel was the alternative to—or aftermath of—repeated gang rape, and where being even the leavings of a regiment was the alternative to eventual starvation.

Some women did confront just such circumstances. Others, however, were on the margins of their home communities for illegitimate pregnancy; ideas inappropriate to their gender, such as rejecting their parents' choice of a husband; or simple poverty. Still others fell victim to the kind of sweet talk that has led maids to follow men since the dawn of time.[11]

An early modern regiment should not be confused with a traveling brothel. In the *Landsknechte*, for example, the train was under the charge of a *Hurenweibel*. The common translation of this word as "whores' sergeant" is misleading. The *Hurenweibel's* rank approximated that of a modern warrant officer, and his responsibilities strongly resembled those of a quartermaster in a British regiment circa World War I. He was responsible not only for keeping order, but for maneuvering the train, keeping it out of the regiment's way, and keeping it safe, even in the face of the enemy: a focal point in victory or defeat. Like his British successor, the *Hurenweibel* was usually a canny veteran chosen for his ability to get things done without fuss. He was paid appropriately— about as much as a captain-proprietor of a company.

Critics may suggest that the text has painted an excessively rosy picture of women's lot, and certainly the surviving records contain accounts of every conceivable abuse. Those same records suggest, however, that the ordinary soldier under ordinary circumstances was neither a sadist nor a brute. Kept fed and loved—after a fashion—he was reasonably content. He was constrained, moreover, by the provost's men and the *rumormeisters* of the *Hurenweibel*, who patrolled the camp to keep the women and children in order but who could also intervene in a domestic dispute that was getting out of hand. Most women found their lot hard, but those who made the best of it rather than the worst also found compensations in enlarged horizons and expanded choices; protection under established law rather than custom that favored the powerful; and not least, freedom from the boredom of routine that had led them to consider a fundamental life change in the first place.

MEDICINE, SEXUAL DISEASES, AND SANITATION

Once the camp was a going concern, the security officer arranged for guarding the perimeter and the baggage train, the latter usually given its own area for hygienic and aesthetic reasons. The doctors opened for business, with company medics dealing with blisters, toothaches, stomach distress, and other routine sicknesses as well as checking the state of healing wounds if the regiment had been in action. More serious matters were referred to the regimental surgeon, who, if ignorant of germ theories of infection, was usually an artist in treating battle traumas and equivalent nonbattle injuries. Surgeons developed sophisticated means of removing bullets and fragments. Even before the introduction of explosive shells, iron cannonballs generated deadly splinters when they hit stone or wood. Black powder wounds also mangled limbs so badly that soldiers were increasingly ready to take the one big risk of amputation rather than face the alternatives for the sake of retaining an arm or leg rendered grotesquely useless.

Army surgeons responded in the familiar spirit of "nothing venture, nothing have" by developing instruments and techniques for removing mangled limbs quickly, before the patient died of shock, and completely, so that there was at least a chance of avoiding gangrene. The procedure was not gentle. Alcohol was the usual anesthetic, when it was used. A good few surgeons believed a man kept conscious through the surgery, or most of it, had a better chance of surviving than someone whose vitality was diminished by intoxication. Cauterization with hot oil or metal was the usual means of closing the wound, with most sufferers lapsing into unconsciousness at that point. But the variety of artificial limbs, some crudely jointed, appearing on the market indicated that amputation was both common and ameliorative, with evidence that the procedure left survivors whose traumas did not exclude concern for their personal appearance.[12]

Some healers stand out. Ambroise Paré was a sixteenth-century barber surgeon, self-taught (with the more or less willing participation of his patients) and willing to learn from experience. On one occasion, when he ran out of the oil used for cauterizing bullet wounds, he noticed that the men left untreated suffered less pain, inflammation, and infection than those treated conventionally. He learned from peasant women that burns cause by gunpowder were best treated leaving them open and lightly dressed. For amputations Paré reintroduced the Roman practice of ligature, tying off individual veins and arteries, as opposed to cauterization.[13]

There was only one Paré, but he was often imitated. Armies also developed collective treatment of disease and injury. Hospitals had been understood as places where one went to die. Army hospitals had a motive to cure: It was cheaper than recruiting a replacement. The Spanish Army of Flanders opened a permanent hospital in 1585, with a capacity of over 300 patients, and achieved good results curing wounds, disease, and even emotional trauma—the last, apparently, by appealing to religious faith.[14] Seventeenth-century France developed a network of large stationary hospitals at least as good as their civilian counterparts. Where surgeons' appointments were considered venal offices, however (i.e., offices for sale), it was unlikely that overall care of the sick and wounded soldiers would improve exponentially.[15]

Army surgeons were responsible for another health issue as well. It remains disputed whether syphilis originated in Europe, crossing the Mediterranean from Africa, or whether it was brought back from North America as Montezuma's real revenge. It is generally agreed, however, that its first major outbreak was diagnosed in the camp of a French army besieging Naples in 1494. From there it spread across Europe like wildfire, with armies playing a major role in its transmission.

The sexual promiscuity associated with early modern warmaking was only one element in that process. The virulence of the early forms of syphilis owed something to the favorable opportunities for mutation generated by the tight-fitting, hugely padded hose fashionable among soldiers. In its early years, syphilis was correspondingly more susceptible of transmission by nongenital contact: kissing, for example, at the time common behavior among battle comrades, or sharing a drinking cup in a subculture where refusing to do so could cause a death duel.

The disease proved far easier to diagnose than to treat, though its direct lethality has been exaggerated. Army doctors helped pioneer the use of mercury (poisonous in large quantities) and extended the already familiar concept of quarantine for fever to syphilis cases. What success there was, however, reflected more the development of a survivor's immunity—genetically susceptible lines died out—combined with lifestyle modifications. If the eighteenth-century grenadier was not as spectacular a roisterer as his sixteenth-century predecessor, prudence may have played a role as well as discipline.[16]

The surgeon and his staff were also responsible for collective sanitation, which was better than frequently described by external observers. It took only a little experience of the consequences of neglect for the men to enforce latrine discipline themselves, often with vigorous methods that could include throwing a persistent offender into a latrine pit and leaving him to find his own way out. Personal hygiene was another matter, best left to an imagination that is unlikely to exaggerate if working from a contemporary mind-set. Suffice it to say that there was a reason *Landsknechte*, mercenaries, and grenadiers spent a good deal of their discretionary income on scents and pomades.

REWARDS OF THE JOB

Pay and the Soldier

Any romantic illusions held by soldiers or their women were likely to be dispelled quickly and permanently by the most constant element of an early modern soldier's life: pay, or better expressed, the lack of pay. No state, not even Spain when it commanded the wealth of the New World, was able to keep to anything resembling the agreed-on pay schedules. Arrears ran for months, sometimes years. A German regiment in Spanish service received full pay when enlisted in 1572 but waited seven years for the next payday.[17] That may well have been a record, but in 1647, a major French army was six months in arrears, and in 1706, another French commander reported his fear that lack of pay would "tear his army apart."[18]

When even part of the sums owed were paid in cash, the troops were likely to squander it in compensation for previous months of deprivation. Even the most sober planners for the future, if such were to be found in the ranks, were confounded by two other problems. The expanding time frame and declining scale of wars led to the long-term distribution of troops in stable garrisons, thus creating a stable matrix for supplies. No longer could a regiment hope to be transferred to "somewhere else," the proverbial virgin territory where the wine was strong, the bread cheap, and the merchants gullible. Europe in general, moreover, and particularly its economically developed areas, experienced a general rise in prices during the sixteenth and seventeenth centuries. One might better speak of a price explosion. Food prices in the Netherlands, for example, increased by 400 percent in a century when the base pay of the ordinary infantryman, the backbone of the Army of Flanders, was raised once, from three escudos a day to four.

Supplements, bonuses, and the escudo's eventually rising value helped bridge the gap but could not close it, any more than it could be closed for other armies in other places. The obvious immediate response was to seek credit; the obvious source of credit was the company commander. He was the most likely man in the regiment to have ready access to cash. He was also the leader of his men in battle, the embodiment of their collective valor. And in practice, whatever his nationality and service, opportunity turned him into both a loan shark and a spectacular manipulator of official financial records to his own advantage. One of the most common, and most profitable, involved putting false names on the roster and pocketing their wages. Should a muster be held, there was seldom a problem finding stand-ins for a day, ready enough to perform the service for a drink and a few cents.[19] The scam indeed helped define a word in the English language: A *faggot* in eighteenth-century slang was one of these false soldiers and therefore a make-believe man.

When cash was available, delivering it was often a problem. Letters of exchange and government promissory were heavily discounted by the local institutions that cashed them. Shipping hard money had its own risks, ranging from the weight of the specie, the money in coin, to the risk—at times, the probability—that a percentage of the coins would disappear en route.[20] The most obvious solution was for the state to provide the soldiers' material requirements directly, with pay expected to finance only small personal expenses. Spanish policies are indicative. Beginning toward the end of the seventeenth century, clothing, bread, arms, and shelter became the army's responsibility. Such fringe benefits as medical care and marriage allowances, even a service for managing wills, were furnished as well. By 1630, about half of the soldiers' wages were paid in kind, and the other half paid directly to the men, thereby putting an end to what amounted to a garnishee system, by which captains received the cash and settled back debts before paying out what remained.[21]

Economic Issues in the Early Modern Era

The erosion, then the breakdown, of payment and supply systems during the Thirty Years War has been analyzed so often, and from so many perspectives, that it is necessary to do no more than summarize the main factors involved. First, the armies tended to campaign in the same areas year after year, with correspondingly devastating effects on already vulnerable infrastructures. Second, all the combatants tended to raise forces larger than their systems could support, in the hope that this time, this campaigning season would bring decisive results. Third, the armies grew increasingly symmetric by mutual imitation, which meant that none could gain a significant superiority in effectiveness. Finally, the comprehensive spectrum of broken agreements and broken faith generated among the common soldiers an ethic of self-help that evolved into a sense of "to hell with the rest of you; we've got ours." This set soldiers against civilians, soldiers against other soldiers, and in extreme situations, even soldiers against the followers upon whom they depended, in what amounted to a Hobbesian situation of all against all. It was barely kept in check by what remained of the officers' authority, until a peace of exhaustion was finally arranged by the Peace of Westphalia in 1648.[22]

Religion and the Soldier

As suggested in Chapter Five, God as well as gold played a role in soldiers' lives. Particularly in the Reformation era, soldiers seemed to have been, to a considerable extent, believers as well. Their concepts of Christianity may have been muscular in the extreme but were no less internalized for that. French Huguenot Henri IV, the Protestant who converted to Catholicism in 1593 in order to win Paris and unify France, may have decided that Paris was worth a Mass, but his insouciance sat poorly with many of his rank and file.[23] The Spanish army's grim Catholicism was by no means the top-down product of pulpit exhortation.[24]

Religious impulses in many soldiers probably reflected Sunday morning repentance: fear of an eternal damnation chaplains described as in good part foreshadowed by activities central to a soldier's life. Among both Catholics and Protestants, a historic, pragmatic toleration for behavior considered natural to men and involving liquor, women, and brawling was being challenged by more conventionally pious—perhaps even feminine—patterns of observance, such as the cult of the Virgin Mary and the revival of the Rosary in Catholicism.[25] Killing the proverbial heretic for Christ was one way of rebalancing a spiritual account likely to be seriously in arrears.

Individual religiosity might also be enhanced by collective experience. The regiment was home to most early modern soldiers, even if they might change addresses through the military version of reformation, the disbanding or combining of units, or less formally by decamping and reenlisting. A good part of acceptance in any environment is adjustment to its particular mores. A free-living reprobate might correspondingly not only become a psalm singer or an amulet wearer but internalize the principles behind the practices, at least for a time.

The religious experience of soldiers could run deeper than the comfort of conformity or the fear of eternal damnation. Their medieval forebears had some sense, however attenuated it might have become, of serving a purpose greater than themselves. By the beginning of the early modern period the soldier had become a solipsist who found meaning in a lifestyle. But courage, honor, and comradeship had their limits as motivators. The religious revivals of the seventeenth century gave, if only for a while, a higher moral purpose to a calling that was becoming a craft. But if craft was all it was, what was the difference between dying a soldier and dying a blacksmith?[26]

THE CREATION OF STANDING ARMIES

The development of permanent standing armies is usually presented in the general context of an early modern military revolution, in which varying combinations of tactical and technological developments were best implemented by highly trained and well-disciplined soldiers organized in smaller, more flexible units. Specifically, standing armies are usually linked to a Dutch Republic condemned to a forever war with a richer and stronger Habsburg Spain, yet also concerned with fostering the Calvinist/bourgeois values of a genuine "calling" within an urban, market-based economy. Compared to its Scottish and French counterparts, Dutch Calvinism incorporated a visible thread of pacifism. Well before the Enlightenment, the Dutch mentality valued a rational approach to problem solving. Small wonder that the Dutch Republic's military and political leaders perceived early on the value of a disciplined army serving indefinitely under a reliable paymaster.[27]

Experience as well as reason played a role in the rise of standing armies. In the Low Countries a combination of broken terrain, the rapid introduction of modern fortifications, and the persistence of religious elements combined to increase the time frame and reduce the scale of warmaking. Long sieges were expansive as well as expensive, absorbing land as well as money. Large-scale field operations tended to bog down of their own weight—and sometimes literally as well, in the water wilderness that so de-fined the Netherlands. Spain's Army of Flanders, outnumbered and far from its pri-mary bases, responded in a way comparable to the French during the First Indochina War from 1945 to 1954. Where the French used their paratroopers and the Foreign Legion, the Spanish combined companies from different regiments into task forces of between 1,000 and 3,000 men. These "squadrons" of seasoned veterans were dispro-portionately effective in what Geoffrey Parker calls the "skirmish and surprise" fighting characteristic in the Netherlands in the later sixteenth century.[28] They correspondingly suggested the disproportionate worth of units formed in a common system, able to work together easily and smoothly.

Drill

In *The Face of Battle* John Keegan repeatedly raises the question why men fight when the common sense of self-preservation urges running. The conditions of early modern battle often made flight, or even passivity—simply remaining in position—a more dan-gerous action than aggression. *Homo sapiens* appears to have no genetic predisposition against killing a submitting fellow human—indeed, he seems quite capable of enjoying the process. For some, the ultimate purpose of an attack is not to kill the enemy face-to-face, but to compel him to run and then kill him—less costly and more satisfying. If casualties for an army that stood its ground could be murderously high, breaking in the face of an enemy might well prove annihilating, particularly at the end of a long and bitter day, when mercy was unlikely to be a common emotion. Discipline, in short, was a survival mechanism whose utility surpassed those offered by the obvious alternatives of flight or capitulation.

Underlying the question of discipline is a general characteristic of early modern so-ciety. It was more hierarchic than deferential. The kinds of grass-roots, small-group cooperation engendered by the factory system, compulsory schooling, and team sports was foreign to ordinary people even in the Age of Reason. Bowing to the landlord and the pastor was a given and understood. Taking orders from someone of one's own so-cial standing and close to one's own age because of a few lines of braid on his sleeve was a much more dubious proposition. The authority of the noncommissioned officers who supervised an army's daily routines, in other words, could not be taken for granted. It had to be sustained and reinforced at every turn, in ways even the most hardheaded rear-ranker could understand.[29]

Discipline had a broad meaning in the Dutch approach to war. Soldiers were required to dig as well as fight and received systematic instruction in using the spade. They were required to drill as well. The new organization was based on smaller companies, 120 men or so, with a greater number of officers to assist with control. They were designed to increase firepower through a movement called the countermarch: the front rank fir-ing, then retiring to the rear of a formation to reload and move up in turn to deliver a second volley, and so on.

The countermarch resembled the cavalry caracole, with its successive ranks of troop-ers firing their pistols, then wheeling away to reload and return, and it required more skill from the infantry than anything since the days of Rome. Ranks were more open, yet they had to be rigidly maintained for the countermarch so as not to disintegrate into a collection of individuals. Reloading had to become an automatic process. Yet at the same time the soldier had to develop the kind of courage that enabled him to break contact, however briefly, then rally and return to the firing line—not all at once, but a rank at a time. This was something different from the hot blood necessary to mount a musket-and-pike charge or to meet one head-on and reckon the losses when the fighting was over. It was correspondingly questioned, in Holland and elsewhere, if it could be inculcated, much less sustained, among the lowest classes of the common people.[30]

The Benefits of Drill

The success of the new structure owed a great deal to the soldiers' acceptance of drill. Twenty-first-century readers, accustomed to dismissing drill as a mindless hut-two-three-four process intended to break down individual consciousness, may find it unlikely that soldiers whose ancestors refused to soil their hands with digging would turn

out willingly, even enthusiastically, for a turn on the parade ground. Several factors were involved. One was pragmatism. The value of the innovations was clear enough that professionals quickly recognized their worth as survival mechanisms—particularly in holding men together in the new, more open ranks. From the beginning of his service, every early modern infantryman had one truth hammered into him from every quarter: The unskilled or unwilling soldier in a firing line directly endangered his comrades as well as himself. A musket out of alignment when firing by ranks could mean a burst eardrum for the man in front of it. One man who flinched or ran could be the first step in the destruction of an entire battalion by a cavalry charge. Any recruit who did not understand drill's practical importance was likely to become the subject of direct and uncomfortable enlightenment by the old soldiers of his company.

A second factor in drill's popularity was its role as a social bond. Anthropologists debate the extent to which common movement of large muscle groups arouses echoes of primitive hunting groups. Drill was also likely to be the first systematic example of play—in the sense of an activity undertaken without immediate purpose—that many seventeenth-century men had experienced

Pike drill from *The Principles of the Art Military* by Henry Hexham. © HIP/Art Resource, New York.

in their lives. Especially when executed to music, as was increasingly the case, drill performed many of the same functions as dance, in the complex, highly structured forms of the period, did in the ballrooms and courts of early modern Europe.[31]

Drill was also a source of status. The private soldier who mastered the arcana of military movements and military bearing tended to take pride in the accomplishment. His chances for tangible signs of approval, such as promotion to corporal, depended heavily on his ability to meet the standards of his community—standards, it may be noted, no more artificial than their civilian counterparts and a good deal more survival-enhancing.

Finally, drill was an alternative to the boredom accompanying service in a standing army during peacetime. Initially, the soldier of early modern Europe had been consistently on the move. Even if in one place for months, there was always the promise of change tomorrow, the promise that brought so many men into the ranks and the promise expressed in such soldiers' songs as "Over the Hills and Far Away." Now the peacetime soldier found himself increasingly "cribb'd, cabined, and confined" to the narrow limits of a garrison town. Boredom and anomie contributed at least as much as brutal treatment in the ranks to desertion rates in the new standing armies. The sutlers, the entertainers, and the women were long gone or usually well out of range of an enlisted man's newly adjusted pay. Where during war he had been at the top of the camp life's pecking order, the soldier now found himself a marginal figure in communities that considered him dangerous and alien. Drill offered some compensations—at least it had a narcotic effect.

TRAINING, PUNISHMENT, AND AT EASE

Training Methods

Training methods evolved in specific ways along lines particular to armies in the century after 1648. Their general forms, however, remained essentially similar. Prussia, whose army proved master of so many stricken fields in the eighteenth century, is a useful focal point. Like all of its contemporaries, the Prussian army received relatively few recruits at any one time. Its system was correspondingly based on a degree of individual instruction impossible to the mass armies of a later generation, with their large intakes and small cadres. A common practice was to pair a raw recruit with a reliable old soldier, who, for a share of whatever the recruit might possess or receive from home, provided basic instruction in dress, grooming, and behavior. The details of drill and uniform were left to the noncommissioned officers, but even they were instructed to deal patiently, if not always gently, with recruits who showed good will. It represents no whitewash of Prussian discipline to note that many of the more vivid horror stories of abusive treatment were reported either by officers advocating a discipline based on mutual honor and mutual respect or by men whose experiences in Prussian service were unhappy or unfortunate. Most men who were tractable and learned quickly enough did not find life in the ranks unduly harsh.

Correction and Punishment

In Prussia and throughout Europe, the instruction and correction of young men was likely to be accompanied by a blow or a slap to drive home the point. It was part of the system, no more to be resented than the laps and push-ups ordered by high school coaches in a later century; it was rather, indeed, something to be endured as part of the process of being accepted as a man. In any army a disproportionate amount of the serious punishment fell to a disproportionately small number: the dull-witted and the loud-mouthed, the sullen, the vicious, and those unfortunate enough to be made scapegoats by their superiors or their fellow soldiers. Sober and well-conducted men often tended to accept the need for strong sanctions against the others, whose behavior could do much to make regimental life far worse than it needed to be. Collective punishment, moreover, was not a usual feature of eighteenth-century armies in peacetime—a fact serving to reduce sympathy for men whose fate was understood as a consequence of their own derelictions.[32]

Desertion

Desertion was the principal military crime. It tended to be less a social or political statement than a means of changing employment in a system where contracts were decidedly one-sided. From the state's perspective, desertion's costs were financial, involving the expenses of obtaining a replacement and outlays for clothing or equipment that might have disappeared with the runaway. Trained soldiers were scarce and therefore valuable as commodities. Such sanctions as setting men to watch each other, paying generous bounties for a fugitive's capture, and Draconian punishments on return were intended as deterrents as well as penalties.

Deserters were less likely than might be expected to simply disappear into the civilian population. The deserter might well spend some time on the road or as a casual laborer. But when jobs grew scarce or the weather bad, he was likely to find himself in uniform again, probably under a different flag, but even in his original service. That process seldom involved more planning than choosing a garrison and a regiment reasonably distanced from one's original, plus offering a new nom de guerre. Officers and sergeants were seldom interested in a volunteer's past, even if the volunteer seemed surprisingly familiar with drill movements.[33]

The Soldier's Life at Ease

Nor was a soldier's life one of unrelieved misery in an alien environment. After his initial training, the Prussian recruit spent as much as ten months of every year at home on furlough. With the regiment, a good part of his time was spent in civilian billets, outside the immediate supervision of his officers and sergeants, with corresponding opportunities to cultivate contacts and relationships that ranged from the romantic to the criminal. Soldiers off duty, cantonists or mercenaries, were left to their own devices to a degree inconceivable in British or American armed forces until recent years. They could dress much as they pleased, seek part-time employment—a practice encouraged by the army—or pursue the arts of idleness. A good many of the often-cited problems of complying with the regulations governing one's uniform and personal appearance on duty seem to have been consequences of previous, avoidable sins of omission and commission regarding uniform, kit, and grooming.

Many of the apparently petty regulations instituted in the Prussian army and its counterparts reflected the need, learned at great cost in previous centuries, to maintain high levels of cleanliness and sanitation among men whose civilian experiences had done little to encourage either quality. Washing and sewing were women's work. Disease could spread like wildfire among men who had to be taught such rudiments as the use of latrines—not always customary among country boys accustomed to seeking a convenient tree.[34]

The Prussian army's culture of competence also fostered morale. Even under modern conditions, field service, let alone battle, takes up a limited part of a soldier's life. Far more important are issues involving everyday circumstances: food, clothing, and shelter, delivered with a reasonable minimum of regularity and efficiency. An army able to meet such conditions will often survive flagrant mismanagement in combat: the Union Army of the Potomac during the U.S. Civil War and the British Expeditionary Force of World War I, 1914–1918, are two prime examples. In most eighteenth-century armies the uniforms were durable and the pay regular. Such points did not make a soldier's lot happy, only acceptable in the context of reasonable alternatives.

BILLETS AND QUARTERS: LIVING OUTSIDE OF CAMP

Experience with supply suggested the wisdom of a similar solution to lodging: the construction of buildings specifically designed to house large numbers of men in a way facilitating observation and control. The costs of such construction, however, led states during this period to fall back on the time-tested practice of billeting. It might better have been called boarding, for where the earlier process involved soldiers coming and soldiers going, usually with some time elapsing until the next arrivals, this situation was permanent—"the soldier in the parlor," to borrow a phrase from a leading authority on the phenomenon.[35]

Quartering Soldiers in Town

Communities could derive advantages from quartering. France, for example, allowed collective costs to be charged against taxes, both those in arrears and those yet to be levied. Temporary quartering of soldiers in public buildings—even churches and taverns—could also be sources of profit. Taken as a whole, however, exemption from quartering was everywhere prized. Communities tried to buy themselves free. Even in towns and villages, the better off were often willing to pay premiums to neighbors willing to assume their unwanted guests. Tavern keepers found soldiers readier to pick fights with the inn's civilian customers than to pay their own scores—and what might be negotiated with one or two men was usually impossible when a dozen were involved and none wished to lose face before the rest by seeming to back down. Soldiers demanded food and drink above the amounts specified. They smashed plates and glasses. They put their boots on chairs and beds. They were a source of physical infection, bringing with them alien germs and strange diseases. Soldiers brought moral infection as well: the strong language and swaggering attitudes that so impressed young boys; the open contempt for systematic work that was every parent's nightmare when considering their children. Soldiers broke hearts, and worse. For every "maid of Fif-e-o" who refused her martial suitor and sent him into a terminal decline, there were too many like the

Captain bold in Halifax
Who dwelt in country quarters

[and] Seduced a maid who hanged herself
One Monday in her garters. . . .[36]

The laws governing quartering and billeting offered ample room for everyday friction. In France they dated back to the days of Joan of Arc and provided soldiers with
firewood, salt, and vinegar, a bed and a candle, linens, cookware, and wine as a matter
of course. Increasingly, items of consumption were compensated in cash. That made
the system no more popular. Most of its friction involved domestic disputes rather
than pregnant daughters. In the German city of Göttingen, for example, a soldier
enjoyed puttering around in the kitchen, to the growing anger of his involuntary
hostess. One day, when he attempted to warm a dish in the oven, he was informed
that he was interfering with the preparation of dinner for the family. He called the
housewife a "sassy, brutal broad." She kicked him in the shins. He pushed her into
the wall. The husband and son appeared and told the soldier to shut his big mouth.
Words like *ox*, *villain*, and *jackass* were freely exchanged among all participants. The
pattern was universal. The townsmen saw themselves unjustly exploited. The soldiers
felt cheated by people who did not care enough to treat them properly.

An alternate solution developed in the lesser German states, whose armies were
seldom large enough, and whose budgets seldom stretched far enough, to encourage
barracks construction. In the relatively quiet circumstances of German "home towns,"

Soldiers Occupy a Village during the Thirty Years War by Nicholaes van Eyck. © Erich Lessing/Art
Resource, New York.

local authorities had more practice dealing with minor domestic squabbles. One solution involved civilians—at least those who could afford it—paying the soldiers assigned to them a cash sum equal to the legal billeting costs. The soldiers then sought other quarters in the poorer sections of town, but as renters, making their own terms. In these circumstances a bed and a chest was often enough to satisfy them—it left more money for important things like beer. Meanwhile, their landlords were pleased to have the extra income.

Thus far, so good. But the pressures the system put on low-rent housing did nothing to increase the soldiers' popularity among apprentices and day laborers. Small wonder that Austria, for example, shifted responsibility for quartering troops to the state in 1749, and even before then, preferred to house its men in barracks or quasi-barracks, such as abandoned monasteries. Even in Prussia, where most of the soldiers lived at home most of the time, most garrison towns featured so-called private barracks, which were essentially rooming houses for soldiers.

Relationships with Civilians

Soldiers quartered among civilians often found useful social niches. Like their predecessors of the *Landsknechte*, and the Spanish *tercios* (see Chapter Three) who succeeded them as Europe's toughest soldiers, they were reasonably decent men most of the time. In Germany's increasingly "well ordered police states," where every form of commerce was regulated, soldiers worked off the books, making doors and cupboards for their hosts and helping out craftsmen, from tailors to carpenters. Soldiers were useful in other ways as well. Responsible for guard duty at town gates, soldiers could facilitate smuggling on a large scale—grain, cloth, and brandy were common items. With production, consumer sales, and business dealings largely conducted in family homes, quartered soldiers provided security and muscle, both the literal and the euphemistic kind. Two or three burly grenadiers carrying cudgels sent an unmistakable message to neighborhood busybodies and officious constables. And since these were widely regarded as victimless crimes, good citizens seldom found moral problems in buying at reduced costs "off the back of a wagon."

Acculturation was easier in small states and city-states, which tended, as a rule, to attract an herbivorous species of soldier, more concerned with bed, board, and a quiet life than with seeking reputation at the cannon's mouth or getting into payday fights. In Germany, local authorities regularly sought veterans of the Prussian service to smarten up their somewhat ragtag contingents. These men, however, tended to consider service in the smaller states and city-states as a form of active retirement, with the result that things went on pretty much as before.

Marriage between soldiers and civilians was everywhere legally restricted or forbidden, less because of what soldiers did than because they were outsiders. Nevertheless, in Göttingen between 1721 and 1755, almost two-thirds of the soldiers who married legally wed civilian spouses. Other forms of bonding remained open. The most common was standing as godparents at a time when that office had major secular as well as spiritual connotations. Again, in Göttingen, three-fourths of the godparents of soldiers' legitimate children were civilians. Soldiers occasionally were able to accumulate the money to buy a house and to acquire the civic rights accompanying the ownership of property.

Without seeking to generalize from a single example, it seems reasonable to suggest that similar patterns obtained across western Europe—at least when conditions were such that troops were not frequently shifted from garrison to garrison, a project sufficiently expensive that few states undertook it, except from necessity.

AFTERWARD: VETERANS

Eighteenth-century soldiers could be surprisingly long-lived. In Prussia, for example, peacetime death rates from 1713 to 1740 were under 1.4 percent, a figure comparing quite favorably with the percentage for the counterpart male civilian population. As a rule, veterans were valued substantially higher than recruits. They were less likely to fall ill and more likely to recover from wounds. Old hands seldom fell prey to panic or despair—or to the heedless enthusiasm that could have even worse results once the adrenalin died out. The elite grenadier companies organized by most armies in the eighteenth century, consistently given the most dangerous missions, were disproportionately drawn from the upper age levels of the regiment.[37]

Old soldiers in turn often grew deeply attached to the name, the number, and the flag under which they had not merely served time, but made a life. Eventually, however, they faced the hard fact of demobilization at the end of a war or the harder one of no longer being equal to the demands of regimental service. Those unable or unwilling to give it one more try somewhere else faced proverbially uncertain futures. Some ex-soldiers took to banditry or smuggling. Others turned to begging—though in England, at least, a fair number of beggars falsely claimed to have been soldiers. Prussia maintained garrison battalions for men still able to stand watch and man the walls. Prussian regulations also provided that when a soldier finally left from age or disability, his name must be reported to the king. The noncommissioned officers and some of the more fortunate privates found jobs in government offices. Others were settled as colonists on reclaimed wasteland. A few received small monthly pensions; a few others—about 600—were settled in the Potsdam Invalid House. Too many contented themselves with a license to beg.[38]

France did better by its old soldiers. As early as the sixteenth century, they had been objects of royal concern. An early attempt at solving the problem by assigning needy veterans to monasteries proved—predictably, one would think—uncongenial to all involved. In 1674, Louis XIV founded the Hôtel des Invalides. Still one of the geographic attractions of Paris today, it became the focal point for a network of initiations and agencies designed both to provide for the veteran's welfare and to control his behavior. As the original building grew overcrowded, the less infirm were encouraged to join "detached companies of invalids." By the end of the Seven Years War, there were about 150 of them, with a total strength of about 15,000 men. As the number of applicants for support continued to increase, those unable or unwilling to enter one of the institutions could request an invalid pension—full pay after twenty-four years of service, half-pay after sixteen.

Each veteran was supposed to be able to choose. The cash pensioners, however, posed a problem. In their late thirties and older, many were unwilling to settle down.

Many were unable to do so because of physical or psychological trauma. The pension was at best subsistence level. The Comte de Saint-Germain, war minister from 1775 to 1777, sought to deemphasize the Hôtel des Invalides in favor of smaller "hospices" in the provinces, where living costs were cheaper. Underfunded and implemented haphazardly, the reforms had the effect of forcing hundreds of old soldiers—plus, it must be said, a good number of freeloaders—onto the streets of Paris.[39] The images thus created did nothing to enhance the monarchy's popularity—but that is part of the story of the next volume in this series.

NOTES

1. "Over the Hills and Far Away" is a soldier's song dating to Marlborough's era, with many verses. This verse is from the version developed by John Tams for the "Sharpe" TV series.

2. The above account follows John Richards, *Landsknecht Soldier, 1486–1560* (Oxford, UK: Osprey, 2002), another in the high-standard Warrior series offered by this press. For more detailed accounts, cf. Reinhard Baumann, *Das Söldnerwesen im 16. Jahrhundert im bayerischen und süddeutschen Beispiel* (Munich, Germany: Woelfle, 1978); and *Landsknechte: Ihre Geschichte und Kultur vom Spaten Mittelalter bis zum Dreissigjaehrigen Krieg* (Munich, Germany: Beck, 1994).

3. James B. Wood, *The King's Army: Warfare, Soldiers, and Society during the Wars of Religion in France, 1562–1576* (Cambridge, UK: Cambridge University Press, 1996), 51.

4. Gervase Phillips, *The Anglo-Scottish Wars, 1513–50: A Military History* (Woodbridge, UK: Boydell Press, 1999).

5. Wood, *King's Army*, 55 ff., is a good case study.

6. Michael Roberts, "The Military Revolution, 1550–1660," in *The Military Revolution Debate: Readings on the Transformation of Early Modern Europe*, ed. Clifford J. Rogers (Boulder, CO: Westview, 1995), 30–31 n.10.

7. See the general history by Ken Albala, *Food in Early Modern Europe* (Westport, CT: Greenwood Press, 2003).

8. The best discussion, though with a later focus, is Marcel Reinhard, "Nostalgie et service militaire pendant la Revolution," *Annales historiques de la Revolution française* 30 (1958): 1–15.

9. Geoffrey Parker, *The Army of Flanders and the Spanish Road, 1567–1659: The Logistics of Spanish Victory and Defeat in the Low Countries' Wars* (Cambridge, UK: Cambridge University Press, 1972), remains definitive and detailed.

10. Except where otherwise specifically referenced, the following account of sixteenth-century camp life is reconstructed from the sources cited in note 2. Other forces and armies during the same period differed from the pattern only in details.

11. A good survey of the subject is Barton Hacker, "Women and Military Institutions in Early Modern Europe: A Reconnaissance," *Signs: Journal of Women in Culture and Society* 6 (1981): 643–671.

12. See Lorraine White, "The Experience of Spain's Early Modern Soldiers: Combat, Welfare, and Violence," *War in History* 9 (2003): 1–38.

13. Ambroise Paré, *The Apologic and Treatise of Ambroise Paré* (New York: Dover, 1968); J. F. Malgalgne, *Surgery and Ambroise Paré* (Norman: University of Oklahoma Press, 1965).

14. Parker, *Army of Flanders*, 168–169.

15. John A. Lynn, *Giant of the Grand Siècle: The French Army, 1610–1715* (Cambridge, UK: Cambridge University Press, 1997), 420–426.

16. William H. McNeil, *Plagues and Peoples* (Garden City, NY: Anchor, 1976), discusses the early years of the syphilis plague in Europe.

17. Parker, *Army of Flanders*, 160 n. 1.

18. Lynn, *Grand Siècle*, 155.

19. Parker, *Army of Flanders*, 161.

20. Lynn, *Grand Siècle*, 165–166.

21. Parker, *Army of Flanders*, 161 ff.

22. David A. Parrott, "Strategy and Tactics in the Thirty Years' War: The 'Military Revolution,'" in Rogers, *Military Revolution Debate*, 227–251.

23. For background, see N. M. Sutherland, *The Huguenot Struggle for Recognition* (New Haven, CT: Yale University Press, 1980).

24. White, "Experience," 30–31.

25. The essays in F. Van Liebing, ed., *Confessionalism and Pietism: Religious Reform in Early Modern Europe* (Mainz, Germany: von Zabern, 2006), are suggestive. Cf. Christine Peters, *Patterns of Piety: Women, Gender, and Religion in Late Medieval and Reformation England* (Cambridge, UK: Cambridge University Press, 2003).

26. See the general discussion by Carlos M. N. Eire, *From Madrid to Purgatory: The Art and Craft of Dying in Sixteenth-Century Spain* (Cambridge, UK: Cambridge University Press, 1995).

27. M. C. 't Hart, *The Making of a Bourgeois State: War, Politics, and Finance during the Dutch Revolt* (Manchester, UK: University of Manchester Press, 1993).

28. Parker, *Army of Flanders*, 12–16.

29. This issue is addressed in various contexts of the French Revolution in Bryan T. Ragan and Elizabeth Williams, eds., *Re-creating Authority in Revolutionary France* (New Brunswick, NJ: Rutgers University Press, 1992). Cf. as well Robert Darnton's *The Great Cat Massacre and Other Episodes in French Cultural History* (New York: Basic Books, 1984), especially the title essay.

30. Barry Nickle, "The Military Reforms of Prince Maurice of Orange" (PhD diss., University of Delaware, 1975). Cf. Harald Kleinschmidt, "Using the Gun: Manual Drill and the Proliferation of Firearms," *Journal of Military History* 63 (1999): 601–629.

31. William H. McNeill, *Keeping Together in Time: Dance and Drill in Human History* (Cambridge, MA: Harvard University Press, 1995); Kate van Orden, *Music, Discipline, and Arms in Early Modern France* (Chicago: University of Chicago Press, 2005).

32. Dennis Showalter, *The Wars of Frederick the Great* (London: Longman, 1996), 22 ff.

33. Michel Sikora, *Disziplin und Desertion: Strukturprobleme in militärischer Organisation im 18. Jahrhundert* (Berlin: Duncker and Humblot, 1996).

34. Showalter, *Wars*, 23 passim.

35. The following presentation is based on Ralf Proeve, "Der Soldat in der 'guten Bürgerstube': Das frühneuzeitliche Einquartierungssystem und die sozioökonomischen Folgen," in *Krieg und Frieden. Militär und Gesellschaft in der Frühen Neuzeit*, ed. B. Koerner and R. Proeve (Paderborn, Germany: Schoeningh, 1996), 191–217; and *Stehendes Heer und städtisch Gesellschaft im 18. Jahrhundert* (Munich, Germany: Oldenbourg, 1995). The anecdote is from Proeve, "Der Soldat," 207–208.

36. "Unfortunate Miss Bailey" is usually considered a traditional folk song but actually was composed by George Coleman for "Love Laughs at Locksmiths," an eighteenth-century play.

37. Willerd Fann, "Peacetime Attrition in the Army of Frederick William I," *Central European History* 11 (1978): 323–334; and "Foreigners in the Prussian Army, 1713–56: Some Statistical and Interpretive Problems," *Central European History*, 23 (1990): 76–84.

38. Christopher Duffy, *The Army of Frederick the Great* (New York: Hippocrene Books, 1974), 60–62.

39. Isser Woloch, *The French Veteran from the Revolution to the Restoration* (Chapel Hill: University of North Carolina Press, 1979), 3 ff.

Seven

✳ ✳ ✳

EUROPEANS IN A WORLD OF WAR

Beginning with the sixteenth century, it becomes not merely possible, but necessary to establish Europe's soldiers in a global context.[1] Previous encounters between "the West and the rest" had been episodic. Europe's relative isolation in the world of war reflected problems of access, projection, and sustainability. A peninsula at the far end of the Eurasian land mass, Europe was difficult to reach from any external centers of power. Much of its internal geography was a tangle of mountains and hills, swift-flowing rivers, and thick forests—uncongenial to prospective conquerors accustomed to the easy access of open spaces. The Roman Empire had indeed not been built in a day. Conquest in Europe was slow work, and it is questionable whether either Mongol or Islamic empire builders would have had the institutional endurance and fortitude to repeat the process. The centuries-long Muslim offensive against Europe that formed the commonly overlooked framework for the Crusades was impelled, particularly in its Ottoman version, by a consistent and religiously based urge to conquest. Jihadist energy and Muslim power, however, could only be mobilized in surges. Able to make significant progress on the periphery of the West, able to fight largely on Western ground, after the fall of Constantinople in 1453, Islamic empires were nevertheless unable to threaten the heartland of Europe in a consistent fashion.[2]

The same geography that inhibited invaders of Europe also restricted prospective European empire builders. Alexander the Great's conquests in the fourth century B.C.E. reflected the genius and willpower of a single man. Rome's boundaries were set in the north by the warriors and forests of Germany, and in the east by the horsemen of Parthia and Persia.[3] No matter how warlike Europe's inhabitantslater became—and their development in that respect was nothing if not impressive—they were unable, prior to the early modern period, to move outward with any strength and were even less able to sustain themselves away from their base area. Deep, endemic rivalries among the maritime powers limited the effects of Western sea power. With the development of riverine defenses, amphibious and so-called brown-water operations (using riverine systems and other inland waterways to support operations at a distance from actual coastlines) in the Viking style were, in the absence of support from a local faction or community, generally restricted toephemeral, if nonetheless destructive, coastal raids; the Norman conquest of England in 1066 stands as a heroic exception. The medieval Crusades are similarly best understood in military terms as a series of unsustainable surges by Christian Europe to the eastern Mediterranean littoral, never able to penetrate very far inland, even had there been a compelling strategic interest in doing so.[4]

EUROPEAN RECONNAISSANCE AND INITIAL CONQUESTS

It was during the early modern period, specifically in the Age of Reconnaissance (c. 1450–1600), when they deployed cannon-armed, oceangoing galleons, that Europe demonstrated a sustainable strategy of maritime power projection.[5] Efficient sailing ships mounting effective shipboard artillery, operating individually, then as small squadrons, eventually as high seas fleets, enabled Europeans, from the beginning of the sixteenth century, to engage and suppress local systems successfully. By the last quarter of the seventeenth century, European states were extending their own wars into the Caribbean, the Indian Ocean, and even the Pacific. Initially, the Westerners enjoyed what amounted to a free hand, able to evade boarding parties launched from hostile shores by sailing out of their reach, while crippling their opponents' ships with long-range gunfire. When locals developed effective shipboard artillery of their own, the Europeans regularly found their hands full tactically. By that time, however, Europeans had established a sufficient global presence that they could fall back on developed regional base areas to lick their wounds.[6]

That development reflected Europe's growing ability to project land power halfway around the world. The qualities that enabled Western ships to make long voyages and defend themselves when they arrived were synergistic: neither the ships nor the guns they carried required large crews to work them. But the small crews of the Age of Reconnaissance were far less capable of sustained effort onshore. Even fairly large squadrons of ships could spare only token landing parties. The early modern sailor, moreover, might be formidable enough in a ship-to-ship action, whether as a gunner or in hand-to-hand combat. But he possessed neither the training nor the mentality to make him effective in the long term on land. The West's first non-European ground operations were thus generally limited to securing and fortifying harbors and bases along coastlines or on islands. If that could be done without a fight, by occupying unsettled land, as was frequently the case as Portugal established the East African link in its south Asian commercial network, so much the better. On the other hand, Portuguese expeditions into the interior of Africa, conducted independently or, far more usually, in the context of regional politics, seldom turned out well enough to become established as policy.[7]

The same was true on the other side of the African continent. The extensive logistic and security requirements of the trade in slaves and gold that was the key to the Euro-African connection required Europeans to maintain a military presence in African territory. They did so, however, with the consent—sometimes at the sufferance—of local rulers, at the cost of substantial and ongoing rents and fees. European slave traders encouraged local and regional disputes within Africa by offering to purchase the captives made should war result. Periodically, European garrisons participated in local politics as clients, auxiliaries, or even mercenaries. Except for the Portuguese in Angola, however, these small forces never made any conquests, nor sought to, nor were they encouraged to, and Portugal's control over Angola remained marginal into the twentieth century.

European technology did influence warmaking in West Africa. European muskets, for example, steadily replaced the natives' bows, leading to the abandonment of earlier forms of hand-to-hand combat. Direct European influence on the process was, however, minimal, apart from the occasional presence of a few of what would later be called "military advisors." Not until the synergistic development, in the later nineteenth century, of a spectrum of manpower-saving devices, ranging from steamboats to tropical medicines to magazine rifles and automatic weapons, were Western soldiers able to leave a permanent mark on Africa.[8]

Neither of those lines of developments had much to do with the European soldiers who festered and died in cramped coastal fortresses. Before Westerners were able, after 1820, to extract and mass produce quinine to combat malaria, the death rate for British soldiers garrisoned along the West Coast of Africa hovered around 50 percent. One famous expedition led by William Bolt in 1777 went into Africa with 152 men; only 20 survived. The high death rate of Europe's exploratory and imperialistic efforts inspired H. G. Wells to pen *War of the Worlds* (1898), the story of a bellicose alien people possessing superior technology brought low by common microbes, to which they had no natural immunity. European soldiers anticipated the plight of Wells's Martians in a contemporary doggerel: "Beware, beware the Bight of Benin! There's few come out/Though many go in."[9]

Despite surface appearances, the dramatic overthrow by Spain of the Aztec and Inca empires in the Western Hemisphere (to Europeans, the "New World") during the sixteenth century confirms the generalization of the initial marginalization of Western soldiers.[10] Both operations depended heavily on the presence of nearby bases. Hernán Cortés (1485–1547), the famous Spanish conquistador, had no hope of reaching Mexico in force or staying there for any length of time had he not been able to draw logistical support from the Spanish Caribbean. Once ashore in Mexico, the Spaniards sustained their efforts at conquest by forging local alliances. In Peru, Francisco Pizarro and his band of 168 conquistadores also took advantage of the factionalism never too far from the surface in an Inca polity itself little over a century old, seeking to govern dozens of formerly independent societies and their corresponding ethnic groups.[11]

In terms of warmaking, the Spanish conquests in the Americas, impressive as they were, are best understood as wildly successful filibustering expeditions in the style replicated by William Walker, the notorious American military adventurer who briefly gained the presidency of Nicaragua in the 1850s. Small numbers of military adventurers with at best tangential backing by their government sought to overthrow existing native institutions and seize control by force of arms. The conquistadores saw themselves not as professional soldiers in state service, but as a combination of crusaders and entrepreneurs.[12] They journeyed to the New World, as that genial hardcase and historian Bernal Díaz del Castillo candidly put it, to honor God by increasing the number of his subjects, to serve their monarch by enlarging the size of his domains, and above all, "to grow rich, as all men desire to do."[13] God, gold, and glory was the cry, but gold was the most consistent motivator.

Helpful as well to the success of Europeans in Mexico and Peru was the fact that Amerindian peoples were ignorant of horses, firearms, and steel. Western technology and techniques contributed heavily to the cultural shock experienced by Amerindian peoples. So did Aztec beliefs. The first sighting of Spanish galleons was widely interpreted by the Aztecs as the fulfillment of apocalyptic prophecy; thus they initially accorded Cortés and his men considerable deference and respect.

Spaniards attacked by the Aztecs in Tenochtitlán during *La Noche Triste* ("The Sad Night"), 1520. © North Wind Picture Archives.

By the time Spanish motives of greed and conquest became painfully clear, it was too late for the Aztecs to eject their enemy from their great capital city of Tenochtitlán (site of present-day Mexico City). But if superior armament, and discipline honed over eight centuries of war with Spain's Muslims, were important "force multipliers" to the conquistadores, it was mainly Amerindian allies and European diseases, working in terrible concert with Aztec myths, that proved decisive as empire destroyers.[14] The Aztecs were overcome not by European power projection, but by the potentialities and terrors created by their own beliefs and practices, by their susceptibility to Old World diseases—and not least by a war of liberation waged by subject peoples fed up with the insatiable demands of their Aztec overlords, especially victims for ritual sacrifice.[15]

PEBBLES IN A FLOOD: EUROPEANS IN ASIA

Europe's difficulties with power projection did not end at the waterline of the Yucatan peninsula. The changing nature of Europe's coastal geography and the water-related location of its major cities had combined, over the previous five or six centuries, to produce high levels of experience and expertise in what today is called littoral warfare: operations on rivers, lakes, and estuaries. English attacks against Ireland beginning in the sixteenth century depended heavily on a spectrum of coastal and inland amphibious operations. The sixteenth-century Dutch-Spanish Wars were characterized, if not defined, by web-footed fighting over boggy or flooded terrain. The long series of operations by the French crown against the Protestant stronghold of La Rochelle from 1570 to 1626 were directed largely against the port city's water-based inland geography. Both specialized amphibious material and specialized amphibious skills were developed to a significant degree when Europe burst on the world during the sixteenth century.[16]

As a result, Europeans achieved some notable early successes in direct amphibious assaults. In 1511, for example, Afonso de Albuquerque took the port city of Malacca in the Malay peninsula against ten-to-one odds—a remarkable achievement, even given the absence of fixed fortifications.[17] Nevertheless, with the obvious exception of Cortés's success in the lagoons of Mexico City, Westerners found themselves consistently on the short end of brown-water operations in Africa and Asia. To some degree, this reflected the unsuitability for inshore fighting of the big ships with heavy guns that brought the Europeans to those continents and kept them there. It reflected as well the presence of local forces adapted to local conditions. From the Cameroons of West Africa to Burma's Arakan in the Bay of Bengal to the Indonesian archipelago, Europeans faced enemies whose expertise they could not match, under conditions where their firepower was at a discount.

A factor often overlooked, yet significant from the perspective of this volume, involved marines or similar specialized amphibious troops. Even in European waters, the number of men a sailing ship could detach for a landing party was limited. The ad hoc combination of improvised forces, moreover, invited high-risk levels of confusion in sea-land operations demanding precise execution. Experiments with marines date to the mid-seventeenth century, but for decades earlier, soldiers had been supplementing and complementing ships' crews in littoral fighting. In the Spanish Army of Flanders, some companies, repeatedly called upon for such missions, seem to have developed reputations as what today are called commandos.[18]

Such specialized units were significantly underrepresented in European orders of battle in the Southern Hemisphere. The ordinary garrison forces that sometimes attempted to replace them possessed neither the numbers nor the skills to match their indigenous opponents. Blue-water sailors called on by default to bear the brunt of brown-water operations were quickly rendered content with their control of the open ocean. Projecting and sustaining power inland remained a high-risk proposition, a fact that encouraged Europeans to seek alternative arrangements with local peoples and systems.

Well aware of Westerners' limitations on land, Asian rulers countered their superiority at sea with, in Geoffrey Parker's words, "the permit and the prison," paying protection money for their own inferior ships and punishing Western captains who failed to honor the bargain with imprisonment—or worse.[19] A major reason for European willingness to strike deals rather than fight wars was that Europeans had come to Asia not to conquer native peoples, but to profit from trade with them. The Dutch were an exception, having been convinced by decades of experience dealing with Spain that trade could only prosper when properly defended. Even then, ground forces played a secondary role. The Dutch East India Company, founded in 1602, put its major military emphasis on ships and fortresses—and the latter were something of a strategic necessity reflecting the Indonesian archipelago's geography of small islands, each needing a Dutch military presence to secure such highly portable and profitable products as nutmeg and other spices.[20]

When Europeans fought, it usually involved extensions of wars at home. The long struggle between the Dutch and the Portuguese for mastery of Indonesia in the seventeenth century as well as the Anglo-French duel for primacy in India were essentially political conflicts. They had only secondary connections to the paramount commercial interests that brought Europeans halfway around the world in the first place. Robert Clive, conqueror of Bengal, began his career as a clerk and was periodically called to account for neglecting his business responsibilities in order to play soldier. Fighting indeed was often so bad for business that trading company executives in Europe paradoxically saw total military victory as desirable: driving commercial rivals from the disputed region altogether, thereby producing the stability and security essential to profitable trading relationships.[21]

From a European soldier's perspective north Asia was an even less congenial environment than Africa. The extension of Europe's influence was essentially a maritime, commercial process. It was also contested. The Japanese were especially quick studies, making rapid and extensive use of European-style firearms after these were introduced to them in 1543 by Portuguese castaways. Soon they were making their own high-quality muskets that, in contrast to their European counterparts, sacrificed rate of fire for better accuracy. Japanese armies and Japanese tactics were increasingly structured around firepower, so much so that Tokugawa Ieyasu, Japan's first shogun, declared that he desired guns and gunpowder more than gold. The great battles for control of the Japanese empire, Nagashino (1575) and Sekigahara (1600), matched in operational sophistication and tactical virtuosity anything in the early modern Western experience.[22] Only the greatest of European captains, someone like a Gustavus Adolphus with his full army at his back, would have had a chance of victory against the Japanese—and then only on a very good day. If Japanese fortifications were not built along the lines introduced by the *trace italienne* in Europe, they were arguably even more proof against siege and bombardment, to the point where most fell by negotiation—or treachery, if one prefers to be harsh. Small wonder that Westerners accepted Japan's instructions and injunctions, right down to the eventual closing off of the island empire (with the lone exception of Dutch traders at Nagasaki), without significant challenge from the West until the mid-nineteenth century.[23]

China as well, although it never adopted Western military technology with Japan's initial enthusiasm, was a far too effective military power to be challenged on its own ground. The famed Middle Kingdom was, for much of this period, in the process of changing rulers, as the Mandate of Heaven passed from the Ming Dynasty to the Qing (still better known as Manchu outside academic circles) in the seventeenth century. In the Chinese context of land campaigns and battles involving tens and even hundreds of thousands of men, the few hundred Western soldiers who might be brought to China would have had the impact of a pebble on a flood.

European soldiers did develop an offshore presence in the Far East, but it was never a stable one during this period. During the first half of the seventeenth century, the Dutch established the island of Taiwan as one of the most prosperous parts of their overseas empire. But they defended the island with only two small fortresses. In 1660, the Chinese pirate king Coxinga led an invasion force that captured the larger fort after a nine-month siege involving Western cannon and Western methods. Coxinga then sent envoys to the Spanish-occupied Philippines, demanding tribute. With only around 600 troops in the entire archipelago, prospects for successful resistance were limited. Only Coxinga's unexpected death in 1662 kept the Spanish flag flying over Manila.[24]

THE SEPOY EXCEPTION IN INDIA

Wherever one looks in the Southern Hemisphere during the early modern period, the European soldier's footprint is limited, more often found in the sand and mud of a coastline than the terra firma farther inland. The single exception is the subcontinent of India. And yet so powerful alike in myth and history is that experience that it largely continues to define, particularly in popular culture, the military presence of the West in the non-Western world.

It began at the outer limits of "permit and prison," as Western merchants sought greater security for their goods and warehouses than payments and native promises. They began by hiring small numbers of guards and security personnel from among local civilian toughs and unemployed soldiers. These forces remained small, in good part for the sake of amiable relations with local rulers who permitted trade. Not until the 1740s did the French Compagnie des Indes begin raising company-sized units of sepoys (from the Persian *sipahi*, "soldier"). The sepoy model of Indian units commanded by European officers and trained on European lines was initially defensively oriented: a search for security against the increasing scale and number of raids launched in defiance of the declining Mughal Empire by regional enemies seeking financial gain and political autonomy. When the French used their new native troops to capture British Madras in 1746, Britain's Honourable East India Company (which had been trading in the subcontinent more than a century, since 1600) began recruiting counterparts, and the sepoy race was on.

Westerners initially used Indian troops in their own quarrels. Not until the *nawab* (provincial governor) of Bengal captured Calcutta in 1756 and demanded as ransom

Sepoys. © HIP/Art Resource, New York.

increased payments for trade concessions were sepoys turned systematically against other Indians. They proved remarkably successful under a series of commanders like Robert Clive and Eyre Coote—successful to the point where crown and company alike took notice. The British East India Company had periodically sought to build a European ground force in India, but death and desertion rates proved prohibitive. So too did the costs of recruiting and transporting these men, and so the company asked the British government to contribute to their upkeep. Thus it was that the Thirty-ninth Regiment of Foot came to India in 1754, first of a long line of such deployments, its status commemorated by its motto *Primus in Indis* (first in India). But the escalation of Europe's wars in the mid-eighteenth century made British regulars in India no better a military bargain than company-enrolled Europeans. Faced with a manpower shortage, the company's directors, in April 1760, allowed its authorities in Calcutta to enlist so-called blacks (Indian natives) at discretion.[25]

In evaluating the efficacy of the sepoy model, a well-developed triumphalist thread has emerged that trumpets the wisdom of the company's decision. According to it, the British enlisted hundreds, then thousands, of native Indians, gave them uniforms, armed and trained them in the European fashion, and led them to victory after victory—to the point where local Indian rulers were constrained to imitate Western methods blindly in order to survive. Even in the most modern of the Indian armies, however, Western-style formations were embedded—sometimes literally—in an Indian military culture based on political alliances at the top and warrior virtue at the cutting edge. The fundamental challenge for these "mixed" forces was to fight as a cohesive body rather than as aggregates. Efforts to develop cohesiveness in turn put a premium on centralized command and control—control that was, according to an emerging sepoy paradigm, best provided by European officers and methods.

Sepoy triumphalism asserts that European training and discipline provided cohesion and community to Indians who had previously fought as warrior individuals, no matter how large the army to which they belonged. European tactics proved exponentially superior to the cavalry-and-elephant systems of the Mughal-style armies. "John

Company" (the nickname for the Britain's East India Company) provided fair pay to "Jack Sepoy" on time. It saw to the establishment of a bazaar-based supply system, which, albeit cumbersome, provided the sepoy's necessities, supplemented by a few luxuries. The British officers at the core of the newly formed battalions set an example of courage in battle and provided objective external supervision of the Indian caste system. Finally, the sepoy system made men of outcasts, showing them that by standing together and holding their ground, they could defeat the men on horseback who had been, for generations, their masters.[26]

Like most myths, this one is not without substance. Western military technology, the musket/bayonet combination and mobile field artillery in particular did prove master of south Asian battlefields time and again. The drill that enabled men to face superior numbers with calmness, if not equanimity, and endure in the face of danger, as opposed to charging to meet it head-on, was the necessary complement to the musket and bayonet weapon system, which was most effective when employed in controlled masses. Regular pay, and supplies obtainable without scouring the countryside, helped create a sense of community vital to unit effectiveness in any army—a force composed primarily of Indian sepoys was no exception.

Another major facilitator of sepoy socialization was the European introduction of direct recruitment. Indian armies were historically formed on a variation of the military enterpriser pattern. In the Indian version a chief or landowner negotiated with a larger contractor or directly with a ruler to provide a certain number of men with a certain level of equipment. The result was, as had been the case in Europe during the fourteenth and fifteenth centuries, to develop primary loyalty to a relatively small primary group. The British, seeking to enlarge the scope of sepoy loyalty, instead sent recruiting parties to villages and enlisted individual applicants for service in a particular regiment. They did everything possible to make the regiment the center of the sepoy soldier's identity. His oath of enlistment was sworn on the colors. His regiment's history was commemorated in feasts and holidays. His British officers served for years at a time and took the lead in battle, exhibiting a level of commitment and courage that facilitated their acceptance by the sepoys as legitimate counterparts of more traditional leaders.[27]

At the same time a successful sepoy system depended on incorporating south Asian traditions and mentalities. India's Hindu and Muslim cultures attached great importance to birth and occupation and the duties accompanying them. The Hindu warrior caste was second only to the Brahmin in a theoretical religious context. What counted practically was membership in a specific, recognized group that carried with it ideas of right conduct and collective loyalty. It was not particularly difficult for a man wearing the *Kampani bahadur*'s (as the East India Company was known) uniform to perceive himself, and to be generally understood by his peers, as fulfilling his *karma* and his *dharma* (duty) within Hinduism in exemplary fashion.

Both Hindu and Muslim cultures also laid great value on personal and collective honor and on loyalty to the provider of a livelihood. The East India Company's pay and pension systems were generous. Victory followed its banners. And at this period of history at least, European officers understood and responded to local concepts of honor. A sepoy's language, faith, and customs were respected, along with his personal dignity. That made service in the Company particularly attractive to diverse groups of men, especially in southeast India, which was not as caste-conscious as Bengal. Men knocked loose from their villages or blown into south India by the winds of war found opportunities to regain a sense of belonging, purpose, and status, both at personal and community levels. They included masterless and clanless men from a dozen subcultures: Tamils from the Coromandel Coast and Afghans from the Hindu Kush. Christians, without standing in either Hindu or Muslim systems, also served the company in its early years, often standing randomly in its ranks. The elaborate distinctions among martial classes and martial races would come later.[28]

As the eighteenth century progressed, sepoy regiments formed an ever-increasing proportion of the British order of battle, frequently executing operations without the European "stiffening" that would become a matter of course in later centuries. The regiments of British regulars or British East India Company Europeans never quite fell into the "nice to have" category, especially for major campaigns. Nevertheless, sepoys provided the backbone of British conquest and expansion on the Indian subcontinent. They became full-time professionals who achieved and maintained in arms their position at the top of India's military effectiveness tables, winning a wide reputation among Europeans as "the best black troops in the world."

Flattering the British by imitation, the French and Dutch raised sepoys as well, the Dutch primarily in what is now Indonesia. They never matched the British success, and the reasons remain obscure. One strong possibility is that the other Western states sought to westernize their recruits too comprehensively. Even as the British East India Company evolved into a governing body, enough of its initial commercial character remained to sustain a healthy dose of common sense. In dealing with sepoys, as with so many other things in British India, pragmatism overruled dogmatism: *that* something worked was far more important than *why* it worked.

The attention paid here to sepoys—a decidedly specific military subculture—may seem disproportionate. But for two centuries the West's position in the world depended heavily on successfully creating local military forces loyal to the imperial order, effective both internally and outside their homelands. The sepoy model, applied in many variations, proved by far the best means to that end, but its very complexity and cultural specificity made it difficult to replicate. "Cohesion and motivation within native battalions," John Lynn concludes, "depended on focusing the force of indigenous community identity and honor."[29] With the sepoys the British succeeded in creating soldiers who bought into a system serving colonial interests because that system respected their beliefs, and because it gave them honorable identities that were linked to and nurtured by established societal norms. The sepoy model succeeded because it was a syncretic process, synergistically combining elements of European military practice with native Indian beliefs and customs and creating in the bargain something new and resilient. Contemporary events in Iraq suggest that the sepoy exception may yet still have its uses—and that its inherent cultural complexities may yet prove too difficult to replicate.

WESTERNERS: OPPORTUNISTIC ENTREPRENEURS OR NATURAL BORN KILLERS?

In creating the sepoy model, Europeans showed sensitivity to local conditions and ability to forge alliances with local elements. But wherever they went in the world,

Europeans also acquired a common reputation for ferocity—ferocity of a unique kind.[30] African and Asian societies were no strangers to large-scale killing. Nor did they lack cultural insight into battle madness—what one might call "heroic rage" or "berserkers' fury," which could motivate individuals, and sometimes formations, to extraordinary heights of courage and corresponding depths of brutality. Europeans nevertheless seemed different. The historian Victor Davis Hanson ascribes this to a unique "Western way of war" dating back to ancient Greek hoplite armies, combining self-critical rationalism, technological proficiency, and commitment to military decision, even at extreme cost.[31] Scholars of the Iberian expansion focus on the hardihood and ferocity of Spanish warriors, fueled by religious enthusiasm, acquired in the centuries of bitter war with Muslims on both sides of the Straits of Gibraltar. A temporally extended version of that argument suggests that European soldiers, and particularly the British officers who set the tone for locally raised imperialist armies, forged a professional military subculture that eschewed imagination in favor of unreflective and enduring commitment to violence unmatchable by less militarized peoples.

A rational actor variant on this cultural approach suggests that, particularly in the initial stages of encounter, Westerners hopelessly outnumbered turned consciously to ferocity both as a force multiplier and as a deterrent. On his first voyage to Asia in 1498, for example, Vasco da Gama burned Arab captives alive and sent their ears and noses ashore with the tide. The counterargument that European nastiness had nothing to teach Aztecs with their bloodthirsty practice of large-scale human sacrifice, or south Asian cultures, where individual torture could be an art form and mass atrocity a commonplace, has merit. Da Gama's behavior, for example, was at least matched by the Ottoman Turks in 1571, when the Venetian governor of Famagusta in Cyprus, in retaliation for a stubborn defense, was flayed alive and his skin stuffed and displayed as a trophy.[32]

Perhaps a way around the "you're another" argument is to suggest that European violence differed less in degree or imagination from non-European cultures than in contexts. Aztecs, for example, regarded taking captives for sacrifice as a major war aim. To the Spaniards, prisoners who could neither be ransomed nor safely guarded, whose word not to escape meant nothing to Christians, were burdens best avoided by taking no prisoners. Similarly, most African and some Asian cultures sought captives as slaves or for labor. In societies far less mechanized than even preindustrial Europe, muscle power was too valuable to be wasted indiscriminately. Lacking domestic traditions of transferable servile labor (serfs were tied to the soil they cultivated, by law and custom), and perceiving that all indigenous peoples were more alike than different, Europeans appear to have had fewer concerns for the economic consequences of large-scale killing.

The major element of European success, however, seems to have involved alternative military value systems. Non-European military cultures, far from being inward looking and stagnant, tended strongly toward cosmopolitan models. War on all scales was sufficiently a feature of the African coasts, south Asia, Japan, and even China, that ideas, techniques, and weapons passed freely among regional combatants. Successive rulers of Mysore, the south Indian state that mounted the most effective challenge to British power, drafted prisoners of war and recruited European technicians. Its sultans organized infantry on Western lines and with Western armament, requiring the men to drill three hours a day—also a Western standard. Mysore even developed its own armament industries, importing skilled craftsmen directly from France.[33]

Non-European military systems also proved capable of independent innovation. To cite one example, the Maratha Confederacy that ruled much of central India in the eighteenth century developed field artillery as an antipersonnel weapon and possessed an infantry culture that antedated the often-cited employment of European mercenaries as technical advisors and formation commanders.[34] The Afghan army that invaded India in 1760 and crushed the Marathas at the Third Battle of Panipat a year later was as far from a tribal *lashkar* (a loosely organized "camp" army) as can be imagined. Its disciplined, musket-armed infantry and effective heavy field artillery provided a structural focal point for the Muslims who rallied to Ahmad Shah Durani and an operational one at Panipat in 1761.[35]

The long-alleged Western superiority in drill and discipline has also recently come under scrutiny and criticism. Asian military cultures were well accustomed to the use of firepower weapons in masses: firing arrows on a signal is not essentially different from firing muskets in volleys. China's Han Dynasty fielded large bodies of disciplined crossbowmen in the first century C.E. African armies as well, particularly on the west coast, had significant independent traditions of disciplined infantry acting in coordinated bodies. The African slave trade with Europe provided ample money for firearms, and while the quality of the flintlock "Dane guns" thus obtained was widely denigrated by Western authorities, long-range accuracy was far less important in the African bush than shock power and rapid fire. Not until the second half of the nineteenth century were European forces able to move beyond the coastal regions, and even then, the British were impressed by Ashanti marksmanship, small arms drill, and discipline. The French drew similar conclusions from their later experiences in Dahomey and elsewhere in West Africa.[36]

As early as the sixteenth century, *Topasses*, men of mixed Portuguese and Indian ancestry, were serving with European forces, learning drill and gunnery procedures and taking their knowledge to market. As the number of sepoys increased, so too did the number of locals with experience in European-style forces willing to serve in the "new model" regiments being organized everywhere in the Indian states. At higher levels Europeans who had served in their own armies or the forces of the trading companies were readily available for hire. A mythology that still tends to depict them as society's losers, unable to meet the demands of European soldiering, is countered by a large body of evidence that these "mercenaries" were in fact the heirs of a long and honorable Western heritage of changing military employment for advancement—one that has only recently given way to a more nationalist perspective of lifelong service under the same flag.[37]

Non-Western combatants fought to win whenever they fought—but their definitions of victory were, as a rule, different from those prevailing in Western military culture. Strategies and tactics tended to emphasize cost effectiveness: care in expending limited resources, whether human, material, or political. Opportunity and survival were key words throughout south Asia and sub-Saharan Africa. War was a business opportunity. Merchants with goods to sell, whether cloth, grain, or luxury items; bankers and moneylenders; soldiers and would-be soldiers all valued open, flexible markets.

Social opportunities existed as well. An Indian peasant with a weapon could pass for a warrior. A man with a horse was even more employable in raiding cultures. In Japan, generally regarded as a highly stratified culture, many a samurai began, as the saying had it, "with paddy mud between his toes."[38]

The risks involved in living a warrior's life were acceptable in African and Asian cultures for the same reasons that they were acceptable in Europe. Participation in the culture of war represented a chance for advancement. Death in battle was honorable, even in China, where the familiar proverb that one does not use good iron to make nails nor good men to make soldiers owed as much to Manchu conquerors as to Confucian philosophy—each had an interest in maintaining a docile population.[39] One of the reasons for Japan's shutting down the use and importation of gunpowder weapons involved the growing social pretensions of the men who led the growing contingents of arquebusiers who were changing the nature of war culturally as well as operationally. The mightiest feudal lord and the boldest samurai warrior could alike be brought down by an anonymous bullet.

Ultimately, however, what counted was maintaining the system. Victory did not normally entail annihilating an enemy people or destroying their social order. It involved gaining a place in the structure, buying into it through force of arms, after which new power-sharing arrangements could be negotiated with the other players. Europeans often appeared as newcomers to the game, sometimes marginal in terms of resources available, but correspondingly willing to participate on existing terms.

A similar point can be made in a political context regarding the Aztec and Inca empires. Inca authority was shaky at best; reorganization along what, in contemporary terms, would be called federal lines was a distinct possibility, even if Pizarro's military adventurers had not intervened. Certainly the central Inca authority at Cuzco failed to mobilize regional support to any permanent degree in the face of the Spanish threat.

In Mexico the Spanish overthrow of the Aztecs was initially processed not as an example of genocidal annihilation, but as part of a political continuum. The Amerindian victors saw the future in terms of making new alliances and redistributing power. Militarily, gunpowder technology plus steel weapons and armor made the Spaniards desirable allies. Locals viewed them as expendable shock troops, willing and able to break through Aztec lines with a regularity impossible for Mesoamerican technology. Politically, the conquistadores appeared, if not exactly rootless, then lacking the staying power to compete effectively in the long run. Their internal relationships, so heavily influenced by friction and faction, also did not suggest long-term staying power to Mesoamericans.

Both calculations, of course, were fundamentally mistaken. The Spanish sought conquest in what amounted to an ideological sense: subjugating entire populations, installing new rulers down to town levels, introducing a new religion, diverting the wealth of the New World to Spain's benefit—and, of course, their own. None of the great European conquerors of the past had come even close to this model in aspiration, much less achievement. By many accounts, as Amerindian peoples could not effectively process their fundamentally changed circumstances, cultural shock triggered a biological and ecological catastrophe that the conquistadores themselves little understood and could not control.[40]

The other aspect of Western success was economic: specifically, credit. African and Asian states were well aware of the link between economic and military development. Mysore's Tippoo Sultan sought to improve agriculture directly by subsidizing the cultivation of new land and indirectly by constructing irrigation systems. He established banking houses to facilitate making loans. Similar native measures were widely adopted in India as the eighteenth century progressed. But Britain was an economic superpower, able to use international capital resources to dominate a still-developing south Asian military economy, directly by hiring away troops through better wages and indirectly by choking off funding sources to rivals and enemies.[41] Where that approach was inapplicable, as in China and West Africa, albeit for opposite reasons, the Western military model remained marginal—at least until new sources of expertise and energy were unleashed by the Industrial Revolution of the nineteenth century.

THE AMERICAN EXPERIENCE: SOUTHERN HEMISPHERE

The experiences of early modern Europe's soldiers in the New World's Southern Hemisphere can be subdivided into two categories, both marginal. On the land frontiers the dominant military system was some variant of what Spain called the "presidio." Presidios in their developed form were military fortresses, but with major religious, economic, and social functions as well. They originated in mid-seventeenth century Mexico as a supplement to private defensive measures, such as walled towns and strongly built churches, which proved increasingly vulnerable to Amerindians not intimidated by the Spanish Conquest. Despite their small garrisons, usually around 50 men or so, plus between 200 and 300 dependents and laborers, presidios were bases for offensive operations, while providing protection for local residents, friendly natives included, and acting as a secular arm in support of missionary activity.

Unlike the posts the U.S. Army would later establish on the Great Plains, presidios were usually actual fortresses, constructed somewhat along the lines of a late medieval castle and correspondingly almost impregnable to any siege or assault techniques available to the locals. That did not avert a general pattern of small, deadly conflicts that stretched garrisons to the limit and made service on any presidial frontier a last option for the desperate, such as exiled convicts or criminals on the run. Presidio garrisons also included the desperately upwardly mobile. In Spanish America, mestizos, men of mixed Spanish and Indian heritage, found military service one of the few openings for social advance, despite the "stain" of their birth in a culture emphasizing a Peninsular heritage that valued "purity of blood" (*limpieza de sangre*). As the status of the frontier army increased, soldiers qualified for special privileges while on active service: the *fuero militar*, or military code of justice and privilege. On discharge they could request pensions and land grants. Given New Spain's ratio of ready cash to open land, land grants were more likely. Some of them provided the basis for the great land-and-cattle empires of the north—and even for an officially sanctioned redefinition of racial identity.

While frontier service offered fewer opportunities in central and South America, the structural patterns were essentially the same. The presidial system's successes were remarkable, particularly given the limited resources it consumed. Indeed, that limitation was part of its success: it proved nearly impossible for newcomers to swamp existing Amerindian social and economic orders. Realizing that they could not overthrow the system, they became players in it. Periodic threats of fire and sword issued by fire-breathing governors or overstuffed generals remained largely empty. Only occasionally did the Spanish, or in Brazil, the Portuguese, pose the kind of direct challenge to local institutions and arrangements that led to uprisings along the lines of the Pueblo Revolt of 1680—and then only in local contexts. Even the intra-European wars waged in these regions during the early modern period involved small numbers. Dispatching large forces safely and supplying them systematically was beyond the logistical and financial capacity of the powers involved, usually Spain, France, and Portugal, nor was it necessarily in their best commercial interest.[42]

The relative marginality of European soldiers on southern land frontiers was replicated in the Caribbean basin. Here the economic stakes of warfare were exponentially higher: As late as 1763, retaining the sugar islands of Guadeloupe and Martinique was, for France, worth the sacrifice of all Canada to Britain. In the Caribbean the conduct of war was shaped by sea power and fortresses: the ability of fleets arriving from Europe to maintain themselves in secure base areas. The generic indecisiveness of early modern naval battles was increased in this situation by the difficulties of repairing and replacing ships. That in turn enhanced the importance of the fortresses that protected harbors and their facilities.[43]

The islands of the West Indies, with their confined areas, broken terrain, and often deadly climate, offered unpromising hinterlands for European-style sieges. Under these difficult conditions, sieges took the form of amphibious operations: a ground force delivered to the objective by sea and sustained by sea power until the opponent's fortress capitulated or the attackers were worn down by disease and privation. In consequence, European states tended to allocate a high proportion of their Caribbean military spending to building fortifications able to endure long sieges with their own resources. Here Spain in particular excelled: Cartagena, for example, and above all Havana, whose capture by the British in 1762 was a triumph of determination and technique in the face of a hostile climate, treacherous terrain, and stubborn defense.[44]

That was where European soldiers came in: as mosquito fodder for landing operations and as garrisons doing the kind of internal security work to be expected on Caribbean islands, whose populations consisted overwhelmingly of slaves, many of recent vintage.[45] Spaniards on Cuba and, to an extent, Britons on Jamaica benefited relatively from more space, higher ground, and wind currents that at least changed the atmosphere. But on the smaller islands in particular, European mortality rates were so high that an assignment to the islands amounted to a death sentence in slow motion. The situation was exacerbated by a spectacularly unhealthy lifestyle built around a general belief among Europeans that liquor was a sovereign preventative of tropical disease. Not until the wars of the French Revolution were large forces of European troops committed to the Caribbean. Their contribution to military history was little more than to provide statistics on how long it took to die of whatever diseases were endemic to the region. Faced with debilitating death tolls, Britain, dominant in the region after the turn of the century, increasingly replaced its European garrisons by black slaves, purchased directly from Africa and manumitted on discharge, organized sepoy-style into battalions stiffened by European cadres.[46]

THE NORTHERN HEMISPHERE AND
THE FIRST WAY OF WAR

Events in the Northern Hemisphere, particularly in British North America, presented an entirely different spectrum of problems. Settlers found themselves in a decidedly hostile physical environment, inhabited by a people whose everyday ways of living were significantly alien and whose principles of warmaking in particular seemed barbaric.[47] They had, however, the beginnings of a model and a method for meeting the challenge. The model was Ireland: another alien environment, and for Britons, another "unworthy" race, able to achieve liberty only at the price of submission. The method was unlimited war. This "first way of war" meant pitched battles when possible and "little war" when they were not; no significant distinctions drawn between combatants and noncombatants; and the use of shock and awe—or simply, terror—to break not merely the capacity, but the will of the Native American warrior peoples, thereby forcing them "to fight no more forever" and to accept fully the consequences of that decision.[48]

John Ferling's use of the word *feral* to describe warfare in North America is entirely appropriate. At a time when Europe's wars were becoming more focused, with less collateral damage away from the battlefields themselves, warfare waged in the British colonies grew increasingly violent and increasingly comprehensive, targeting infrastructure like villages and agricultural resources, accepting casually the deaths of children on the grounds that "nits make lice," and even considering germ warfare by introducing smallpox-infected blankets to Native American communities.[49] Rationalization of these techniques, when it was needed, in some senses anticipated the rhetoric U.S. soldiers would employ 300 years later during the Vietnam Conflict, when officers paradoxically declared that they had to destroy villages to save them.

Other rationalizations for such a strategy fell under three categories: pragmatic, economic, and moral. In the first category the reciprocal passing of primal blame tends to obscure the fact that Native American ways of war were at least as susceptible to atrocities as European ones, particularly at micro levels, where small-scale raids and skirmishes were often motivated by individual grievances and grudges. "Stone dead has no fellow" and its successors like "rubble never gives you trouble" are even more readily applicable when the combatants seem to have no exploitable body of common ground and interests. In economic terms Native American and European ideas of what to do with the same country were sufficiently incompatible to facilitate belief that one or the other people must either submit or vanish. And a distinctively New World synergy of classical learning, religious identity, and cultural shock provided ample—or at least sufficient—rationale for primal war against an Other so uniquely and malevolently alien that in extreme cases Europeans concluded that Native Americans were literally in league with Satan.[50]

The operational approach that emerged from the strategy has been described as incorporating three elements.[51] One was extirpation: a pattern of burning towns and killing noncombatants imported from the fringes of the Thirty Years War and Europe's border wars with the Ottoman Empire, then refined over decades in the New World because Native American cultures, from a European perspective, offered no other worthwhile military targets. The second characteristic, bounty systems, again had European antecedents in a history of paying ransoms and bounties for captives. The American variant, however, was more or less original. Under European conditions of warfare, live prisoners were worth something, even if only as potential recruits for one's own armed forces. Corpses were worth nothing at all. In British North America, just the reverse was true. Prisoners had no value as objects of ransom, little for exchange purposes, and not much more when sold as slaves—especially in competition with an increasingly flourishing African slave trade.

Gruesome bounty systems emerged that were supported by colonial governments offering money or goods for proof of death. Fingers, ears, and similar body parts were too easily misrepresented. As proof of high body counts, scalps were readily preserved, easily carried, and traceable to a single in-dividual. But they were too primal a medium of exchange to be judged acceptable to emerging colonial societies that believed themselves to be "civilized" and "enlight-ened." Under the often chaotic and con-fused conditions of wilderness warfare, the ability to seize scalps was also too problem-atic to serve as a reliable means of compen-sation, just as booty had proven unreliable in the late medieval and early modern pe-riods. Instead, governments offered boun-ties based on taxes raised and land claimed. Often, these too proved ephemeral. Nev-ertheless, cash in hand on enlistment and promises of land on discharge were an appealing combination to ambitious and adventurous men. "Nothing ventured, nothing have" was the mantra of many a recruit to the Indian Wars from Georgia to Massachusetts.[52]

Extirpation of Native Americans and sys-tems of bounty in turn developed the third characteristic, the one most important to the present narrative: the concept of irregu-lar war practiced by "rangers." The data of the preceding paragraphs logically suggests that British North America should have developed as a martial, even a militarized, society along the lines of Austria's military border, the Anglo-Scottish frontier, or the No Man's Land of the Cossack steppe. What happened instead was just the opposite.

*An Indian Warrior
Entering his Wigwam with a Scalp.*

Western image of Native American "savagery," depicting the taking of scalps. Courtesy of the Library of Congress.

Colonial militias based on general manhood service rapidly gave way to specialized strike forces composed of and led by men who knew what they were doing in the operationally complex conditions of wilderness warfare existing from the St. Lawrence Valley to the swamps of Georgia and South Carolina. To a degree, "ranging war" developed as Native American populations diminished and Native American peoples abandoned frontier zones for the ostensible security provided by distance. It was facilitated as well by the growing cultivation of the warrior aspects of Native American cultures, making them exponentially more formidable as combatants. One might also suggest that the extirpation of natives was to a degree an acquired taste, less easily nurtured as colonial society stabilized. The farmer, the blacksmith, and the shopkeeper were well content to abide at home and compound for their service with money.[53]

Colonial rangers—the practitioners of ranging war—were formidably effective, but only within limits. One set of limits was institutional. Particularly in the South, their discipline was ragged to the point of nonexistence. Time and again, an exchange of insults and challenges to each others' manhood took Europeans headlong into ambushes prepared by Native Americans, who emerged as the rational actors in the scenario. A second problem was operational. Ranger companies could wage war but could not decide it, even before the French began furnishing arms, ammunition, and base areas to Native American clients. Ironically, in that context, ranging tactics arguably exacerbated the problem of suppressing the natives by forcing most of the Northeast Indians to seek French protection as the lesser evil as well as the better commercial prospect. Finally, rangers were too far outside the mainstream of developing colonial societies to make comfortable defenders and protectors. There was always some concern as to just where a ranger's allegiance might abide when put to an ultimate test. This concern furnishes subtext, for example, to such fictional works as *The Last of the Mohicans*, where Hawkeye repeatedly proclaims himself "a man without a cross"—that is, of unmixed blood and of unchallengeable loyalty.

Increasingly, then, British colonists in North America demanded the presence of regular troops. That preference for regulars vis-à-vis rangers remained unaltered by such catastrophes as the near-annihilation of Braddock's column at the Monongahela or the costly failure to storm Fort Ticonderoga in 1758. The colonies were quite content to have their own "provincial" regiments relegated to second-line and labor missions. After all, they were not professional men of war, but civilians in all but formal definition.[54]

Colonial acquiescence was facilitated by the British professionals' admirable and rapid adaptation to North American conditions.[55] As mentioned previously, irregular war or *petite guerre* (little war), as it was called, had entered Europe from the east as a feature of Habsburg-Ottoman frontier zones and the Ukrainian steppes. Feuds and hatreds ran deep there, motivated by ethnic and religious tensions. A noncombatant was usually considered someone who had forgotten to pick up his weapon. As little-war techniques moved westward, the accompanying antagonisms tended to be replaced by grudging mutual respect. From destroying as much property and killing as many people as possible, the purpose of partisan war came to be seen as checking the other side's partisans: keeping them away from one's own supply convoys and rear areas.

British regiments who served on the continent during the ongoing wars of the seventeenth and eighteenth centuries played their part in that fighting. They faced different circumstances at home, where both Ireland and Scotland fostered something closer to partisan war as understood in North America: enemies who saw themselves as having nothing to lose and therefore bound by none of the restraints that helped to limit the barbarity of warfare among nation-states. The military response involved campaigns of suppression so brutal that the nine of diamonds still carries the nickname "curse of Scotland" on the mythic grounds that Cumberland wrote on that playing card his order for no quarter at the battle of Culloden in 1745. Much of the dirtier work was done not by professionals, but by local irregulars, motivated by anything from traditional antagonism toward neighbors, like the Campbells in the west of Scotland, to a simple exchange of shillings.[56]

The British army thus had something of a playbook when it deployed to North America in force during what was called, on this side of the Atlantic, the French and Indian War (1757–1763). If regular officers continued to slight the military skills of provincial regiments, they made increasing use of rangers for raiding and screening. Any potential for the rangers' development along the lines of Grenzer, Cossacks, or the independent companies who became the ancestors of the Black Watch was checked, however, by the regulars' increasingly comprehensive acculturation to frontier warfare under North American conditions. The British raised an entire regiment, the four-battalion Royal Americans, from German and Swiss settlers in western Pennsylvania, supplemented by overseas recruits. While not light infantry in the strict sense, these men did receive extra instruction in marksmanship and movement. Each regular battalion also raised a light company, in theory composed of the most alert and agile men, specially trained in skirmishing and given uniforms better adapted to rough country than the traditional long-skirted scarlet coats. "Battalion companies," counterparts of today's grunts, also found themselves fighting in fewer ranks and looser formations than prescribed by drill books designed with the open and ordered fields of Europe in mind.

French Canada's military system too was regularized. Canada, though hardly a pacific society, for a variety of reasons—not least the relatively small size of its population vis-à-vis the First Canadians—had never fought indigenous people on the scale or with the enthusiasm of their southern neighbors. The locally recruited Canadian militia, the woods-runners or *coureurs des bois*, and the colonial service companies raised by the Naval Ministry were sufficiently acculturated to be formidable bush fighters. Yet the near-token regular regiments, white coats and all, that the home government managed to send at too-long intervals soon became the backbone of Canada's long rear guard struggle. This reflected in good part their status as the only troops in Canada who could stand against the reconfigured British regulars with fair prospects of success in anything like a stand-up fight.[57]

The American preference for regular soldiers at the sharp end of war persisted through the American War of Independence (1775–1783). For all the recent focus on that conflict's revolutionary aspect an emerging America's first-line Continental Army was a force recruited in good part from the marginalized, the disadvantaged, and the ambitious. Patriotism was certainly a motive, but increasingly, generous bonuses in cash, land, and even goods appealed as well to self-interest in a synergy that can be described as uniquely American, remaining central to the character of the contemporary professional armed forces of the United States. In contrast to their European counterparts,

Idealized depiction of the Continental Army during the American Revolution. Courtesy of the Library of Congress.

American regulars were limited-service troops. Enlistment for "three years or for the war," George Washington's preference, remained a theoretical norm. Constant personnel turnover handicapped a force whose effectiveness was more or less directly related to its acculturation to the professional methods developed in Europe. The Continental Army nevertheless developed to a point where its better units, particularly its corps of light infantry formed from the picked men of all the regiments, proved consistently a match for the best British and German troops they faced. Despite their title, the light infantry were considered shock troops rather than skirmishers, and proved their worth in this role from Stony Point to Yorktown as an alternative to presumably less "republican" grenadiers.

The American rebels' second line, the state militias, depended heavily on the services of patriots with property. They proved more effective in support roles, such as organizing men and supplies, rather than as field forces.[58] It must be noted, however, that compared to Europe, individual militiamen freely shifted between militia and continental service. An important military result was that by the end of the war, particularly in the South, militia regiments gave good accounts of themselves under commanders who understood how to use them.[59] In social and cultural contexts the early modern pattern of military professionalization never became as pronounced in America as it did in Europe—a fact illustrated by, among many other points of evidence, the Second Amendment to the U.S. Constitution and the persistence, even today, of organizations like the National Rifle Association, whose bumper stickers and publications continue to celebrate the putative virtues of an armed citizenry.

NOTES

1. Previous studies that place European developments in world context include Jeremy M. Black, *War and the World: Military Power and the Fate of Continents, 1450–2000* (New Haven, CT: Yale University Press, 1998); and J. H. Parry, *The Establishment of the European Hegemony: 1415–1715* (New York: Harper and Row, 1961). William H. McNeill's *The Pursuit of Power: Technology, Armed Force, and Society since* A.D. *1000* (Chicago: University of Chicago Press, 1982) is indispensable, as is Geoffrey Parker's *The Military Revolution: Military Innovation and the Rise of the West, 1500–1800* (Cambridge, UK: Cambridge University Press, 1988).

2. John F. Guilmartin Jr., "Ideology and Conflict: The Wars of the Ottoman Empire, 1453–1606," *Journal of Interdisciplinary History* 18 (1988): 721–747; Norman Itzkowitz, *Ottoman Empire and Islamic Tradition* (Chicago: University of Chicago Press, 1980).

3. Arther Ferrill, *Roman Imperial Grand Strategy* (Lanham, MD: University Press of America, 1991).

4. Cf. the essays in D.J.B. Trim and M. Fissell, eds., *Amphibious Warfare 1000–1700: Commerce, State Formation and European Expansion* (Leiden, Netherlands: Brill, 2006). On the Crusades themselves, see Christopher Tyerman, *God's War: A New History of the Crusades* (Cambridge, MA: Harvard University Press, 2006).

5. Carlo Cipolla, *Guns, Sails, and Empires: Technological Innovation and the Early Phases of European Expansion* (New York: Pantheon, 1966).

6. Peter Padfield, *Tide of Empires: Decisive Naval Campaigns and the Rise of the West, Vol. 1, 1481–1654* (London: Routledge, 1979).

7. Bailey W. Diffie and George D. Winius, *Foundations of the Portuguese Empire, 1415–1580* (Minneapolis: University of Minnesota Press, 1977).

8. Daniel Headrick, *The Tools of Empire: Technology and European Imperialism in the Nineteenth Century* (New York: Oxford University Press, 1981).

9. John Thornton, *Warfare in Atlantic Africa, 1500–1800* (London: UCL Press, 1999).

10. Cf. Hugh Thomas, *Rivers of Gold: The Rise of the Spanish Empire from Columbus to Magellan* (New York: Random House, 2004), and Henry Kamen, *Empire: How Spain Became a World Power, 1492–1763* (New York: Harper Collins, 2003).

11. Steve J. Stern, *Peru's Indian Peoples and the Challenge of Spanish Conquest: Huamanga to 1640* (Madison: University of Wisconsin Press, 1982).

12. James Lockhart, *The Men of Cajamarca: A Social and Biographical Study of the First Conquerors of Peru* (Austin: University of Texas Press, 1972), concludes that no more than three or four of the Europeans had prior military experience.

13. Bernal Díaz del Castillo, *The Conquest of New Spain,* trans. J. M. Cohen (New York: Penguin Books, 1978).

14. A recent study documenting the ecological and biological disaster of the "Columbian Exchange" is Charles C. Mann, *1491: New Revelations of the Americas Before Columbus* (New York: Knopf, 2005).

15. Ross Hassig, *Mexico and the Spanish Conquest* (London: Longman, 1994). On the Aztec practice of human sacrifice, see Inga Clendinnen, *Aztecs: An Interpretation* (New York: Cambridge University Press, 1991).

16. D.J.B. Trim, "Medieval and Early Modern Inshore, Estuarine, and Lacustrine Warfare," in Trim and Fissell, *Amphibious Warfare,* 357–419.

17. Malyn Newitt, "Portuguese Amphibious Warfare in the East in the Sixteenth Century (c. 1500–1520)," in ibid., 103–122.

18. Geoffrey Parker, *The Army of Flanders and the Spanish Road, 1567–1659: The Logistics of Spanish Victory and Defeat in the Low Countries' Wars* (Cambridge, UK: Cambridge University Press, 1972), 15–16.

19. Geoffrey Parker, *The Military Revolution: Military Revolution and the Rise of the West, 1500–1800* (Cambridge, UK: Cambridge University Press, 1988), 108.

20. George D. Winius and Marcus P. M. Vink, *The Merchant-Warrior Pacified: The VOC (The Dutch East India Company) and Its Changing Political Economy in India* (New York: Oxford University Press, 1991), is a case study in relative demilitarization.

21. Bruce Lenman, "The Transition to European Military Ascendancy in India, 1600–1800," in *Tools of War: Instruments, Ideas, and Institutions of Warfare, 1445–1871*, ed. John Lynn (Urbana: University of Illinois Press, 1990), 100–130, remains a useful overview.

22. The Japanese use of volley fire at Nagashino to defeat traditional samurai on horseback is memorably depicted in Akira Kurosawa's epic film *Kagemusha* (1980).

23. Noel Perrin, *Giving Up the Gun: Japan's Reversion to the Sword, 1543–1879* (Boston: Godine, 1979).

24. F. Wakeman Jr., *The Great Enterprise: The Manchu Reconstruction of Imperial Order in Seventeenth-Century China* (Berkeley: University of California Press, 1985); Jonathan King, *Pirate King: Coxinga and the Fall of the Ming Dynasty* (Phoenix Mill, UK: Sutton, 2004).

25. J. P. Lawford, *Britain's Army in India: From Its Origins to the Conquest of Bengal* (London: Allen and Unwin, 1978); Amiya Barat, *The Bengal Native Infantry: Its Organization and Discipline, 1796–1852* (Calcutta, India: Firma K. L. Mukhopadhyay, 1962).

26. The best expression of this perspective is Philip Mason, *A Matter of Honour* (New York: Holt, Rinehart, and Winston, 1974).

27. Channa Wickenremesekera, *"Best Black Troops in the World": British Perceptions and the Making of the Sepoy, 1746–1808* (New Delhi: Manohar, 2002); Seema Alavi, *The Sepoys and the Company: Tradition and Transition in Northern India, 1770–1830* (New Delhi: Oxford University Press, 1995).

28. John Lynn, "Victories of the Conquered: The Native Character of the Sepoy," chap. 5 in *Battle: A History of Combat and Culture* (Boulder, CO: Westview, 2003), 145–178, may be supplemented by Douglas M. Peers, *Between Mars and Mammon: Colonial Armies and the Garrison State in Early Nineteenth Century India* (London: Tauris, 1995).

29. John Lynn, "Heart of the Sepoy: The Adoption and Adaptation of European Military Practice in South Asia, 1740–1805," in *The Diffusion of Military Technology and Ideas*, ed. Emily O. Goldman and Leslie C. Eliason (Stanford, CA: Stanford University Press, 2003), 33–62: 59.

30. Parker, *Military Revolution*, 117–118.

31. Victor Davis Hanson, *The Western Way of War: Infantry Battle in Classical Greece* (New York: Knopf, 1989).

32. John F. Guilmartin Jr., "The Military Revolution: Origins and First Tests Abroad," in *The Military Revolution Debate: Readings on the Transformation of Early Modern Europe*, ed. Clifford J. Rogers (Boulder, CO: Westview, 1995), 317.

33. Irfan Habib, *Confronting Colonialism: Resistance and Modernization under Haidar Ali and Tippoo Sultan* (London: Anthem, 2002).

34. R.G.S. Cooper, *The Anglo-Maratha Campaigns and the Contest for India* (Cambridge, UK: Cambridge University Press, 2003), 15–61.

35. T. S. Shejwalkar, *Panipat 1761* (Poona: Deccan College, 1946).

36. Alan Lloyd, *The Drums of Kumasi: The Story of the Ashanti Wars* (London: Longmans, 1964), is a serviceable popular narrative.

37. Shelford Bidwell, *Swords for Hire: European Mercenaries in Eighteenth-Century India* (London: Murray, 1971).

38. The above follows the argument of Cooper, *Anglo-Maratha Campaigns*, 57 ff.

39. See Wakeman, *Great Enterprise*, passim.

40. See Ross Hassig, *War and Society in Ancient Mesoamerica* (Berkeley: University of California Press, 1992); and *Time, History, and Belief in Aztec and Colonial Mexico* (Austin: University of Texas Press, 2001).

41. Cooper, *Anglo-Maratha Campaigns*, 299 ff.

42. Max L. Moorhead, *The Presidio: Bastion of the Spanish Borderlands* (Norman: University of Oklahoma Press, 1975), provides the basics of the presidial system.

43. Given the economic and strategic significance of the Caribbean, its neglect by military historians of the early modern period is striking. The best overview is Christian Buchet's intellectually formidable *La lutte pour l'espace caraïbe et la façade atlantique de l'Amérique centrale et du sud (1672–1762)*, 2 vols. (Paris: Librairie de l'Inde, 1991). Richard Harding's case study, *Amphibious Warfare in the Eighteenth Century: The British Expedition to the West Indies, 1740–1742* (Suffolk, UK: Boydell Press, 1991), is badly in need of company.

44. David Syrett, *The Siege and Capture of Havana, 1762* (London: Navy Records Society, 1970), is a document collection.

45. Roger N. Buckley, *The British Army in the West Indies: Society and the Military in the Revolutionary Age* (Gainesville: University Press of Florida, 1998), is a valuable source on military routine, despite being outside the time period covered by this book.

46. Roger N. Buckley, *Slaves in Red Coats: The British West India Regiments, 1795–1815* (New Haven, CT: Yale University Press, 1979).

47. Patrick M. Malone, *The Skulking Way of War: Technology and Tactics among the New England Indians* (New York: Madison, 1991).

48. John Grenier, *The First Way of War: American Warmaking on the Frontier, 1607–1814* (Cambridge, UK: Cambridge University Press, 2005), and Armstrong Starkey, *European and Native American Warfare, 1675–1815* (London: UCL Press, 1998), are the best overviews.

49. John Ferling, *A Wilderness of Miseries: War and Warriors in Early America* (Westport, CT: Greenwood Press, 1980).

50. John Dederer, *War in America to 1775: Before Yankee Doodle* (New York: New York University Press, 1990); David S. Lovejoy, "Satanizing the American Indian," *The New England Quarterly* 67 (1994): 603–621.

51. The structure of the following paragraph is a modification of Grenier, *First Way of War*, 29 ff.

52. The standard case study is Fred Anderson, *A People's Army: Massachusetts Soldiers and Society in the Seven Years' War* (Chapel Hill: North Carolina, 1984). Cf. Harold Selesky's complementary *War and Society in Colonial Connecticut* (New Haven, CT: Yale University Press, 1990).

53. But see Stephen C. Eames, "Rustic Warfare and the Provincial Soldier on the Northern Frontier, 1689–1748" (PhD diss., University of New Hampshire, 1989).

54. Fred Anderson, *Crucible of War: The Seven Years' War and the Fate of Empire in British North America* (New York: Vintage, 2001), is a masterful contextualization of the particular material discussed here.

55. Cf. King Parker, "Anglo-American Wilderness Campaigning 1754–1764: Logistical and Tactical Developments" (PhD diss., Columbia University, 1970); and Stephen Brumwell, *Redcoats: The British Soldier and War in the Americas, 1755–1763* (Cambridge, UK: Cambridge University Press, 2002).

56. Cf. Johannes Kunisch, *Der kleine Krieg: Studien des Heerwesen des Absolutismus* (Wiesbaden, Germany: Franz Steiner, 1973); and Martin Rink, *Vom Partheygaenger zum Partisanen: Die Konzeption des kleinen Krieges in Preussen 1740–1813* (Frankfurt, Germany: Lang, 1999)—the latter with a European dimension that belies its title. Jeremy M. Black, *Culloden and the '45* (New York: St. Martin's Press, 1990), is solid.

57. Cf. W. J. Eccles, "The Social, Economic, and Political Significance of the Military Establishment in New France," *Canadian Historical Review* 52 (1971): 1–22; and Martin L. Nicolai, "A Different Kind of Courage: The French Military and the Canadian Irregular Soldier during the Seven Years' War," *Canadian Historical Review* 70 (1970): 53–75.

58. Charles Royster, *A Revolutionary People at War: The Continental Army and American Character, 1778–1783* (Chapel Hill: University of North Carolina Press, 1979); Charles Neimeier, *America Goes to War: A Social History of the Continental Army* (New York: New York University Press, 1996).

59. A point developed in John Buchanan, *The Road to Guilford Court House: The American Revolution in the Carolinas* (New York: Wiley, 1997).

Eight

✳ ✳ ✳

CONCLUSION

The conclusion to this work begins with two negatives. First, the European soldier was not yet a universal soldier, in the sense of being master of the world's battlefields. Even in India, sepoys played a relatively larger role than would be the case in later periods. George Raudzens makes a telling case that maritime evolution, the ability to transport and supply consistently, was more important than military revolution in establishing European influence during the early modern period.[1] At its end, in the eighteenth century, France's ability to maintain its transatlantic communications was vital in first sustaining, then losing, its North American empire. Sustaining command of the sea was similarly critical for Britain during the American Revolution. Soldiers went where ships could take them and stayed where ships could support them.[2]

The second negative shaping this work is the near-universal dislike felt for the soldier by contemporaries and scholars alike. He is presented as everything from a brute and a rapist, sustained by an insatiable appetite for plunder, to an automaton, mind and spirit deadened by drink, held in ranks only by a discipline so brutal that it debased even those enforcing it. Geoffrey Parker speaks harshly of the *picaro* values, idleness, brutality, and violence, which "invaded" Spanish society through discharged soldiers. Other scholars are no less critical of veterans' influence in other countries.[3]

It is worth suggesting that the choices and behaviors congenial to respectable early modern bourgeoisie, and to contemporary academicians with a near-visceral distaste for even the diluted masculinity of student cultures, are not necessarily normative. Nor are they always congruent with the values of young men whose nerve and ambition exceed their opportunities. Without understating the burdens early modern armies laid on civil society, the common soldier of the period, the subject of this book, was more than a brigand in state pay. That fact involved a crucial, complex process: the development from serf to warrior to soldier.

The serf fights because a weapon is thrust into his hand on the command of his lord. He lacks the agency that fosters commitment. By the beginning of this book he had been replaced in armies' ranks by the warrior. The warrior may fight for cause or comrades, for pay or for sport. He may fight from ambition, seeking honor or wealth, or because fighting is a condition of group acceptance. He may, like many warriors, simply be imitating his social superiors. At seventh and last, he fights because it is his choice: his will to do so.

As the early modern era progressed, the warrior was increasingly supplanted—though never entirely replaced—by the soldier. The soldier may be motivated by the considerations inspiring the warrior. He may also be motivated by hunger, coercion, or necessity. Compulsion to serve in the armies of early modern Europe, however, was usually indirect, and sufficiently collective-oriented that an individual's chances of sidestepping military service were good even in authoritarian states like Prussia and Russia. Comprehensive moral and institutional coercion was a product of later times and stronger states: the white feathers of World War I Britain or the risk of a death sentence in Nazi Germany. They obscured but did not invalidate the principle developed between the sixteenth and eighteenth centuries. The soldier fights because he has agreed to fight: He has given his word.

That pledge can involve pay—indeed the word *soldier* derived from the coins used to pay the professional armies of Rome. The pledge can involve patriotism: the most common coin of the nineteenth and twentieth century. Religious idealism might well provide a focus of agreement in the twenty-first century. The key to a soldier's identity nevertheless remains commitment: to comrades, to regiment, and ultimately, to cause—commitment based on the word of a self-respecting individual.

Will and word are frequently cast as opposites, and never more so than in early modern Europe. Toward the end of the period, Friedrich Schiller highlighted the debate in "Wallenstein's Camp." A sergeant and a rifleman, both veterans, take the stage:

> SERGEANT: . . . Must a soldier then be made
> By driving this riotous, roaring trade?
> 'Tis drilling that makes him, skill and sense—
> Perception, thought, intelligence.
>
> RIFLEMAN: 'Tis liberty makes him! Here's a fuss!
> That I should such twaddle as this discuss. . . .
>
> Idle and heedless I'll take my way, hunting for novelty every day;
> Trust to the moment with dauntless mind,
> And give not a glance before or behind.

Sergeant and rifleman, grenadier and *Landsknecht*, drill and drive: The juxtaposition seems perfect. Yet as this chapter has shown, the worth of discipline was never denied on one hand, nor the spirit of risk abandoned on the other. Instead, we have witnessed a synergy of the two among the rank and file that in turn shaped the professional armies that emerged from the Military Revolution, and informed, to an extent only now achieving recognition, the citizen armies of the Revolutionary and Napoleonic eras—and their nineteenth- and twentieth-century successors as well.

NOTES

1. George Raudzens, "Military Revolution or Maritime Evolution? Military Superiorities or Transportation Advantages as Main Causes of European Colonial Conquests to 1788," *Journal of Military History* 65 (1999): 631–641.

2. Kenneth Banks, *Chasing Empire across the Sea: Communications and the State in the French Atlantic, 1713–1763* (Cambridge, UK: Cambridge University Press, 2006); David Syrett, *Shipping and the American War 1775–83: A Study of British Transport Organization* (London: University of London/Athlone Press, 1970).

3. Geoffrey Parker, *The Army of Flanders and the Spanish Road, 1567–1659: The Logistics of Spanish Victory and Defeat in the Low Countries' Wars* (Cambridge, UK: Cambridge University Press, 1972), 180, 183. For an even harsher critique of veterans' civic impact, see J. H. Hale, *War and Society in Renaissance Europe, 1450–1620* (Baltimore: Johns Hopkins University Press, 1985), 115 ff.

BIBLIOGRAPHY

GENERAL STUDIES

Addington, Larry H. *The Patterns of War through the Eighteenth Century.* Bloomington: Indiana University Press, 1990.

Anderson, Matthew S. *War and Society in Europe of the Old Regime, 1618–1789.* New York: St. Martin's Press, 1988.

Black, Jeremy M., ed. *The Origins of War in Early Modern Europe.* Edinburgh: J. Donald, 1987.

Black, Jeremy M. *A Military Revolution? Military Change and European Society, 1550–1800.* London: Macmillan, 1991.

Black, Jeremy M. *The Cambridge Illustrated Atlas of Warfare: Renaissance to Revolution, 1492–1792.* Cambridge, UK: Cambridge University Press, 1996.

Black, Jeremy M., ed. *War in the Early Modern World, 1450–1815.* London: UCL Press, 1999.

Brodsky, G. W. Stephen. *Gentlemen of the Blade: A Social and Literary History of the British Army Since 1660.* New York: Greenwood Press, 1988.

Cameron, Euan, ed. *Early Modern Europe: An Oxford History.* Oxford, UK: Oxford University Press, 1999.

Childs, John C. R. *Armies and Warfare in Europe, 1648–1789.* New York: Holmes and Meier, 1982.

Clark, G. N. *War and Society in the Seventeenth Century.* Cambridge, UK: Cambridge University Press, 1958.

Clark, J. C. D. *The Language of Liberty, 1660–1832: Political Discourse and Social Dynamics in the Anglo-American World.* Cambridge, UK: Cambridge University Press, 1994.

Corvisier, André. *Armies and Societies in Europe, 1494–1789.* Bloomington: Indiana University Press, 1979.

Delbrück, Hans. *The Dawn of Modern Warfare.* Lincoln: University of Nebraska Press, 1990.

Delumeau, Jean. *Sin and Fear.* Translated by Eric Nicholson. New York: St. Martin's Press, 1990.

Duffy, Michael, ed. *The Military Revolution and the State, 1500–1800.* Exeter, UK: University of Exeter, 1980.

Earle, Edward Mead. *Makers of Modern Strategy: Military Thought from Machiavelli to Hitler.* New York: Atheneum, 1966.

Ehrenreich, Barbara. *Blood Rites: Origins and History of the Passions of War.* New York: Henry Holt, 1997.

Ertman, Thomas. *Birth of the Leviathan: Building States and Regimes in Medieval and Early Modern Europe.* Cambridge, UK: Cambridge University Press, 1997.

Garrett, Clarke. *Spirit Possession and Popular Religion: From the Camisards to the Shakers.* Baltimore: Johns Hopkins University Press, 1987.

Howard, Michael. *War in European History.* Oxford, UK: Oxford University Press, 1976.

Huntington, Samuel P. *The Soldier and the State: The Theory and Politics of Civil-Military Relations.* New York: Random House, 1957.

Jones, Archer. *The Art of War in the Western World.* Urbana: University of Illinois Press, 1987.

Kaiser, David. *Politics and War: European Conflict from Philip II to Hitler.* Cambridge, MA: Harvard University Press, 1990.

Kamen, Henry. *European Society: 1500–1700.* London: Hutchinson, 1984.

Keegan, John. *The Mask of Command.* New York: Viking Penguin, 1987.

Keegan, John. *A History of Warfare.* New York: Alfred A. Knopf, 1994.

Keegan, John. *Fields of Battle: The Wars for North America.* New York: Alfred A. Knopf, 1996.

Kiernan, Victor G. *The Duel in European History: Honour and the Reign of Aristocracy.* Oxford, UK: Oxford University Press, 1989.

Lovejoy, David S. *Religious Enthusiasm in the New World: Heresy to Revolution.* Cambridge, MA: Harvard University Press, 1985.

Lynn, John A., ed. *Feeding Mars: Logistics in Western Warfare from the Middle Ages to the Present.* Boulder, CO: Westview, 1993.

Marini, Stephen A. *Radical Sects of Revolutionary New England.* Cambridge, MA: Harvard University Press, 1982.

McNeill, William H. *Keeping Together in Time: Dance and Drill in Human History.* Cambridge, MA: Harvard University Press, 1995.

Paret, Peter, ed. *Makers of Modern Strategy from Machiavelli to the Nuclear Age.* Princeton, NJ: Princeton University Press, 1986.

Paret, Peter. *Imagined Battles: Reflections of War in European Art.* Chapel Hill: University of North Carolina Press, 1997.

Roberts, Michael. *Essays in Swedish History.* London: Weidenfeld and Nicolson, 1967.

Rogers, Clifford J., ed. *The Military Revolution Debate: Readings on the Transformation of Early Modern Europe.* Boulder, CO: Westview, 1995.

Strachan, Hew. *European Armies and the Conduct of War.* London: Allen and Unwin, 1983.

Tallett, Frank. *War and Society in Early-Modern Europe: 1495–1715.* London: Routledge, 1992.

Thomson, Janice E. *Mercenaries, Pirates, and Sovereigns: State-Building and Extraterritorial Violence in Early Modern Europe.* Princeton, NJ: Princeton University Press, 1994.

van Creveld, Martin. *Supplying War: Logistics from Wallenstein to Patton.* Cambridge, UK: Cambridge University Press, 1977.

van Creveld, Martin. *Command in War.* Cambridge, MA: Harvard University Press, 1985.

Weigley, Russell F. *The Age of Battles: The Quest for Decisive Warfare from Breitenfeld to Waterloo.* Bloomington: Indiana University Press, 1991.

Wilson, Peter H. "The German 'Soldier Trade' of the Seventeenth and Eighteenth Centuries: A Reassessment." *International History Review* 18 (1996): 757–792.

WARFARE FROM 1494 TO 1648

Aberth, John. *From the Brink of the Apocalypse: Confronting Famine, War, Plague, and Death in the Later Middle Ages.* London: Routledge, 2001.

Adams, Simon. "Tactics or Politics? 'The Military Revolution' and the Hapsburg Hegemony, 1525–1648." In *Tools of War: Instruments, Ideas, and Institutions of Warfare, 1445–1871,* ed. John A. Lynn. Urbana: University of Illinois Press, 1990.

Barker, Thomas Mack. *The Military Intellectual and Battle: Raimondo Montecuccoli and the Thirty Years' War.* Albany: State University of New York Press, 1975.

Barnes, Robin Bruce. *Prophecy and Gnosis: Apocalypticism in the Wake of the Lutheran Reformation.* Stanford, CA: Stanford University Press, 1988.

Bayley, Charles C. *War and Society in Renaissance Florence: The De Militia of Leonardo Bruni.* Toronto, ON: University of Toronto Press, 1961.

Cunningham, Andrew, and Ole Peter Grell. *The Four Horsemen of the Apocalypse: Religion, War, Famine, and Death in Reformation Europe.* Cambridge, UK: Cambridge University Press, 2001.

De Gheyn, Jacob. *The Exercise of Armes: A Seventeenth Century Military Manual.* London: Lionel Leventhal, 1986. Original published 1607.

Dunn, Richard S. *The Age of Religious Wars, 1559–1689.* New York: W. W. Norton, 1970.

Fallon, Robert Thomas. *Captain or Colonel: The Soldier in Milton's Life and Art.* Columbia: University of Missouri Press, 1984.

Fissel, Mark Charles. *English Warfare, 1511–1642.* London: Routledge, 2001.

Gardiner, Samuel R. *The Thirty Years' War, 1618–1648.* New York: Greenwood Press, 1969.

Gentles, Ian. *The New Model Army in England, Ireland and Scotland, 1645–1653.* Oxford, UK: Blackwell, 1991.

Gunn, Steven. "War, Religion, and the State." In *Early Modern Europe*, ed. Euan Cameron. Oxford, UK: Oxford University Press, 1999.

Guthrie, William P. *Battles of the Thirty Years War: From White Mountain to Nordlingen, 1618–1635.* Westport, CT: Greenwood Press, 2002.

Hale, John R. *Renaissance War Studies.* London: Hambledon, 1983.

Hale, John R. *War and Society in Renaissance Europe, 1450–1620.* Baltimore: Johns Hopkins University Press, 1985.

Hale, John R. *Artists and Warfare in the Renaissance.* New Haven, CT: Yale University Press, 1990.

Hale, John R. "How War Fed War: The Tax of Violence and Contributions during the *Grand Siècle.*" *Journal of Modern History* 65 (1993): 286–310.

Harari, Yuval Noah. *Renaissance Military Memoirs: War, History, and Identity, 1450–1600.* Woodbridge, UK: Boydell Press, 2004.

Hibbert, Christopher. *Cavaliers and Roundheads: The English Civil War, 1642–1649.* London: Harper Collins, 1993.

Hill, Christopher. *The World Turned Upside Down: Radical Ideas during the English Revolution.* New York: Viking Press, 1972.

Hill, Christopher. *The English Bible and the Seventeenth-Century Revolution.* New York: Penguin, 1993.

Kamen, Henry. *Philip of Spain.* New Haven, CT: Yale University Press, 1997.

Kingra, Mahinder S. "The *Trace Italienne* and the Military Revolution during the Eighty Years' War, 1567–1648." *Journal of Military History* 57 (1993): 431–446.

Koch, H. W. *The Rise of Modern Warfare, 1618–1815.* Englewood Cliffs, NJ: Prentice-Hall, 1981.

Langer, Herbert. *The Thirty Years' War.* London: Dorset Press, 1990.

Machiavelli, Niccolò. *The Art of War.* New York: Bobbs-Merrill, 1965. Original published 1521.

Mallett, Michael E. *Mercenaries and Their Masters: Warfare in Renaissance Italy.* London: Bodley Head, 1974.

Mallet, Michael E. "The Art of War." In *Handbook of European History, 1400–1600: Late Middle Ages, Renaissance, and Reformation.* Vol. 1, *Structures and Assertions*, ed. Thomas A. Brady Jr., Heiko A. Oberman, and James D. Tracy. Grand Rapids, MI: William B. Eerdmans, 1996.

Mallett, Michael E., and John R. Hale. *The Military Organization of a Renaissance State: Venice c.1400–1617.* Cambridge, UK: Cambridge University Press, 1984.

Moxey, Keith. *Peasants, Warriors, and Wives: Popular Imagery in the Reformation.* Chicago: University of Chicago Press, 1989.

Parker, Geoffrey. "The 'Military Revolution, 1560–1660'—A Myth?" *Journal of Modern History* 48 (1976): 195–214.

Parker, Geoffrey. *The Thirty Years' War.* New York: Military Heritage Press, 1987.

Parker, Geoffrey. *The Grand Strategy of Philip II.* New Haven, CT: Yale University Press, 1998.

Parrott, David. "Strategy and Tactics in the Thirty Years' War: The 'Military Revolution.'" *Militärgeschichtliche Mitteilungen* 18 (1985): 7–25.

Parrott, David. "The Military Revolution in Early Modern Europe." *History Today* 42 (1992): 21–27.

Parrott, David A. *Richelieu's Army: War, Government and Society in France, 1624–1642.* Cambridge, UK: Cambridge University Press, 2001.

Phillips, Gervase. "To Cry 'Home! Home!': Mutiny, Morale, and Indiscipline in Tudor Armies." *Journal of Military History* 65 (2001): 313–332.

Quatrefages, René. *Los Tercios.* Translated by E. Jarnes Bergua. Madrid: Colección Ediciones Ejército, 1983.

Redlich, Fritz. *The German Military Enterpriser and His Work Force: A Study in European Economic and Social History.* 2 vols. Wiesbaden, Germany: Franz Steiner, 1964–1965.

Roberts, Michael. *Gustavus Adolphus: A History of Sweden, 1611–1632.* 2 vols. London: Longmans Green, 1953–1958.

Roberts, Michael. *Gustavus Adolphus.* 2nd ed. London: Longman, 1992.

Rogers, Clifford J. "The Military Revolutions of the Hundred Years' War." *Journal of Military History* 57 (1993): 241–278.

Rothenberg, Gunther E. "Maurice of Nassau, Gustavus Adolphus, Raimondo Montecuccoli, and the 'Military Revolution' of the Seventeenth Century." In *Makers of Modern Strategy: From Machiavelli to the Nuclear Age,* ed. Peter Paret. Princeton, NJ: Princeton University Press, 1986.

Showalter, Dennis E. "Caste, Skill, and Training: The Evolution of Cohesion in European Armies from the Middle Ages to the Sixteenth Century." *Journal of Military History* 57 (1993): 407–430.

Smythe, John. *Certain Discourses Military.* Edited by John Hale. Ithaca, NY: Cornell University Press, 1964. Original published 1590.

Vale, Malcolm. *War and Chivalry: Warfare and Aristocratic Culture in England, France, and Burgundy at the End of the Middle Ages.* London: Duckworth, 1981.

Wedgwood, C. V. *The Thirty Years War.* New Haven, CT: Yale University Press, 1939.

Williams, Roger. *The Actions of the Low Countries.* Edited by D. W. Davies. Ithaca, NY: Cornell University Press, 1964. Original published 1618.

WARFARE FROM 1648 TO 1792

Asprey, Robert B. *Frederick the Great: The Magnificent Enigma.* New York: Ticknor and Fields, 1986.

Barnett, Correlli. *The First Churchill: Marlborough, Soldier and Statesman.* New York: Putnam, 1974.

Black, Jeremy. *European Warfare, 1660–1815.* New Haven, CT: Yale University Press, 1994.

Chandler, David. *The Art of War in the Age of Marlborough.* New York: Hippocrene Books, 1976.

Chandler, David. *Marlborough As Military Commander.* 2nd ed. London: Batsford, 1979.

Duffy, Christopher. *The Army of Frederick the Great*. New York: Hippocrene Books, 1974.

Duffy, Christopher. *The Army of Maria Theresa: The Armed Forces of Imperial Austria, 1740–1780*. New York: Hippocrene Books, 1977.

Duffy, Christopher. *The Military Experience in the Age of Reason, 1715–1789*. New York: Atheneum, 1988.

Dwyer, Philip G., ed. *The Rise of Prussia, 1700–1830*. London: Longman, 2000.

Gat, Azar. *The Origins of Military Thought: From the Enlightenment to Clausewitz*. Oxford, UK: Clarendon Press, 1989.

Kopperman, Paul E. "'The Cheapest Pay': Alcohol Abuse in the Eighteenth-Century British Army." *Journal of Military History* 60 (1996): 445–470.

Langins, Janis. *Conserving the Enlightenment: French Military Engineering from Vauban to the Revolution*. Cambridge, MA: MIT Press, 2003.

Lund, Erik A. *War for the Every Day: Generals, Knowledge, and Warfare in Early Modern Europe, 1680–1740*. Westport, CT: Greenwood Press, 1999.

Luvaas, Jay, ed. *Frederick the Great on the Art of War*. New York: Free Press, 1966.

Lynn, John A. *Giant of the Grand Siècle: The French Army, 1610–1715*. Cambridge, UK: Cambridge University Press, 1997.

Lynn, John A. *The French Wars 1667–1714: The Sun King at War*. Oxford, UK: Osprey, 2002.

Nosworthy, Brent. *The Anatomy of Victory: Battle Tactics, 1689–1763*. New York: Hippocrene Books, 1990.

Quimby, Robert S. *The Background of Napoleonic Warfare: The Theory of Military Tactics in Eighteenth-Century France*. New York: Columbia University Press, 1957.

Reinhard, Marcel. "Nostalgie et service militaire pendant la Révolution." *Annales historiques de la Révolution française* 30 (1958): 1–15.

Rothenberg, Gunther. *The Art of Warfare in the Age of Napoleon*. Bloomington: Indiana University Press, 1978.

Showalter, Dennis E. "Tactics and Recruitment in Eighteenth Century Prussia." *Studies in History and Politics* 3 (1983–1984): 15–41.

Showalter, Dennis E. *The Wars of Frederick the Great*. London: Longman, 1996.

Starkey, Armstrong. *War in the Age of Enlightenment, 1700–1789*. Westport, CT: Greenwood Press, 2003.

WEAPONRY AND EARLY MODERN WARFARE

Alder, Ken. *Engineering the Revolution: Arms and Enlightenment in France, 1763–1815*. Princeton, NJ: Princeton University Press, 1997.

Baumgartner, Frederick J. *From Spear to Flintlock: A History of War in Europe and the Middle East to the French Revolution*. New York: Praeger, 1991.

Cipolla, Carlo M. *Guns, Sails, and Empires: Technological Innovation and the Early Phases of European Expansion, 1400–1700*. New York: Pantheon Books, 1966.

De la Croix, H. "The Literature of Fortification in Renaissance Italy." *Technology and Culture* 4 (1963): 30–50.

Duffy, Christopher. *Fire and Stone: The Science of Fortress Warfare, 1660–1860*. London: David and Charles, 1975.

Duffy, Christopher. *Siege Warfare: The Fortress in the Early Modern World, 1494–1660.* London: Routledge/Kegan Paul, 1979.

Duffy, Christopher. *The Fortress in the Age of Vauban and Frederick the Great, 1660–1789.* London: Routledge/Kegan Paul, 1985.

Esper, Thomas. "The Replacement of the Longbow by Firearms in the English Army." In *Technology and the West,* ed. Terry S. Reynolds and Stephen H. Cutcliffe. Chicago: University of Chicago Press, 1997.

Guerlac, Henry. "Vauban: The Impact of Science on War." In *Makers of Modern Strategy: Military Thought from Machiavelli to Hitler,* ed. Edward Mead Earle. New York: Atheneum, 1941.

Hale, John R. *Renaissance Fortification: Art or Engineering?* London: Thames and Hudson, 1977.

Hall, A. Rupert. *Ballistics in the Seventeenth Century.* Cambridge, UK: Cambridge University Press, 1952.

Hall, A. Rupert. "Gunnery, Science, and the Royal Society." In *The Uses of Science in the Age of Newton,* ed. John G. Burke. Berkeley: University of California Press, 1983.

Hall, Bert S., and Kelly DeVries. "The Military Revolution Revisited." *Technology and Culture* 31 (1990): 500–507.

Hall, Bert S. *Weapons and Warfare in Renaissance Europe: Gunpowder, Technology, and Tactics.* Baltimore: Johns Hopkins University Press, 1997.

Henninger-Voss, Mary. "Between the Cannon and the Book." Ph.D. diss., Johns Hopkins University, 1995.

Hughes, Basil P. *Firepower: Weapons Effectiveness on the Battlefield, 1630–1850.* New York: Scribner, 1974.

Lavin, James D. *A History of Spanish Firearms.* New York: Arco, 1965.

Lynn, John A., ed. *Tools of War: Instruments, Ideas, and Institutions of Warfare, 1445–1871.* Urbana: University of Illinois Press, 1990.

Lynn, John A. "The *Trace Italienne* and the Growth of Armies: The French Case." *Journal of Military History* 55 (1991): 297–330.

McNeill, William H. *The Pursuit of Power: Technology, Armed Force, and Society since A.D. 1000.* Chicago: University of Chicago Press, 1982.

McNeill, William H. *The Age of Gunpowder Empires, 1450–1800.* Washington, DC: American Historical Association, 1989.

Oakeshott, R. Ewart. *European Weapons and Armour: From the Renaissance to the Industrial Revolution.* London: Lutterworth, 1978.

Oakeshott, R. Ewart. *The Archaeology of Weapons: Arms and Armor from Prehistory to the Age of Chivalry.* Woodbridge, UK: Boydell Press, 1994.

Ochs, Kathleen H. "The Failed Revolution in Applied Science: Studies of Industry by Members of the Royal Society of London, 1660–1688." Ph.D. diss., University of Toronto, 1981.

O'Connell, Robert L. *Of Arms and Men: A History of War, Weapons, and Aggression.* Oxford, UK: Oxford University Press, 1989.

Parker, Geoffrey. *The Army of Flanders and the Spanish Road, 1567–1659: The Logistics of Spanish Victory and Defeat in the Low Countries' Wars.* Cambridge, UK: Cambridge University Press, 1972.

Parker, Geoffrey. *The Military Revolution: Military Innovation and the Rise of the West, 1500–1800.* Cambridge, UK: Cambridge University Press, 1988.

Pepper, Simon, and Nicholas Adams. *Firearms and Fortifications: Military Architecture and Siege Warfare in Sixteenth-Century Siena.* Chicago: University of Chicago Press, 1986.

Peterson, Harold L. *Arms and Armor in Colonial America, 1526–1783.* Harrisburg, PA: Stackpole Books, 1956.

Rogers, Hugh C. B. *A History of Artillery.* Secaucus, NJ: Citadel Press, 1975.

Roland, Alex. "Technology and War: The Historiographical Revolution of the 1980s." *Technology and Culture* 34 (1993): 117–134.

Steele, Brett D., and Tamera Dorland. *The Heirs of Archimedes: Science and the Art of War through the Age of Enlightenment.* Cambridge, MA: MIT Press, 2005.

Stone, John. "Technology, Society, and the Infantry Revolution of the Fourteenth Century." *Journal of Military History* 68 (2004): 361–380.

van Creveld, Martin. *Technology and War: From 2000 B.C. to the Present.* New York: Free Press, 1989.

INTERNET RESOURCES

The following Internet sources are arranged from general to specific.

EuroDocs: Online Sources for European History
Richard Hacken, Brigham Young University, Provo, Utah
   http://eudocs.lib.byu.edu/index.php/Main_Page
A wealth of primary historical documents on Europe, many related to military history.

International Seminar on the History of the Atlantic World
Atlantic History Seminar, Harvard University, Cambridge, Massachusetts
http://www.fas.harvard.edu/~atlantic/atlanbib.html
Comprehensive bibliography of recent works related to the Atlantic World in the early modern period that includes links to book reviews.

Eighteenth-Century Resources—History
Jack Lynch, Rutgers University, New Brunswick, New Jersey
http://www.andromeda.rutgers.edu/~jlynch/18th/history.html
Outstanding resource on early modern history that includes both European and American sources.

Documents in Military History
Dave Stewart, Hillsdale College, Hillsdale, Michigan
http://www.hillsdale.edu/personal/stewart/war/
Wide-ranging collection of primary documents related to military history, including the early modern period.

The Arquebus and Matchlock Musket Page
J. E. Quest
http://www.geocities.com/Yosemite/Campground/8551
A reenactors' site with excellent technical information on matchlock weapons.

Join the British Army!
Adi Neuman and Yoni Brenner
http://www.umich.edu/~ece/student_projects/soldier/
Comprehensive discussion of the eighteenth-century army from the soldiers' perspective.

Polish Renaissance Warfare (1450–1699)
S. A. Jasinski
http://www.jasinski.co.uk/wojna/index.htm
Colorful depiction of the Polish army and its enemies, with good links.

The Seven Years War Web Site
Military Heritage and the Discriminating General
http://www.militaryheritage.com/7yrswar.htm
Comprehensive Web site about the Seven Years War that includes scholarly
    articles, maps, and sound clips.

English Civil War Publications/Thirty Years War Publications and Other
    Information
L. E. Pearson
http://www.lukehistory.com/resources/ecwpubs.html
http://www.lukehistory.com/resources/30yrswar.html
Primary sources related to the English Civil War from both Royalist and Parlia-
    mentarian perspectives as well as informative documents related to the battle
    of Breitenfeld in 1631.

Frederick the Great's Military Instructions
Ed Allen, Stanford University, Stanford, California
http://www.au.af.mil/au/awc/awcgate/readings/fred_cavalry.htm
An English translation of Frederick's "Particular Instruction of the King of
    Prussia to the Officers of His Army, and Especially Those of the Cavalry," a
    sixteen-article summary for his officers, and "The King of Prussia's Military
    Instruction to His Generals," a twenty-eight-article list to Frederick's gener-
    als on how to prepare for and fight battles.

The Spanish "Tercios" 1525–1704
Dr. Pierre Picouet and Dr. Susana Pombo
http://www.geocities.com/ao1617/TercioUK.html?200610
Impressively detailed, scholarly overview with an extensive set of links.

INDEX

Adolphus, Gustavus (King of Sweden), 12–14, 37, 45, 83, 104; cavalry under, 72; tactical innovations of, 64

Africa: European trade with, 9; Portugal in, 142–43

Age of Chivalry, laws of war in, 29

Age of Discovery, 5

Age of Entrepreneurs (1494–1648), 80–84

Age of Noblemen (1648–1740), 84–88

Age of Reason, military academies in, 60

Age of Reconnaissance, 5, 142

Age of the Officer (1740–1789), 88–94

Allotment system, of Sweden, 45

American Revolution, 19; French Revolution *vs.*, 107; nationalism and, 107; religious motivation for, 106–7

Americas, Europe and, 154–60

Amphibious assaults, 145

Anglo-Dutch Wars (1652–1674), 15

Aristocracy: French feudal service and, 39–40; in heavy cavalry, 30

Army of Flanders, 59, 130

Army surgeons, 125–27

Arquebus, 35

Artillery: cavalry *vs.*, 73; French production of, 70; importance of, 69–70

Asia: Europe and, 146–47, 149; military cultures in, 152

Aztec and Inca empires, Spanish conquest of, 143–44, 153

Ballistics, 70

Battles: Breitenfeld (1631), 84; Culloden (1745), 159; Formigny (1450), 53; Kunersdorf (1759), 91; Lützen (1632), 104; Malplaquet (1709), 67; Nördlingen (1634), 64; Zorndorf (1758), 91

Bernhard of Weimar (Duke), 82

Billets and quarters, 134–37

Black Death, 25–26

Bolt, William, 143

Breitenfeld (1631), battle of, 84

British East India Company, 147–48

Brown Bess musket, 65

Callot, Jacques, 103

Calvinism, 10, 101, 104

Camisards, 106

Canada, military system, militia of, 159

Candide (Voltaire), 99

Canons, 53

Capitalistic entrepreneurs, in military, 82–83

Caracole, 36

Caribbean basin, French Revolution and, 155
Carnot, Lazare, 107
Catholic Reformation, 12
Cavalier, Jean (Colonel), 106
Cavalry: Adolphus's use of, 72; aristocracy in,
    30; artillery *vs.*, 73; Cromwell's Ironsides, 104;
    infantry *vs.*, 52; specialization, 72–74;
    subsidiary combat arm of, 71
Cavendish, Charles, 87
Cervantes, Miguel, 111
Charles V (Emperor of Spain), 10–11, 102
Charles VIII (King of France), 11; invasion of
    Italy by, 54
China, military power of, 147
Chivalry, gunpowder weapons impact on, 29
Christianity, Islam *vs.*, 5
Churchill, John (Duke of Marlborough), 68, 82,
    87–88, 106
Clausewitz, Carl von, 79, 94
Clive, Robert, 146, 148
Close-order drill, 61
A Column of Mercenaries (Schön), 81
Combat, at close quarters, 81
Commanders, 81; attributes of, 89–90, 93–94;
    effective, 94–95; structure of, 69; subordinates
    to, 90–91
Commonwealth of Poland-Lithuania: army
    structure of, 43–44; mounted forces of, 44;
    territories of, 43
Constantinople, Turkish assault on, 5–6
Continental Army, 159–60
Coote, Eyre, 148
Cortés, Hernán, 143, 145
Cosimo I (Duke of Florence), 55
Cossacks, 44
Coup d'oeil, 90
Courage, 31; firepower and, 52
Cromwell, Oliver, 28, 104–6
Crusades, 100
Culloden (1745), battle of, 159

D'Avenant, Charles, 85
Défense du Système de Guerre Moderne (Guibert),
    20–21
Della nova scientai (Tartaglia), 57
Dell'arte militare (Montecuccoli), 85
Desertion, 67, 133
D'espirit geometrique, 16–17
Discipline, 61–62, 118–19, 130, 166;
    punishment and, 94
Don Quixote (Cervantes), 111
Dragoons, 72
Drill, 61–71, 130–32
Dueling, formal codes of, 26

Dutch East India Company, 146
Dutch Wars, French militias in, 40
Dynasties, 14–21

Eastern Europe, army development in, 43–45
Edict of Nantes, 103; Louis XIV's revocation
    of, 106
Eighty Years War, Dutch fortresses and, 58–59
Elizabeth I (Queen of England), 103–4
Empire, faith *vs.*, 9–14
England: militia system of, 42–43; Spain's
    Elizabethan era policy towards, 7
English army, as parliamentary instrument, 106
English Civil Wars, 43, 105
English longbow, matchlock muskets *vs.*, 62
Essai général de tactique (Guibert), 20
Euler, Leonhard, 70
Europe: African trade of, 143; Americas and,
    154–60; amphibious skills of, 145; artil-
    lery revolution in, 53; Asia and, 145–47,
    149; conquest in, 141; globalization by, 5–9;
    homogenization of armies in, 17–18; maritime
    power of, 8–9, 142, 146, 165; mid-eighteenth-
    century infantry battalion in, 69; Muslim
    offensive against, 141; Ottoman Empire *vs.*, 5;
    projection of power by, 142–45; recruitment
    throughout, 38–39. *See also* Eastern Europe;
    Medieval Europe

The Face of Battle (Keegan), 130
Faith, empire *vs.*, 9–14
Farquhar, George, 38
Ferdinand II (Emperor), 56, 104
Feudal service, militias and, 39–42
Field fortifications, pike charges and, 35
Firearms, 35; arquebus, 35; Brown Bess
    musket, 65; flintlock muskets, 65; smoothbore
    muskets, 63, 66; wheel lock pistol, 36. *See also*
    Gunpowder weapons
Firepower, 146; courage and, 52; maximizing, 66;
    shock action *vs.*, 52
Fiscal-military state, 2–4; under
    Louis XIV, 4
Flintlock muskets, 65–66
Formigny (1450), battle of, 53
France: aristocratic feudal service in, 39–40;
    artillery production in, 70; Camisards of, 106;
    defeat at Pavia of, 71–72; military reformers
    of, 70–71; militias of, 40; religious wars in, 10;
    veterans treatment by, 137–38; Wars of
    Religion and, 40
Francis I (King of France), 11
Frederick II (King of Prussia), 18, 89
Frederick William I (King of Prussia), 46

French and Indian War (1757–1763), 159
French Revolution: American Revolution *vs.*, 107; Caribbean basin and, 155

Gage, Thomas, 69
Garrisons, 55–56
Germany: mercenary soldiers of, 81; Peasant's Revolt, 9, 26; religious dispute in, 9
Globalization: of conflict, 9; Europe's, 5–9; sea power and, 8–9
Gloire, 14–17, 20, 72, 100
The Glorious Revolution (1688), 8, 106
Graham, James (Marquis of Montrose), 28
Greene, Nathanael, 19–20
Gribeauval, Jean-Baptiste Vaquette de, 70
Grotius, Hugo, 84
Guibert, Compte Jacues de, 20, 71
Gunpowder weapons, 52; canons, 53; chivalry impact by, 29. *See also* Firearms; Muskets
Günzburg, Johann Eberlin von, 81

Habsburg Spain, 4, 10, 55, 58–59
Harley, Robert, 87
Henry II (King of England), 10
Henry of Navarre, 10
Henry VII (King of England), 11
Hesse-Kassel, 41–42
Honor, 111–12; gentility and, 92
Hôtel des Invalides, 137–38
House of Orange, 32
Howe, George, 69
Hundred Years War (1337–1453), 53
Hussars, 44–45, 72

Ieyasu, Tokugawa, 146
India: Hindu warrior caste in, 149; Maratha Confederacy in, 152; sepoys in, 147–50
Infantry: cavalry *vs.*, 52; mid-eighteenth-century European, 69; rise of, 61–71
Ironsides, 104
Islam, Christianity *vs.*, 5
Italy, Charles VIII's invasion of, 54

James II (King of England), 8
Japan, 146

Kaunitz, Wenzel (Count of Austria), 17
Keegan, John, 60, 82, 130
Knights of Malta, 5
Kunersdorf (1759), battle of, 91

Lance, pike *vs.*, 35
Lancers, 73

Landsknechte, 33, 34, 117–18, 122, 123, 125; recruitment and, 37
The Law of War and Peace (Grotius), 84
Leadership, 94–95; definition of, 79–80
Limited warfare, for dynastic ends, 85
Logistical supply chains, 65
Logistics, soldiers, 119
Louis XIV (King of France), 56–57, 137; Edict of Nantes revocation by, 106; fiscal-military state under, 4
Louis XV (King of France), 110
Luther, Martin, 9
Lutheranism, 104
Lützen (1632), battle of, 104

Machiavelli, Niccolò, 29, 79, 108
Mal du pays, 120–21
Malplaquet (1709), battle of, 67
Maratha Confederacy, 152
Marion, Elie, 106
Maritime power, 142, 146, 165; European globalization and, 8–9
Martini, Francesco di Giorgio, 57
Matchlock muskets, *vs.* English longbow, 62
Maurice of Nassau, 59, 64, 83
Medici, Catherine de, 10
Medicine, diseases and sanitation, 126–28
Medieval Europe, violence in, 9
Mercenary model, 36–37
Mercenary soldiers, 80–81; German, 81; moral for, 108; political loyalties of, 32–33
Military camp life: camp market, 123; domestic duties and, 124; followers, soldier support, 123; provost-marshal and, 121–23; women, children and, 123–25
Military engineers, 57, 60
Military fortifications: European artillery revolution and, 53; state resources for, 57; *trace italienne*, 31, 54–57
Military heroes, 109
Military professionals, aristocratic, 85–88
Military schools, 31
Military service, 25–29; adult male socialization and, 26; recruitment for, 36–47, 111, 118–19, 149
Military states, financing, 3–4
Militias: appeal of, 40; Canadian, 159; Dutch Wars and, 40; of England, 42–43; feudal service and, 39–42; French, 40; Seven Years War and, 43; standing army strength reduction and, 41; state, 160
Misères de la Guerre (Callot), 103
Montecuccoli, Raimondo, 85
Montluc, Blaise de, 34

Moral and motivation, 134; honor and, 111–12; mercenary soldiers and, 108; of officers, 107–10; patriotism and, 159; plunder and, 108; religious, 106–7; of soldiers, 110–13
Moray, Robert, 86
Muskets, 61–67; Brown Bess, 65; flintlock, 65; matchlock, 62; smoothbore, 63, 66

National Rifle Association, 160
Nationalism: American Revolutionary War and, 107; as motivating, unifying force, 99
Native Americans, 156–58
NCO. *See* Noncommissioned officers
Netherlands: Hapsburg rule in, 6; religious wars in, 10; William of Orange and, 8
New Model Army, 28, 104–6
Noncommissioned officers (NCOs), 63, 88, 93–94
Nördlingen (1634), battle of, 64
North America, British colonists in, 158

Officers: education, training of, 63, 88; moral, motivation of, 107–10; NCOs, 88, 93–94; professional, 88, 109; social contract and, 109
Operational effectiveness, 20–21
Ordinance of Lausanne, 52
Ottoman Empire, 101; Europe *vs.*, 5; support of, 5

Paré, Ambroise, 126
Patriotism, 159
Peace of Augsburg (1555), 101
Peace of Chateau Cambresis, 11
Peace of Westphalia (1648), 13–14, 41, 65, 128
Peasants' Revolt, 9, 102
Peter I (Czar of Russia), 46
Philip II (King of Spain), 6, 7, 58–59, 101, 103–4
Pike weapon, 34–35; demise of, 53; drill with, 131; field fortifications and, 35; lance *vs.*, 35; Swiss tactics, 61
Plunder and ransom, 27–28, 108
Popular unrest, 26
Portugal, in Africa, 142–43
The Prince (Machiavelli), 79
Protestant Reformation, 53, 101
Provost-marshal, 122–23
Prussia: domestic recruiting procedures in, 46–47; foreign policy of, 18
Pueblo Revolt (1680), 155
Punishment, 132; discipline and, 94

The Recruiting Officer (Farquhar), 38
Recruitment, 36–47, 111, 118–19; alternative approaches, 42–47; compulsion and, 39; *Landsknechte* and, 37; in Prussia, 46–47; sepoys and, 149; in Spain, 38; in Sweden, 45–46; throughout Europe, 38–39
Reiters, 36
Religious toleration, between Catholics and Protestants, 103
Religious wars, 9–10, 40, 100–107
Robins, Benjamin, 70
Roger, N.A.M., 8
Royal Society of London, 86
Russia, military establishment of, 46

The Safeguard of the Sea (Roger), 8
Saint Bartholomew massacre, 102–3
Saxe, Maurice de, 68, 82
Schiller, Friedrich von, 37, 166
Schmalkaldic League, 10
Schomberg, Frederick Herman von, 32
Schön, Erhard, 81
Second Amendment, U.S. Constitution, 160
Selective Service System, U.S., 47
Sepoys, 147–50
Seven Years War (1757–1763), 19–20, 70–71, 110; English militia service and, 43; formalized army divisions in, 89
Siege warfare, 5, 53, 55, 58–61; break-in phase of, 59–60; rations for, 58
Smoothbore muskets, 63, 66
Soldiers: acculturation of, 136; camp life, 121–25; civilians and, 136–37; collegiality of, 118; developing, 31; discipline of, 61, 118–19, 130, 166; early days for, 117–19; in global context, 141; job rewards, 127–29; lifestyle of, 27–28, 133; logistics and, 119–21; medicine, diseases, sanitation and, 126–28; mercenary, 32–33; moral, motivation of, 107–13, 134, 159; morality of, 118–19; pay and, 127–28; physical condition of, 120; psychological condition of, 120–21; quartering, 134–37; religion and, 128–29; seasoning, 121; sexual promiscuity of, 126–27; under state auspices, 2; syphilis and, 126–27; uniforms and, 122; veterans, 137–38; warriors and, 166; women, children and, 123–25
Spain: during Elizabethan era, 7; enlistment norms, 38; recruitment in, 38; seventeenth century geopolitical decline of, 7; in Western Hemisphere, 143, 154–60. *See also* Habsburg Spain
Spanish Fury at Antwerp (1576), 59
Spanish *tercios*, 63–64
Standing armies, 129–32

Stoicism, 52
Suleiman the Magnificent, 5
Sulle battaglie (Montecuccoli), 85
Sweden: allotment system in, 45; army
  development in, 45–46; conscription
  system in, 45–46; economic *vs.* military
  development in, 3
Swiss pike tactics, 61
Syphilis, 126–27

Tactics, 52; of Adolphus, 64; battle prepara-
  tion, 67; caracole, 36; European *vs.* Mughal,
  148–49; infantry training and, 66–69; siege
  warfare, 5, 53, 55, 58–61; skirmishes and light
  infantry, 68
Tartaglia, Nicolas, 57
Tartars, 44–45
Tax of violence, 3–4
Taxation, 56
Teil, Chevalier Jean du, 70
Tercios, 63–64
Theresa, Maria (Empress of Austria), 19
Thirty Years War, 12, 14, 56, 104; payment, sup-
  ply systems during, 128
Thirty-ninth Regiment of Foot, 148
Trace italienne, 31, 54–57
Training, 52, 73; during Age of Reason, 60;
  methods, 132; of officers, 88; punishment, at
  ease and, 132–34; tactics and, 66–69
*The Treatise of Architecture, Engineering and
  Military Art* (Martini), 57
Treaty of Câteau-Cambrésis
  (1559), 102

United States (U.S.), Selective Service System
  in, 47
U.S. Bill of Rights, church and state separation
  in, 107
U.S. Constitution, Second Amendment, 160

Vauban, Sébastien le Prestre de, 57
Veterans, 137–38
Violence, in Medieval Europe, 9
Voltaire, François-Marie Arouet de, 99

Walker, William, 143–44
Wallenstein, Albert von, 2, 37, 56, 82–83
Wallenstein's Camp (Schiller), 37, 166
War: in Age of Chivalry, 29; business opportu-
  nity of, 150–52; financing, 3–4; motivation
  for, 99–107; physically and psychologically,
  119–21; religious beliefs and, 100–107
War of Austrian Succession, 68
War of Spanish Succession, 67
Warmaking states, 1–9, 17
Wars of Religion, 40
Wars of the Roses, 2
Ways and Means of Supplying the War
  (D'Avenant), 85
Weapons, 33–36; lance, 35; pike, 34–35, 53, 61,
  131; skill levels and, 35–36; wheel lock pistol,
  36. *See also* Firearms; Gunpowder weapons;
  Muskets
William of Orange, 8
Women and children, 123–25

Zorndorf (1758), battle of, 91

About the Authors

DENNIS SHOWALTER is Professor of History at the Colorado College and has been McDermott Chair at the U.S. Military Academy, as well as a Distinguished Visiting Professor there and at the U.S. Air Force Academy, and H.L. Oppenheimer Professor at the Marine Corps University. Among his publications are *History in Dispute: World War I* (2002) and *History in Dispute: The Second World War* (2000), *The Wars of Frederick the Great* (1996), and *Tannenberg: Clash of Empires* (1990).

WILLIAM J. ASTORE is Associate Provost and Dean of Students, Defense Language Institute Foreign Language Center. With Dennis Showalter, he is the co-author of *Hindenburg: Icon of German Militarism* (forthcoming).